Knowledge, Gender, and Schooling

Critical Studies in Education and Culture Series

Knowledge,
Gender,
and Schooling

The Feminist Educational Thought
of Jane Roland Martin

D.G. MULCAHY

Critical Studies in Education and Culture Series
Edited by Henry A. Giroux

BERGIN & GARVEY
Westport, Connecticut • London

Library of Congress Cataloging-in-Publication Data

Mulcahy, D.G.
    Knowledge, gender, and schooling : the feminist educational thought of Jane Roland
Martin / D.G. Mulcahy
        p.   cm.—(Critical studies in education and culture series, ISSN 1064-8615)
    Includes bibliographical references and index.
    ISBN 0-89789-875-3 (alk. paper)
    1. Martin, Jane Roland, 1929– 2. Education—Philosophy. 3. Feminism and
    education. 4. Women—Education. 5. Education—Curricula. 6. Educational
    change. I. Title. II. Series.
    LB885.M26 M85 2002
    370'.1—dc21   2001058322

British Library Cataloguing in Publication Data is available.

Library of Congress Catalog Card Number: 2001058322
ISBN: 0-89789-875-3
ISSN: 1064-8615

First published in 2002

Bergin & Garvey, 88 Post Road West, Westport, CT 06881
An imprint of Greenwood Publishing Group, Inc.
www.greenwood.com

Printed in the United States of America

∞™

The paper used in this book complies with the
Permanent Paper Standard issued by the National
Information Standards Organization (Z39.48–1984).

10 9 8 7 6 5 4 3 2 1

Copyright Acknowledgments

The author and publisher gratefully acknowledge permission for use of the following material:

Excerpts from *Changing the Educational Landscape* by Jane Roland Martin. Copyright 1994
from *Changing the Educational Landscape* by Jane Roland Martin. Reproduced by permission
of Routledge, Inc., part of The Taylor & Francis Group.

Excerpts from *Coming of Age in Academe* by Jane Roland Martin. Copyright 2000 from
Coming of Age in Academe by Jane Roland Martin. Reproduced by permission of Routledge,
Inc., part of The Taylor & Francis Group.

Excerpts from Jane Roland Martin, *Reclaiming a Conversation: The Ideal of the Educated
Woman* (New Haven: Yale University Press, 1985).

To

Mary
and
Brendan,
Cara,
Donal,
Judith,
and
Laura

Contents

Series Foreword

Educational reform has fallen upon hard times. The traditional assumption that schooling is fundamentally tied to the imperatives of citizenship designed to educate students to exercise civic leadership and public service has been eroded. The schools are now the key institution for producing professional, technically trained, credentialized workers for whom the demands of citizenship are subordinated to the vicissitudes of the marketplace and the commercial public sphere. Given the current corporate and right wing assault on public and higher education, coupled with the emergence of a moral and political climate that has shifted to a new Social Darwinism, the issues which framed the democratic meaning, purpose, and use to which education might aspire have been displaced by more vocational and narrowly ideological considerations.

The war waged against the possibilities of an education wedded to the precepts of a real democracy is not merely ideological. Against the backdrop of reduced funding for public schooling, the call for privatization, vouchers, cultural uniformity, and choice, there are the often ignored larger social realities of material power and oppression. On the national level, there has been a vast resurgence of racism. This is evident in the passing of anti-immigration laws such as Proposition 187 in California, the dismantling of the welfare state, the demonization of black youth that is taking place in the popular media, and the remarkable attention provided by the media to forms of race talk that argue for the intellectual inferiority of blacks or dismiss calls for racial justice as simply a holdover from the "morally bankrupt" legacy of the 1960s.

Poverty is on the rise among children in the United States, with 20 percent of all children under the age of eighteen living below the poverty line. Unemployment is growing at an alarming rate for poor youth of color, especially in the urban centers. While black youth are policed and disciplined in and out of the nation's schools, conservative and liberal educators define education through the ethically limp discourses of privatization, national standards, and global competitiveness.

Many writers in the critical education tradition have attempted to challenge the right wing fundamentalism behind educational and social reform in both the United States and abroad while simultaneously providing ethical signposts for a public discourse about education and democracy that is both prophetic and transformative. Eschewing traditional categories, a diverse number of critical theorists and educators have successfully exposed the political and ethical implications of the cynicism and despair that has become endemic to the discourse of schooling and civic life. In its place, such educators strive to provide a language of hope that inextricably links the struggle over schooling to understanding and transforming our present social and cultural dangers.

At the risk of overgeneralizing, both cultural studies theorists and critical educators have emphasized the importance of understanding theory as the grounded basis for "intervening into contexts and power . . . in order to enable people to act more strategically in ways that may change their context for the better."[1] Moreover, theorists in both fields have argued for the primacy of the political by calling for and struggling to produce critical public spaces, regardless of how fleeting they may be, in which "popular cultural resistance is explored as a form of political resistance."[2] Such writers have analyzed the challenges that teachers will have to face in redefining a new mission for education, one that is linked to honoring the experiences, concerns, and diverse histories and languages that give expression to the multiple narratives that engage and challenge the legacy of democracy.

Equally significant is the insight of recent critical educational work that connects the politics of difference with concrete strategies for addressing the crucial relationships between schooling and the economy, and citizenship and the politics of meaning in communities of multicultural, multiracial, and multilingual schools.

Critical Studies in Education and Culture attempts to address and demonstrate how scholars working in the fields of cultural studies and the critical pedagogy might join together in a radical project and practice informed by theoretically rigorous discourses that affirm the critical but refuse the cynical, and establish hope as central to a critical pedagogical and political practice but eschew a romantic utopianism. Central to such a project is the issue of how pedagogy might provide cultural studies theorists and educators with an opportunity to engage pedagogical practices that are not only transdisciplinary, transgressive, and oppositional, but also connected to a wider project designed to further racial, economic, and political democracy.[3] By taking seriously the relations between culture and power, we further the possibilities of resistance, struggle, and change.

Critical Studies in Education and Culture is committed to publishing work that opens a narrative space that affirms the contextual and the specific while simultaneously recognizing the ways in which such spaces are shot through with issues of power. The series attempts to continue an important legacy of theoretical work in cultural studies in which related debates on pedagogy are understood and addressed within the larger context of social responsibility, civic courage, and the reconstruction of democratic public life. We must keep in mind Raymond Williams's insight that the "deepest impulse (informing cultural politics) is the desire to make learning part of the process of social change itself."[4] Education as a cultural pedagogical practice takes place across multiple sites, which include not only schools and universities but also the mass media, popular culture, and other public spheres, and signals how within diverse contexts, education makes us both subjects of and subject to relations of power.

This series challenges the current return to the primacy of market values and simultaneous retreat from politics so evident in the recent work of educational theorists, legislators, and policy analysts. Professional relegitimation in a troubled time seems to be the order of the day as an increasing number of academics both refuse to recognize public and higher education as critical public spheres and offer little or no resistance to the ongoing vocationalization of schooling, the continuing evisceration of the intellectual labor force, and the current assaults on the working poor, the elderly, and women and children.[5]

Emphasizing the centrality of politics, culture, and power. *Critical Studies in Education and Culture* will deal with pedagogical issues that contribute in imaginative and transformative ways to our understanding of how critical knowledge, democratic values, and social practices can provide a basis for teachers, students, and other cultural workers to redefine their role as engaged and public intellectuals. Each volume will attempt to rethink the relationship between language and experience, pedagogy and human agency, and ethics and social responsibility as part of a larger project for engaging and deepening the prospects of democratic schooling in a multiracial and multicultural society. *Critical Studies in Education and Culture* takes on the responsibility of witnessing and addressing the most pressing problems of public schooling and civic life, and engages culture as a crucial site and strategic force for productive social change.

Henry A. Giroux

NOTES

1. Lawrence Grossberg, "Toward a Genealogy of the State of Cultural Studies," in Cary Nelson and Dilip Parameshwar Gaonkar, eds. *Disciplinarity and Dissent in Cultural Studies* (New York: Routledge, 1996), 143.

2. David Bailey and Stuart Hall, "The Vertigo of Displacement," *Ten 8* 2:3 (1992), 19.

3. My notion of transdisciplinary comes from Mas'ud Zavarzadeh and Donald Morton, "Theory, Pedagogy, Politics: The Crisis of the 'Subject' in the Humanities," in *Theory Pedagogy Politics: Texts for Change*, Mas'ud Zavarzadeh and Donald Morton, eds. (Urbana: University of Illinois Press, 1992), 10. At issue here is neither ignoring the boundaries of discipline-based knowledge nor simply fusing different disciplines, but creating theoretical paradigms, questions, and knowledge that cannot be taken up within the policed boundaries of the existing disciplines.

4. Raymond Williams, "Adult Education and Social Change," in *What I Came to Say* (London: Hutchinson-Radus, 1989), 158.

5. The term "professional legitimation" comes from a personal correspondence with Professor Jeff Williams of East Carolina University.

Acknowledgments

I am most grateful to Jane Roland Martin for kindly offering me an advanced draft of her manuscript, *Cultural Miseducation* (forthcoming from Teachers College Press). A heartfelt thanks is also due to the following friends and colleagues for reading and making helpful comments on various portions of my own manuscript: Liz Aaronsohn, Ronnie Casella, Jim McKernan, Tim Reagan, and Carole Shmurak. A special word of thanks, too, to Pádraig Hogan for helpful suggestions based on a related draft. Needless to mention, they are not responsible for deficiencies that remain. Thanks are also expressed for the editorial assistance provided by Greenwood and for several research grants obtained from Connecticut State University and a sabbatical leave from Central Connecticut State University, without which this work could not have been completed in a timely fashion. Thanks, too, to Tammy Cohen for research assistance provided. A special word of thanks is due to my wife, Mary, for her encouragement and support.

Introduction

The idea of a liberal education in one form or another has shaped thinking in education over the centuries and continues to influence how people understand general education in schools and colleges in our own day. One important outcome is the manner in which general education is perceived as being primarily cognitive in nature, relying on the study of the academic disciplines as the centerpiece of the curriculum. There have been calls for a less academic emphasis, yet the idea of a general education propounded by curriculum theorists in the second half of the twentieth century largely adhered to the academic model of schooling. It is one that is still generally found acceptable in the business, governmental, and professional worlds and is considered indispensable in higher education. So influential is this model, in fact, that the history of curriculum thought up until recent times is to a considerable extent one of its adaptation and maintenance, with departures from the dominant viewpoint being infrequent.

In a well regarded article of the late 1960s, Joseph Schwab said of the curriculum field as a whole that it was moribund, characterized among other ways by a "marked perseveration, a repetition of old and familiar knowledge in new languages which add little or nothing to the old meanings as embodied in the older and familiar language, or repetition of old and familiar formulations by way of criticisms or minor additions and modifications."[1] In the intervening years, a time of unprecedented social and technological change, rather than being correspondingly creative and inventive, mainstream curriculum thinking, and policy making as reflected in governmental thinking in particular, too often lived up to Schwab's characterization. By contrast with innovative thrusts and quests for new ways forward in the field, as shown in the work of Marshall, Sears, and Schubert, and Pinar,[2] for example, mainstream curriculum thinking remained dominant, tradition-bound, and unable to chart a new course.

By mainstream I mean that body of curriculum theory in which the curriculum is viewed in terms of chiefly academic or discipline knowledge and whose philosophical underpinnings received extensive treatment by contemporaries of Jane Roland Martin. Of those to express a divergent opinion and create a new vision, Martin is among the most articulate and persistent. Based on her own early background in teaching, combined with a philosophical training and a feminist perspective, she brings to a debate generally lacking in urgency an appreciation of the long evolution of the idea of a general education. She also expresses sensitivity to aspects of the subject that have often been ignored or overlooked, not least the education of women. Martin has characterized her position as a quest for a gender-sensitive ideal of education, one in which values prevalent in a male-dominated concept of education are infused with and transformed by the assimilation of those associated with women and women's experience. She could claim also to champion a less academically dominated and more action-oriented and person-centered view. The upshot is a forthright challenge to the philosophical support structure of mainstream educational thought and practice at the beginning of the twenty-first century. Simultaneously, a forceful addition is made to what might be termed the minorstream, a less widely hailed tradition in educational thought. This tradition, in which a broader and more practical range of learnings is embraced, may be traced at least as far back as the French social philosopher of the eighteenth century, Jean Jacques Rousseau.

Viewed in the context of women's studies, Martin's position may be characterized as moderate. Sensitive to the many crosscurrents the field of feminist theory has experienced in its relatively short period of historical prominence, Martin seeks to carve out a centrist position between the extremes. A strong advocate of women's rights in both the private and public spheres, she is no less a forceful critic of positions she considers extremist or, in one way or another, hurtful to the advancement of women. Fending off unacceptable charges of essentialism that have been leveled against her, she advocates an eclectic approach to the study of issues affecting women inside and outside of education and does not shy away from advocating attention to what she considers traditionally women's issues such as education itself. In addition to offering a philosophical challenge to traditional thought, she is an advocate of political action in support of the cause of women in education.

The alternative to mainstream thinking in education that Martin lays out has many facets, and an important feature of her approach lies in her critical analysis of the work of others, dating from contemporary writers all

the way back to the earliest philosophers. The stature of such writers provides no protection to them; if anything, it is an invitation to scrutiny as
such figures as Plato, Rousseau, John Dewey, William H. Kilpatrick, Paul
Hirst, and R.S. Peters are taken to task with relish. Many of these thinkers
would also have created a yet broader target for Martin, what she considers
to be the Western, White, male, biased, and discipline-bound concept of
curriculum.[3] A second feature of Martin's work is that the critique lays the
basis for a constructive dimension in her own thought. This dimension has
long been present but has become more pronounced in recent years. It is
found in Martin's critical analysis of Hirst's theory of a liberal education,
when the critique gives way to a number of ideas that point to a new way
forward. In her elaboration upon these ideas in later works, as she spells
out the more positive dimension of her challenge to mainstream curriculum
thinking, Martin draws vital support from the ideas of Maria Montessori,
whose work with the young and the poor is especially important to Martin's elaboration of those constructive elements of her thinking. Through
it, Martin calls into question the failings of dominant theories of curriculum
and schooling and presents an alternative view for consideration. These
elements, developed in *The Schoolhome*[4] and elsewhere, include Martin's
analysis of women's education, her search for a gender-sensitive ideal of
education for all, and her outspoken commitment to the values of care,
concern, and connection, the 3Cs as she calls them.[5]

Martin is more than an important critic of contemporary thinking in
education then; she is an idealist who enlarges the scope of the debate from
a unique perspective, opening up new avenues for exploration. This is why
her work demands notice. In going beyond critique as she does, she engages
a range of issues frequently overlooked or downplayed yet in need of urgent
attention: education for family life, civility, domesticity, social justice, and
the 3Cs; the place of practical education and education for action in general
education; curriculum sensitivity to the needs and interests of the learner;
and the implications of gender, race, and class for education and schooling.
In all cases the ramifications of these issues for education are considered in
terms of aims and purpose, curriculum, teaching, and school organization.
The impact on higher education is also addressed, as is the significance for
social and even economic progress. In terms of scholarship the outcome is
a coherent and reasonably comprehensive theory of education—with a particular focus on curriculum—in the philosophical and feminist molds. For
anyone wishing to examine it closely and to consider its implications for
contemporary educational thought and practice, this work combines sim-
plicity with enrichment. The horrific events of September 11, 2001, sadly
remind one that to these qualities must also be added timeliness.

I was first taken by Martin's work when, as a graduate student at the
University of Illinois in the late 1960s, I encountered her treatment of the
limitations of the academic disciplines as curriculum content. I found com-

mon cause with her once more over a decade later on reading her critique of Paul Hirst's theory of a liberal education, by which time my own views on the curriculum questions she deals with had taken clearer shape. By the time *Changing the Educational Landscape* appeared in the mid-1990s, it was evident that Martin had become a pioneering and powerful voice.[6] Arising out of the critique of prevailing educational thought it provides and, especially the innovative and challenging alternatives it advances, her work called for careful scrutiny, I believed. The study that follows attempts such a scrutiny. It consists of five main parts and is intended as a critical analysis of, and response to, those aspects of Martin's thought that address persistent issues that have accompanied us into the twenty-first century.[7] Chapter 1 treats what I term Martin's epistemological critique of mainstream curriculum thinking. Such thinking is best reflected in the traditional appeal of a liberal education and the academic disciplines that comprise it. Both of these components of contemporary academic education, and the theories of those such as Hirst and Peters that support them, are exposed to an unyielding and highly critical analysis by Martin. It is an analysis that argues to an absence of attention to the goals of education and the consequent, unjustified assumptions on which curriculum decisions in liberal education are based, the narrow scope of liberal education and the academic disciplines upon which it is founded, and its unresponsiveness to student and societal needs and changing social conditions.

Martin's position is examined under three main headings: her critique of Hirst's theory of a liberal education; her critique of the suitability of the academic disciplines as curriculum content; and her critique of the values and ideals upon which the curriculum views of writers such as E.D. Hirsch and Allan Bloom are founded. Particular attention is given to Martin's recognition of what she calls the epistemological fallacy, her insistence that in matters of curriculum decision-making, educational goals ought to take precedence over all other considerations, and her arguments for the need to broaden the curriculum beyond the traditional academic subjects. The conclusion reached in Chapter 1 is that while Martin's analysis supports her critiques and her underlying thesis—namely, that philosophical thinking in curriculum has been too narrowly focused—she has also left many questions unanswered, such as identifying criteria for the selection and pedagogical treatment of curriculum content other than the academic disciplines.

Chapter 2 deals with Martin's gender critique of educational thought. Martin acknowledges that early in her career her interest centered largely on philosophical analysis, focused among other issues on the epistemological dimensions of the curriculum.[8] Having broadened the scope of her own work to include a feminist perspective in the analysis of education and schooling, she extends the critical consideration of contemporary thinking in education by introducing the topic of gender to her analysis. By reex-

amining the thinking upon which the educational theories of Plato and
Rousseau are based and the unquestioned beliefs that lie behind Peters's
concept of the educated man, she has crafted a compelling gender critique
of mainstream curriculum thinking.

Martin's position is analyzed in terms of how she portrays gender issues
in education as being differently perceived by men and women. Examples
of how gender in education is viewed by men are drawn from Martin's
discussion of the treatment of gender in education by Plato, Rousseau, and
Peters. The topics of domesticity and the 3Cs are chosen by Martin as
vehicles through which to examine the perception of gender in education
through women's eyes. Other issues treated include the exclusion of
women's experience from education, the imposition of male models of education upon females, and the repression of domesticity. Existing critiques
of Martin's gender analysis, notably those of Harvey Siegel and James Mc-
Clellan, are also considered and issue is taken with Siegel's and McClellan's
objections to Martin's use of the concept of "male cognitive perspective."
Martin's analysis of domesticity and the 3Cs, and her argument regarding
their centrality to education, are considered to add an important dimension
to the discussion of gender in education. Martin's own analysis is also
found wanting in a number of areas, especially the selective treatment of
the positions of others upon which important aspects of her critique of the
idea of liberal education depends.

The next two chapters examine Martin's attempts to go beyond analysis
and critique by presenting a vision of her own. This vision centers on her
decision to opt for a gender-sensitive educational ideal for all rather than
separate ideals for boys and girls. Chapter 3 begins with an examination
of Martin's study of the historical ideal of the educated woman as portrayed by selected educational writers, including Plato, Rousseau, Mary
Wollstonecraft, Catharine Beecher, and Charlotte Perkins Gilman. It then
turns to Martin's study of the treatment of women in a contemporary setting: what she characterizes as the education-gender system of the academy,
the impediments it places in the way of providing equality of education
and career opportunities in higher education to women, and her proposals
for reform of the academy. Finally, the focus shifts to the clarification of
two ideas central to Martin's overall analysis of education: the distinction
she draws between the productive and reproductive processes in society,
and her claim regarding the exclusion of women from the domain of education.

Chapter 4 considers in depth Martin's ideal of a gender-sensitive education, a complex concept that enables her to address both the knowledge
and gender-related weaknesses she perceives in mainstream educational
thinking. It also enables her to advance a position that aims to overcome
them. It is a concept inspired by Virginia Woolf and derived from Maria
Montessori. The chapter starts out by locating the origins of Martin's

gender-sensitive ideal in her epistemological and gender critiques. There follows an analysis of the elements of gender-sensitive education as set forth notably in *The Schoolhome*. Particular importance is given to Martin's interpretation of the domestic tranquillity clause of the U.S. Constitution upon which she draws in framing her ideal. It is seen as providing her position with a source of justification that was lacking in the critiques and in the portrayals of her ideal prior to its elaboration in *The Schoolhome*. Attention is given to the curriculum by which Martin suggests that her ideal be realized and, importantly, to an analysis of the new problem of the curriculum as it is developed in Martin's as yet unpublished *Cultural Miseducation*.[9] This is followed by a consideration of tensions that exist between two somewhat divergent views of the curriculum espoused by Martin. The conclusion is reached that while tensions exist, especially on the vexing question of a compulsory curriculum core, Martin makes a major contribution to the age-old debates on the purposes and content of education and the school curriculum.

Chapter 5, the final chapter, attempts an overall assessment of the significance of Martin's educational thought in terms of its originality, scope, practicability, consistency, and new directions for the future that it suggests.

NOTES

1. Joseph J. Schwab, "The Practical: A Language for Curriculum," *School Review* 78 (November 1969): 4.

2. See, for example, J. Dan Marshall, James T. Sears, and William H. Schubert, *Turning Points in Curriculum* (Upper Saddle River, NJ: Prentice-Hall, 2000).

3. Jane Roland Martin, *Changing the Educational Landscape: Philosophy, Women, and Curriculum* (New York: Routledge, 1994), especially 212–227.

4. Jane Roland Martin, *The Schoolhome: Rethinking Schools for Changing Families* (Cambridge, MA: Harvard University Press, 1992).

5. For the record, and to avoid confusion, it needs to be pointed out that Martin had earlier used the term "3Cs" to refer not to care, concern, and connection but to "the 3Cs of compulsion, coercion, and conformity." See Jane R. Martin, *Choice, Chance, and Curriculum* (Columbus, OH: Ohio State University Press, 1975).

6. The inclusion of Martin among the educators selected for Joy A. Palmer, ed., *Fifty Modern Thinkers on Education: From Piaget to the Present* (London: Routledge, 2001) bears further testimony to this.

7. For a helpful recent overview of Martin's thought, and some personal reflections of a friend and colleague, see Susan Laird, "Jane Roland Martin," *Fifty Modern Thinkers on Education: From Piaget to the Present*, 203–209; and Susan Laird, "Working It Out, with Jane Roland Martin," *Peabody Journal of Education* 71 (1996): 103–113.

8. See, for example, Martin, *Changing the Educational Landscape*, 1–5; and Jane

Roland Martin, *Explaining, Understanding, and Teaching* (New York: McGraw-Hill, 1970).

9. Jane Roland Martin, *Cultural Miseducation: In Search of a Democratic Solution* (Forthcoming from Teachers College Press). In this connection, see also Jane Roland Martin, "The New Problem of Curriculum," *Synthese* 94 (1993): 85–104.

CHAPTER 1

Knowledge and the Curriculum

In the opening pages of "Needed: A New Paradigm for Liberal Education," a sharply focused critique of Paul Hirst's celebrated theory of a liberal education first published in 1981, Jane Roland Martin comes to the point quickly and unequivocally. "Whatever the reason," she writes in a manner reminiscent of Schwab's comments of a decade earlier, "contemporary philosophical investigation of curriculum has for some time been in a rut: it has focused on a very limited range of curricular questions and has endorsed a theory of curriculum that is seriously deficient."[1] Taking what she labels Hirst's "forms of knowledge theory of a liberal education"[2] to be broadly representative of contemporary philosophical thinking in curriculum, she suggests that what is true of mainstream curriculum thinking is true of Hirst's thinking: it, too, is in a rut.

Martin aims at getting out of the rut through a reconceptualization of education that brings her beyond the critique, a position that is closely examined at a later point. In this chapter attention will be confined to Martin's critique of the epistemology of mainstream curriculum thinking. This critique extends beyond Martin's analysis of Hirst's position, and actually predates it by over ten years. It was given an early expression in "The Disciplines and the Curriculum," an article described by Martin as her first venture into the philosophy of curriculum and published in *Educational Philosophy and Theory* in 1969. Shades of the thinking found there reemerge elsewhere in Martin, most importantly as she elaborated her cultural wealth thesis in recent years.[3] The critique was extended in yet another direction in "Curriculum and the Mirror of Knowledge," as Martin drew out the implications for curriculum thinking of Richard Rorty's philosophy that has "challenged the idea that knowledge consists in a unified and justified whole."[4] Accordingly, Martin's epistemological critique of mainstream curriculum thinking is approached here under three main headings that allow for a full treatment of her position: Hirst's theory of a liberal education, the disciplines as curriculum content, and knowledge as the representation of reality in mirror-like fashion. Taken together, these approaches portray the biases, oversights, and other deficiencies of mainstream philosophical thinking in curriculum as seen by Martin. They also lay open the basis for her construction of an alternative vision for education and the school curriculum.

MARTIN'S CRITIQUE OF HIRST'S THEORY OF A LIBERAL EDUCATION

When Martin takes Hirst's forms of knowledge theory of a liberal education to be broadly representative of philosophical thinking in curriculum, she is referring to those views of general education that constituted the mainstream, meaning that body of philosophical thinking in which the curriculum is viewed in terms of chiefly academic or discipline knowledge and that held sway throughout much of the second half of the twentieth century. Important contributions to the theory dating from the 1960s and 1970s when Martin first became interested in the subject, with their inevitable variations and differences of emphasis, include such works by American scholars as *Democracy and Excellence in American Secondary Education* by Harry S. Broudy, B. Othanel Smith, and Joe R. Burnett; *Realms of Meaning* by Philip H. Phenix; *The Process of Education* by Jerome Bruner; and *Science, Curriculum, and Liberal Education* by Joseph Schwab.[5] Important works in the same time frame by English scholars include *Knowledge and the Curriculum* by Paul Hirst, *Ethics and Education* by R.S. Peters, *The Logic of Education* by Hirst and Peters, *The Philosophy of Primary Education* by R.F. Dearden, *Towards a Compulsory Curriculum* by J.P. White, and *Common Sense and the Curriculum* by Robin Barrow.[6] Several of these works from the 1960s and 1970s are singled out for mention by Martin herself. Notable contributions of both a philosophical and more general kind of the 1980s and the 1990s, and with which Martin sometimes takes issue, include *The Paideia Proposal* by Mortimer Adler, *High School* by Ernest Boyer, *The Closing of the American Mind* by Allan Bloom, *Cultural Literacy* by E.D. Hirsch, and *The Dissolution of General Education* by the National Association of Scholars.[7] The thrust of this literature was applied and extended during the 1980s and 1990s as it worked its way into the thinking of governments. It is evident in the curriculum positions advocated in *A Nation at Risk*[8] in 1983 and reflected in *Goals 2000: Educate America Act* of 1994 in the United States. It is also found in the national curriculum adopted and implemented in England during the 1980s and 1990s and in the protracted debate that accompanied these developments, leading to the passage there of the *Education Reform Act* of 1988.

Since Martin places much of the burden of pointing out the weaknesses of this dominant way of thinking upon her critique of the Hirst position, in examining her epistemological critique of mainstream theory it is therefore appropriate to begin with her treatment of Hirst's theory.[9] What is wrong with Hirst's curriculum theory, and that of the mainstream, that it so concerns Martin? After all, the values that are manifest in Hirst's thinking have attained almost universal acclaim in Western educational and social thought. This being so, it is not surprising that in the article on Hirst the main thrust of Martin's critique is not against the advocacy of such values as rationality, logic, breadth of knowledge, and depth of understanding in themselves. Her concern lies rather in the exclusion of other important values, such as those represented by practicality, feelings and emotions, and the 3Cs of care, concern, and connection. Such values, she argues, have been omitted from mainstream curriculum theory, and specifically from Hirst's forms of knowledge theory, because the focus has not been upon the goals of education as the foundation for the curriculum but upon the nature, structure, and uses of knowledge. Accordingly, for Martin, Hirst's curriculum theory is rooted in a fallacy, what she terms the epistemological fallacy. Those of Hirst's own critics who have been duped into a preoccupation with his account of the forms of knowledge as the basis for curriculum theorizing are, as a consequence, equally guilty of this fallacy and of perpetuating the deficient theory of curriculum it supports.

According to Martin, Hirst's critics have directed their energies largely toward an analysis of his forms of knowledge; for Martin, falling foul of the epistemological fallacy is the crucial issue. "Behind Hirst's theory," she writes, "lies a conception of liberal education as the development of mind and the identification of the achievement of knowledge with that development. Upon this foundation rests Hirst's thesis that a liberal education is an initiation into the forms of knowledge."[10] She continues that Hirst has made the "mistaken assumption that the nature and structure of knowledge determines the nature and structure of a liberal education."[11] Hence the epistemological fallacy, namely, "arguing from a theory of knowledge to conclusions about the full range of what ought or ought not to be taught or studied."[12]

In Hirst's view, then, according to Martin, it is epistemological rather than moral considerations that are most fundamental in determining the content and objectives of the school curriculum: what is put into the curriculum depends upon one's theory of the nature and structure of knowledge. According to Martin, Hirst holds in effect that epistemological considerations are decisive, and value judgments are therefore circumvented.[13] The philosopher as epistemologist is merely telling it as it is. While this may simplify life for the curriculum maker—if everyone could agree on one account of the nature and structure of knowledge—Hirst is not actually telling it as it is according to Martin as, she contends, an analysis of Hirst's own argument reveals.

According to Martin, Hirst's theory of a liberal education, according to which a liberal education consists in an initiation into the forms of knowledge, only gives the appearance of dispensing with value judgments.[14] If we choose Hirst's account of knowledge over equally true competing accounts as a basis for curriculum, we do so on the basis of our aims and purposes, and "we cannot choose an account of knowledge to justify them. Their justification will involve value judgments about the kind of life people should lead and the kind of society they should live in." Those who commit the epistemological fallacy "decide what a liberal education should consist in [i.e., in terms of 'the kind of life people should lead and the kind of society they should live in'] and tailor their accounts of knowledge accordingly. . . . In effect, being worthy of inclusion in a liberal education is sufficient for something to be knowledge for them."[15] This is why they go to such lengths to argue that art, religion, and moral judgment are forms of knowledge.

The practical consequences for the curriculum of Hirst's fallacious reasoning are devastating according to Martin for the kind of knowledge that his theory of a liberal education embraces is so narrow that it leads to the formation of lopsided and incomplete human beings. As a result of its exclusive focus upon propositional knowledge and its narrow view of mind, Martin maintains, other values such as "feelings and emotions and other so-called 'noncognitive' states and processes of mind" that one might wish to associate with education, such as caring for others, are omitted. Also ignored—in the theory if not in practice—is "knowledge how" and education for action,[16] and with them such subjects and areas of study as physical education, vocational education, artistic performance, languages, and civic education. In her critique of the disciplines as curriculum content, as we shall see, Martin decries the omission of such subject matter from the curriculum on the grounds that it addresses some of the legitimate needs and interests of students, such as friendship and relationships, not addressed by the theoretical academic disciplines. Not so Hirst. His theory of a liberal education produces what are but caricatures of humankind, what Martin terms "ivory tower people." These people possess knowledge but do nothing: they have no commitment to action and lack "know-how."[17]

While she is slow to do so, Martin recognizes there is a difference between education and schooling,[18] and she is also careful to point out that Hirst does not claim that liberal education is a theory of all education deemed valuable nor deny that there could be other forms of worthwhile education or schooling; they simply would not be liberal education. Yet

Martin is quick to add that not everyone has been so exact on this point and that Hirst's theory has become "the received theory not just of intellectual but of that education deemed valuable," at least in part because of Hirst's own use of the honorific label, "liberal education."[19] Likewise, Martin does not doubt that schooling today also downplays the values excluded by Hirst and that the mindset of education officialdom militates against them, although it is not school practice or officialdom that is the specific object of Martin's critique here but an influential theory of curriculum. If good practice promoting these values is found from time to time it is in spite of the theory. Some who are educated according to Hirst's theory will undoubtedly become competent doers and makers; others will become moral agents and social reformers. From the standpoint of the theory "in its role as paradigm of education deemed valuable, however, this will all be accidental, for what matters is simply that the forms of knowledge be acquired."[20]

The dualism between mind and body that Martin attributes to Hirst's theory separates reason from emotion, thought from action, and education from life, she maintains, by "banishing both knowledge how and noncognitive states and processes from its conception of mind and hence from the realm of liberal education."[21] Yet the theory goes further still and relies on a conception of liberal education that divorces mind from body, thus making "education of the body non-liberal, thereby denying it value. Since most action involves bodily movement, education of and for action is denied value also."[22] This might explain why ivory tower people are apathetic; it has serious social ramifications too. It means that the forms of knowledge theory commits one to political models that require, or at least desire, people "to be passive rather than active participants in the political process."[23] Combine such passivity with a theory of education that separates reason and emotion, mind and body, as does Hirst's, and you are left with people who are both uncaring and inactive. Martin does not go so far as Foucault might and suggest that the connection between liberal education and the development of personal autonomy is a delusion. Rightly or wrongly, she does further characterize such people as politically docile, as Foucault would, and unwilling and incapable of taking action for any cause, however, even in the face of injustice and hardship for themselves and others.[24]

MARTIN'S CRITIQUE OF HIRST CONSIDERED

Hirst has provided a highly articulate reformulation of the traditional ideal of a liberal education and Martin a thoroughgoing critique of this ideal when compared to other conceptions of education. Both positions are classic statements yet both are erroneous. They claim too much: Martin that she discovers what we've known all along; Hirst that his definition of a liberal education is a stipulative one, and, as such, one that departs from

predefinitional usage of the term.[25] Hirst's claim is the crux of the matter
and it invites Martin to repeat his mistake of overlooking what they both
undoubtedly know of the history of a liberal education.

When Hirst draws upon the idea of a liberal education in expressing his
curriculum stance, he locates his thinking within a time-honored tradition.
It is one, as with any rich and powerful line of thought, that includes
differences of understanding, nuance, and interpretation. As he prepares to
set forth his own particular account of a liberal education, Hirst wishes to
make some corrections to earlier views that have shaped the tradition. In
particular, he wishes to make the idea of a liberal education independent
of an Aristotelian metaphysics. This he achieves by departing from the
realism of Aristotle and the claim that knowledge is necessarily a correct
or true account of reality. Such a position he replaces with a view containing elements of Dewey and the postmodernists. According to this view, over
time the human race has constructed the various forms of knowledge as
our way of understanding and talking about reality, whether the account
of reality presented is true or not. Even if it is not a true account, it is an
account to which we can make reference and thereby sustain an objectively
grounded public discourse and publicly verifiable methods of investigation
and proof for the knowledge claims that we do make. Over and above their
being an objective and verifiable basis for public discourse about reality,
the seven forms of knowledge that have been created express how the human mind thinks and comes to know; they also make it possible to initiate
the young into such thinking and knowledge.

The fact that Hirst rejects the Aristotelian underpinnings of a liberal
education does not lead him to reject the value of acquiring knowledge and
the intellectual development that accompanies it; he merely values the acquisition for different reasons. Importantly, he retains the commitment to
the pursuit of knowledge for its own sake rather than for any ulterior
purpose, his search for the forms of knowledge being a search for precisely
that kind of knowledge considered worthwhile in itself, or in Hirst's words,
that knowledge that is logically basic.[26] Hirst is well aware that he is not
the first to seek and characterize such knowledge. Plato's identification of
the knowledge he located in the upper half of the divided line—science,
mathematics, logic, and dialectical reasoning—was an early attempt to formulate such thinking in relation to an educational plan; the organization
and institutionalization of the liberal arts and sciences as the foundation of
university education in medieval Europe was another; and Newman's nineteenth century advocacy of literature, science, and theology as the substance
of a liberal education yet another. It was because such knowledge was
considered logically basic that it was in all cases considered a necessary
foundation for later studies. And it was precisely because it was logically
basic, and simultaneously pure or "theoretical" as distinct from "applied"
knowledge, that many considered it useless. Yet, as Newman would argue,

it was this very uselessness, this logically basic character, that made it also the most valuable in the educational sense. Once mastered, through the knowledge base it provided and the intellectual development which gaining such mastery entailed, it enabled students to see in their learning and lives the connections among the parts, to evaluate their importance in relation to one another, to grow in knowledge and understanding. It was, in a word, a liberal education. It was free and freeing, liberal and liberating: free from the constraints of being shaped by practical ends; freeing in that it empowered the mind.[27]

When Hirst claims to be setting forth a stipulative definition and assigning a new meaning to the term, therefore, he is doing nothing of the kind as it relates to liberal education, whatever one might claim in regard to his rejection of its Aristotelian metaphysical underpinnings. Neither is he merely trading on the term "liberal education," as Martin asserts. He is invoking a tradition stretching all the way back to the Greeks. For these are precisely the claims that he wishes to make in defense of his forms of knowledge theory of a liberal education: it is free and freeing. All that is different is his account of the nature and structure of knowledge—his version of the logically basic forms of knowledge—and the altered nature of the truth claims he attributes to them. This being so, Hirst's theory of a liberal education is as open as any to the equally age-old criticism of it as being of limited value. His theory of the forms of knowledge, being the more novel aspect, not surprisingly attracted the greater critical scrutiny, at least up until the Martin critique.

Hirst's theory of a liberal education is a classic restatement in which he articulates aspects of both its educational and philosophical character, which need to be revealed today in a way not necessary in earlier times. It is in this regard that Martin's critique is valuable too, for it is as much a critique of a twentieth century account of liberal education as it is of Hirst's version of it. The validity of this critique, however, rests largely on the grounds of Martin's comparison of Hirst's theory with that of other possible educational ideals or accounts of what she terms "the whole of education"[28] rather than other theories of a liberal education. It also suggests that the title of Martin's original article, "Needed: A New Paradigm for Liberal Education," is a misnomer, for the proposals for a new way forward contained in the article constitute an outright departure from the historical ideal of a liberal education.

Theories of liberal education have long been based upon theories of the nature and structure of knowledge and to that extent have typically been guilty of the epistemological fallacy; they have long erected a dualism between mind and body and between reason and emotions; and they have long focused on education for reflection rather than action. That is why they were known as theories of a liberal education; to be so labeled meant a particular theory of education was a theory with these characteristics and not a theory of vocational or some other form of education. To suggest, as Martin does, that it is a failing in liberal education to possess such qualities, therefore, is quite beside the point; it is simply an articulation of what it meant. To articulate the distinctive qualities of a liberal education, moreover, with a view to locating it within the context of the whole of education or for some other purpose, is not to deny the necessity or desirability of other forms of education.

Advocates of liberal education did sometimes attempt to locate it within the context of a broader education. According to the widely accepted interpretation, Plato's proposal for the third stage in the education of the philosopher king, namely, the study of those subjects in the upper half of the divided line of knowledge, is a case in point to which Martin repeatedly refers. By the time Plato's future leader or guardian arrives at this stage in the educational process he or she has already completed a basic or elementary education and has been initiated into the values, customs, and mores of the society; so have all other citizens of the state. To view the proposal for the education to follow as not taking place within such a context is therefore to ignore a basic premise. As applied to Martin's critique of Hirst, it is to deny his explicit recognition, and Martin's own acknowledgment of it, that a liberal education does not claim to be the whole of education. Yet Martin proceeds to do just that. She picks out that part of the whole of education that a liberal education claims to be, and then criticizes it for not being the other parts. Hirst knows very well what his theory excludes, and he puts it succinctly himself. His "theory of a liberal education," he wrote in a follow-up piece to his original article,[29]

Can not [sic] be regarded as providing a total education. It explicitly excludes all objectives other than intellectual ones, thereby ignoring many of the central concerns of, say, physical education and the education of character. Even the intellectual ends it seeks are limited. Linguistic skills, for instance, are included only as tools for the acquisition of knowledge in the different forms, and the skills of a second language are therefore completely excluded. To equate such an education with "general education," is also unacceptable if that is taken to be everything a total education should cover other than any "specialist" elements. The lack of concern for moral commitment, as distinct from moral understanding, that it seems to imply, is a particularly significant limitation to this concept's usefulness. Nevertheless, it emphasizes, by drawing them together, precisely those elements in a total education that are logically basic, and the exclusion of all logically secondary considerations gives it importance at a time when the ends of education are often looked at purely pragmatically.

Martin's critique is also misleading in regard to those criticisms of liberal education that focus on the unwillingness and inability of the person of a liberal education to seek justice in the political realm. In Plato's scheme of things, for example, education for this very purpose simply was not possible until the third stage had been completed. That is when the knowledge and understandings that could only be found through theoretical studies were grasped, when the knowledge that was logically basic had been attained. Thereafter there was to be a thoroughgoing education in the skills of a life committed to securing justice for all, a point Martin consistently downplays. Instead she favors the interpretation that because "Plato takes ruling to be a matter of knowing The Good and considers this knowledge to be the most abstract kind there is, he requires the rulers of the Just State to engage in rigorous theoretical study so as to perfect their deductive powers and develop the qualities of objectivity and emotional distance."[30] Now Plato may or may not have been correct in believing that his third stage of education was logically basic to education for action in the pursuit of justice, but he certainly did not overlook the matter of their interrelatedness. Neither did he overlook the need for education for action in the pursuit of justice. This was the whole point of the fourth stage of Plato's plan of education. Nor did he wish his philosophers as kings to be so emotionally distant as to be uncommitted to the ideal and the pursuit of justice. Similarly with the tradition of a liberal education over time, it was because such education—rightly or wrongly—was considered logically basic that it was thought to be a prerequisite for professional studies that embraced education for action along with specialized theory. Sometimes it was also viewed, of course, as the best foundational education for everyone, whatever one's calling in life.

There are other deficiencies in Martin's critique too, as when she concludes that since most action involves bodily movement, education of and for action is also denied value in a liberal education. Arguably, the kinds of action requiring bodily movement are of the less important kind. Political, moral, and religious action may not entail bodily action any more than intellectual activity. President Truman did not have to move the bomb to Hiroshima himself nor President Bush go to the Gulf to take decisive and far-reaching action. Likewise, Gandhi was not exactly a physical activist and neither was Martin Luther King, Jr.; yet they did move mountains. But this is almost to quibble.

So why is Martin's contribution so valuable? Although Martin puts it inaccurately, when she suggests that Hirst is trading on the term "liberal education," she is close to the mark. Hirst is not merely trading on the term "liberal education," as I have already suggested. Along with R.S. Peters, he conceives of liberal education both as education and as general education, his protests to the contrary in the passage just quoted notwithstanding. Martin's contribution is valuable therefore because, firstly, Hirst wants it both ways and she refuses to let him get away with it. That is to say, Hirst wants to hold (a) that his theory of a liberal education does not claim to be a total education and (b) that it is. Martin's contribution is important, secondly, because as she details her objections in terms of the epistemological fallacy, the ivory tower person, and the dualism between mind and body, she articulates forcefully the deficiencies of a theory of liberal education understood as a theory of general education or a theory of the whole of education. Hirst alludes to these deficiencies; Martin elaborates on them with insight and skill. Having alluded to them, and openly stated that his theory of a liberal education is not to be considered a theory of total or general education, Hirst himself ignores this very admonition— notably but not exclusively in *The Logic of Education*.

Between them, Hirst's various references to education, in which he specifically identifies it with liberal education, and general education, make it clear that whatever limitations he acknowledged to exist in his theory of a liberal education by comparison with a broad or total education, he persisted in describing education and general education in terms of his theory of a liberal education.[31] He thereby insinuates, or at least leads others to conclude, that it is the only kind of education that really matters. Martin has made a strong case that it is not. In invoking the epistemological fallacy, moreover, she makes clear that Hirst's insistence in grounding his theory of a liberal education "fairly and squarely on the nature of knowledge,"[32] rather than in the goals and purposes of education, denies his position a source of ultimate educational justification.

Reference to Hirst grounding his theory of a liberal education in the nature and structure of knowledge raises a further issue regarding his view of knowledge and Martin's treatment of it. In his critique of Martin's treatment of both Hirst and Peters in "Genderized Cognitive Perspective and the Redefinition of Philosophy of Education,"[33] Harvey Siegel argues that Martin is unfair to Peters and badly misconstrues his position on the relation between reason and the emotions, on the role of the emotions in education, and on the relationship between thought and action. Siegel writes, "Martin's claims that Peters denies the emotions a legitimate role in education, that Peters divorces reason from emotion, and that he divorces reason (and emotion) from action are simply false. Martin has only selectively attended to Peters here, and has ignored that portion of Peters's work which challenges her interpretation."[34] Martin's treatment of Hirst fares no better in Siegel's view. Her claims that Hirst's conception of the liberally educated person also divorces thought from emotion and action, resulting in ivory tower people, bring a similar response from Siegel. Hirst's liberally educated person, Siegel maintains, like Peters's educated person, has mastered moral judgment which, he further maintains, relies on an appreciation of feelings and emotions. Siegel continues by claiming that Martin's identification of Hirst's and Peters's conceptions as "twins" spells trouble for her analysis of Hirst, "for if the two conceptions are isomorphic, as Martin claims, and if Peters's conception, contrary to Martin, does not divorce reason from emotion or action, then it follows that Hirst's does not either. That is to say, Martin can retain her criticism of Hirst only by retracting her 'twins' analysis."[35]

It is true that Peters has done much work on the role of the emotions in education and on the relationships between the two to which Martin does not refer directly. Of course, Hirst and Peters speak approvingly of moral education and respect for persons, too, and these could also be used to object to Martin's ivory tower criticism. But to say that Martin is lacking in her interpretation of Hirst and Peters on these matters is to overstate the case badly. Martin explicitly recognizes that feelings and emotions enter into the makeup of Peters's educated person when it comes to a commitment to the standards of scientific truth, for example. She is concerned, however, that they do not enter into this person's makeup in regards to people or interpersonal relations.[36] This is an important distinction that is recognized by Scheffler in his discussion of the rational passions. Like Peters, he considers them basic to the rational pursuit of knowledge. While challenging the entrenched opposition of reason and emotion, and recognizing the existence of what he calls the cognitive emotions, namely, the joy of verification and surprise, Scheffler is nonetheless careful to draw boundaries between cognition and emotion.[37] Martin, too, is careful to make such distinctions and to overlook them is unfair to Martin.

While Hirst and Peters dwell upon moral education, it is far from clear that they have as a result been led to depart from their characterization of education as primarily a matter of knowledge and understanding. As Peters puts it in expressly attempting to become clearer about what is involved in the task of educating the emotions, "whatever else we understand by 'education,' at least we think of it as involving a family of experiences through which knowledge and understanding develop."[38] There being no reference here, and on other occasions where a similar view is expressed, to the emotional content or character of education, it is not unreasonable to conclude that in such an account of education, knowledge and understanding is the primary focus, even if secondarily we care for them passionately. This, in turn, would be consistent with Peters's own approach to moral education, in which the primary emphasis appears to be upon the cognitive dimension. Further casting doubt on the significance or at least the clarity surrounding the place of the emotions in Peter's concept of education are the tensions between the role Peters attributes to the emotions in education and, as Martin has pointed out, his rejection, along with Hirst, that child rearing qualifies as education. If child rearing, and the emotional development one associates with it, is to be excluded from education, it surely diminishes the importance attached to the connection between education and the emotions. Even Siegel's suggestion—that the mastery of moral judgment by the educated person, as conceived by Hirst and Peters, relies on an appreciation of feelings and emotions—is contentious in itself, and is further challenged by their view in *The Logic of Education* that "only insofar as one understands other people can one come to care about them."[39] If by "appreciation" of feelings and emotions Siegel means understanding, there is no argument, as long as understanding is not taken to be an emotional state. If such appreciation is understood to imply an emotional dimension, on the other hand, then to say that it can be attributed to the kind of education Hirst and Peters have in mind is largely to beg the question. For such education, as they repeatedly tell us, is concerned with the development of knowledge and understanding; if this entails emotional formation it would appear to be of a limited nature.[40]

Wishing to choose among the nuances in Hirst and Peters, Martin has chosen those that portray education as essentially an intellectual or cognitive enterprise in which primacy is given to knowledge and understanding over emotion and action. It's at least as defensible a choice as any other. Given Hirst's own recitation of the objectives excluded from his concept of a liberal education, including character education and moral commitment as distinct from moral understanding,[41] and given this very concept is the more recent meaning of education with which Hirst and Peters together are at pains to identify, it's the most defensible choice. Given Hirst's own more recent characterization of his earlier view as one in which "education in theoretical forms of knowledge was seen as ultimately fundamental to everything else in education,"[42] it also looks now to be the right choice.

Martin's critique of Hirst's forms of knowledge theory of a liberal education goes a long way to justifying her charge that philosophical investigation of curriculum has endorsed a theory of curriculum that is seriously deficient. While this theory identifies and justifies key aspects of cognitive or intellectual growth required of the educated person, it neglects other crucial aspects pertaining to emotional development, connection to others, and action, aspects that may readily be recognized in a wider concept in which education is viewed as embracing more than just cognitive or intellectual formation. Martin's critique may also have contributed to Hirst's eventual retraction of his original stance for it is notable that he has expressly altered his stance on a number of issues raised as objections by Martin. These include deciding the goals of education or the kinds of lives people should lead based upon a theory of knowledge, highlighting a form of education consisting exclusively of forms of knowledge to the exclusion of practices, claiming cognitive states to be logically basic, focusing exclusively upon propositional knowledge as the content of education, and positing a dualism between mind and body. Although Hirst now favors seeing education as primarily concerned with social practices rather than with knowledge, it is not clear that his altered stance is moving in quite the same direction as Martin.[43] This aside, as Martin points out, his original theory is but one of many in the second half of the twentieth century that are grounded in one or another theory of the nature and structure of knowledge. Others that remain vulnerable to similar critique include those set forth by Broudy, Smith, and Burnett, by Phenix, and by Adler, to mention the more prominent. The position of Hirsch may be included as one that is singled out by Martin. Being strong proponents of academic knowledge as the core, and largely the determinant of much or all of the school curriculum, these theorists are also vulnerable to additional aspects of Martin's epistemological critique of mainstream curriculum theory to which I shall turn now.

MARTIN'S CRITIQUE OF THE DISCIPLINES AS CURRICULUM CONTENT

Martin's treatment of the limits of the academic disciplines as curriculum content in "The Disciplines and the Curriculum" adds an important dimension to her epistemological critique of curriculum theorizing. Set in the context of the writings of Jerome Bruner and the curriculum debate surrounding the nature and structure of school subjects of the 1960s, the main point of the article is to challenge the notion that the school curriculum should be composed of subject matter drawn exclusively from the academic disciplines. Martin contends the claim that in general education only the disciplines or disciplinary content should be taught is mistaken. She does so on the same grounds that led her to charge Hirst with falling foul of the epistemological fallacy, namely, that educational considerations should take precedence when it comes to choosing subject matter for inclusion in the school curriculum. She thereby wishes to create possibilities for the curriculum, such as education for action and emotional growth, that are overlooked or downplayed in Hirst's theory and by strict advocates of the discipline principle of curriculum selection.[44] It is a position that today is as pertinent as ever to those (be they individuals or local and state boards of education) whose concern for standards is largely centered on standards in the academic subjects. It is a view that in an ironic turn of events may also earn the support of Hirst as he now considers "practical knowledge to be more fundamental than theoretical knowledge, the former being basic to any clear grasp of the proper significance of the latter."[45]

By "the disciplines," Martin understands it to mean the theoretical disciplines, such as physics and economics, where the focus is on concepts, laws, and theories, and their interrelations, rather than practical disciplines such as sculpture and the dance.[46] Her main concern about the discipline principle of curriculum selection, accordingly, is that it excludes material from the curriculum that on independent grounds ought to be included.[47] Music is a case in point. Music is not an academic discipline, Martin points out in "The Disciplines and the Curriculum," though it might include music theory, which might be considered an academic discipline. Even so, music theory is not music. Music involves performance and appreciation. Therefore, since it is not an academic discipline as measured by the disciplinary principle, it does not merit inclusion in the school curriculum. Likewise, the subject French might involve grammar, and grammar might be considered an academic discipline but it is not French; literature might involve literary criticism, which might be considered an academic discipline but it is not literature. And so subject matter, such as music, French, and literature, that might be considered valuable on independent grounds, she maintains, is excluded from the curriculum on the basis of the disciplinary principle of selection.[48] Yet, she insists, everything worth teaching or learning does not have to talk or theorize *about* something.[49]

The theoretical disciplines, Martin grants, theorize or make assertions about many matters, and what they say about them may be of some significance to a related area of practice, as in music theory. But there is no guarantee that this is always the case in regard to those matters which, on independent grounds, can be shown to be matters that the young should know about. How much light, she asks, revealing her interest in those affairs characterized by care, concern, and connection that would later come to assume so crucial a place in her writings, do the theoretical disciplines throw on such everyday issues as "war and peace, marriage and divorce, violence and poverty, love and friendship?"[50] She continues a little more assertively, "no doubt some disciplines do speak right now to some of the vital issues with which education should be concerned; that all of them do or that all the things that from the educational point of view need to be illuminated are illuminated by the disciplines seems to me to be quite problematic."[51]

Having suggested that commonsense knowledge, literature and art, practical wisdom, and other nondisciplinary knowledge all have a claim to a place in the curriculum, Martin turns to what she terms "the argument from *verstehen*" to support her claim. To the extent that they do so at all, the disciplines illuminate human conduct from the "outside" by taking the standpoint of a spectator, not of an actor. In economics, for example, consumers are studied from the standpoint of someone—an economist—looking at them; he or she wants to learn more about their behavior. But when studying the consumer there may also be value to put oneself in the place of the consumer, that is to say, in the position of the actor and not the spectator. This may not be necessary if we are to explain and understand what the actor has done, but it may be if we are "to learn to act as he does and if we are to come to see the world as he does."[52] What is objectionable about the discipline principle is not that it is maintained that the disciplines themselves should be studied from the inside, from the standpoint of the inquirer, but that it prevents people from studying activities other than the disciplines from the inside, that is, from the standpoint of the inquirer. Martin argues a case for doing just that. No matter how much value one places on the disciplines, they are not the whole of life, nor ought they be the whole of education, she argues. Artistic practice and appreciation, for example, may contain elements of inquiry within them. Yet neither is reducible to inquiry any more than the professional practice of medicine or law is. Similarly, political, social, and individual moral problems can be inquired into, but the right political and social action is no more reducible to inquiry than is moral behavior. Accordingly, these matters, along with many others such as child rearing, family living, and community action, ought to be candidates "for study from within."[53]

To argue in this way is not to say that the disciplines should have no place in the curriculum. Neither is it to say that anything goes. The moral to be drawn from the consideration of these principles of selection is the same as that drawn from the analysis of Hirst's theory, namely, it is educational considerations ultimately that must be used to determine the content of the curriculum.[54] That being the case, space needs to be made in the curriculum for content other than that admitted by the discipline principle of selection.

Although Martin does not elaborate on this content or attempt to justify it in "The Disciplines and the Curriculum," it does have a certain commonsense appeal; neither does she provide elaboration as to its pedagogy, either here or even in her later, more extensive writings on the matter.[55] She does acknowledge that finding a principle to guide the selection of this kind of material would be difficult to come by. Lacking this, it is upon its commonsense appeal that she largely relies.[56] As to the nature of such subject matter, Martin sometimes hints at it and at other times is a little more expansive. In doing so, she gives a glimpse of her more fully developed views as they will appear in *The Schoolhome* regarding education in the 3Cs and, in other writings, regarding the problem of cultural superabundance. Consider, she writes, a curriculum conceived as embracing a range of human activities and conduct. Such a curriculum would have to include the arts, the professions, various sorts of work, and all sorts of other practical activities. It would also need to include a variety of social activities and roles, such as being a citizen. Neither could it "ignore things in what, for want of a better designation, I will call the personal realm, things such as character development. A curriculum so conceived might well have space for neither distinct disciplines nor families of such disciplines as separate school subjects but might only have space for the theoretical disciplines as a *single* school subject."[57]

Given the already prominent place of the disciplines in the curriculum, this means that they will have to surrender curriculum space. As indicated, if they are to be retained in some form, a new model for doing so will also need to be found, though inevitably, any such model will have its inherent difficulties. Perhaps, Martin suggests, disciplines belonging to the one family, such as the science disciplines, might be grouped together. Instead of being studied individually, the common elements among them could be taught and perhaps special treatment given to one discipline in the group so as to enable the student to experience it as an actor from within. Another possibility would be to offer just one subject called "the discipline" or "the disciplines." Here again, common elements of the disciplines could be emphasized and special treatment given to one discipline to enable the student to experience it from within, to be exposed to the rigors of disciplinary study and learn its ways. What is most important in this regard, whatever its programmatic resolution, is that at some point in the curriculum the disciplines "are taken as important objects to be learned about and as important human contexts to be studied and entered into,"[58] even if they are not the only or the most important ones.

MARTIN'S CRITIQUE OF THE DISCIPLINES CONSIDERED

Martin has shown that there is much in life that is of value other than the disciplines, including the arts, the practice of medicine, good citizenship, and physical activity. One can imagine that there is much else, too, that could be added on, such as laughter, good conversation, and the like. For this reason, and because the disciplines do not address all of the needs and interests of the young, she believes that space ought to be made available for nondisciplinary content in the school curriculum. Once again, commonsense would seem to be on her side. It is difficult to see why elements of medicine or health care, for example, should not be studied just because it is not an academic discipline. Similarly, this is so with technology, business studies, building construction, motor mechanics, and the like, whose status as theoretical disciplines may be considered suspect. Of course, a standard such as "if it's good for you it should be on the school curriculum," does have its downside. If everything good in life were to be included in the school curriculum then why not include a good night's rest or anything from fast food and arcade games to hanging out with one's friends? Martin agrees that anything does not go; but she provides few guidelines for deciding what is desirable and even acceptable. The disciplines, for their part, have provided a tried and tested measure over the years. So, one may ask, why change now?

This question brings us back to Martin's point of departure that knowledge is not a given in the curriculum. The starting point for curriculum selection is the goals and purposes one has for education; it is from here that decisions about the content of the curriculum must flow. If this is the standard, then it is proper to ask if the disciplines ought to be included in the curriculum. To this Martin has already answered yes. But if the disciplines are to be measured by such a standard, so also must all other candidates for inclusion in the curriculum. This is where "partying" and "hanging out with one's friends" could run into some trouble. Yet Martin clearly believes the curriculum ought to address the concerns, needs, and interests of students. These needs undoubtedly include friendship and belonging; if she considers the social well being of young people to be a worthy goal of education, then it is understandable why, for her, such activities may merit a place in the curriculum.

To draw attention to this indicates one set of problems raised by Martin's insistence on putting goals and purpose before the disciplines or knowledge of any kind when it comes to ruling on what goes into the curriculum. Deciding upon goals and purpose is an important and intractable problem for educators and the public alike. Having raised the issue, however, and aside from her obvious leanings toward social unity and inclusion, Martin does not identify here the goals that ought to be adopted or how they might be justified, even as a means of securing a place for content other than the academic disciplines in the curriculum. For that matter, she does not dwell here either on why or by reference to what goals and purposes the disciplines themselves ought to be included. Neither does she consider if a distinction ought to be made between the goals of education and the goals of schooling, and whether and to what extent schooling ought to be expected to attain all of the goals one sets for education. Be that as it may, even if the tricky issue of deciding upon goals and purposes for education and schooling can be resolved, it also raises the question of what curriculum content is necessary and acceptable to promote these goals and purposes. A consideration of the curriculum role of the disciplines can shed helpful light on this question even if, like Martin, one does not accept the discipline principle as the sole basis for curriculum selection.

Whatever the deficiencies of the disciplines as curriculum content, they do have the merit of being serious and considered material. Martin's reservations notwithstanding,[59] it is not at all obvious that they have so little of significance to say to those everyday but important matters that students ought to learn about. As she also argues, however, they do contain gender, racial, cultural, and most likely class biases as well. In addition, the objectivity of which Martin is critical in the disciplines might indeed put them at a remove from the everyday lives of people. Yet, this objectivity brings with it benefits too. Even granting the biases just acknowledged to exist in the disciplines, their methodologies search and root out such bias, unreflective opinion, and personal agendas. Mistakes have been made that must be corrected, not least when it comes to the school curriculum. But this need not blind us to the advances that have also taken place—and evils that have likely been avoided—by embracing the disciplines as a way of gaining new knowledge and understanding. In fact, the recognition of existing biases of the kind to which Martin and others have drawn attention is, in part at least, the outcome of the continuous and painstaking search for the truth that the disciplines, through their systematic and rigorous methodologies, represent. And all of this is still to say nothing on behalf of the potential for intellectual growth and development, including the skills of reasoning and logical argument, typically claimed on behalf of the disciplines as curriculum content.

For all of this, however, the disciplines are not alone in adopting system and rigor. Areas of endeavor, including those that seek knowledge other than the theoretical knowledge of the academic disciplines, also employ methodologies that are systematic and rigorous. This is found, for example, in what Martin calls the practical disciplines, such as the arts, medicine, and law. It is found in bodily endeavors, notably athletic pursuits and skill-based activities. And it is found in making things work, getting things done, tilling the soil, finding the right wine, making friends, having a good time, achieving success in one's career, avoiding pain, seeking legitimate pleasures—even investing in stocks. This being so, and contrary to what those such as Phenix and Hirst appear to claim, the academic disciplines or the forms of knowledge do not have an exclusive claim to having all the right or best answers; neither do they have, in any absolute sense, an objective methodology of getting to them. Likewise, if system and rigor in the pursuit of knowledge is the grounds for being admitted to the curriculum, the theoretical disciplines do not have the exclusive right to that either.

If, as Martin wishes, we allow into the school curriculum content and activities other than the academic disciplines that address the interests and needs of the young, such as home economics, artistic pursuits, and physical education, on the grounds that they too have acceptable methodologies of seeking answers to practical questions, we are still in the domain of knowledge, albeit no longer just theoretical knowledge. Yet both here and in her later writings Martin wants to go beyond even such practical knowledge and include material aimed directly at forming the emotions, attitudes, and values. Assuming that such content can be justified in light of the goals and purposes of education, the question then arises how can one ensure, if at all, that appropriate and suitable methodologies for selecting and dealing with such material in the classroom can be established, for it goes almost unnoticed that little is said by Martin about how the nondisciplinary material that she wishes to introduce is best organized for teaching and learning, not to mention evaluation and grading.

By appropriate and suitable methodologies I mean, for example, teaching methodologies that sanction procedures akin to those followed in the disciplines and practical fields of endeavor to take account of the need for dealing with matters in an ethical and publicly verifiable manner. Here again Martin supplies few answers, and this time it is more difficult to know where to begin looking for them. She does from time to time in her later work pick out specific curriculum elements that she considers valuable in this regard, such as journalism, theater, and activities relating to domestic labor.[60] She also acknowledges that unacceptable material can make its way into the curriculum.[61] She does not elaborate, however, in terms of

the criteria I have just indicated in regard to identifying suitable and jus-
tifiable teaching methodologies. In the absence of satisfactory teaching
methodologies and guidelines for education in the emotions, attitudes, and
values, it would appear necessary that as a minimum some means of excluding trivial and potentially injurious material be established, a position
with which Martin appears to disagree in "Women, Schools, and Cultural
Wealth" and even more strongly disagree in *Cultural Miseducation.*[62] Safeguards may also need to be set in place to guard against material that can
be drawn in at the whim of a teacher, a curriculum project, or a band of
zealots to advance a personal or partial agenda. In the search for safeguards
and guidelines for pedagogy in this sensitive and even uncertain and un-
charted territory, there may be much to be gained from studying areas of
professional practice such as counseling, psychiatry, social work, and ther-
apy in regard to the ground rules pertaining to clients' rights, privacy, individual preferences, independence, safety, and the like. The notion of
teacher as neutral chairperson of student discussion of controversial issues
advocated by Lawrence Stenhouse some years ago also remains as an example of an approach that holds promise in this regard.[63] These are possibilities to which Martin pays little or no attention, however. As a
consequence, there remain serious omissions from her theorizing that are
likely to give practicing teachers and curriculum-makers considerable
doubts about the justifiability and practicability of her ideas and, if not
attended to, will diminish their impact.

Reference also needs to be made to Martin's ruminations concerning the
organization of the academic material in the curriculum. Her suggestion
that curriculum content could be divided into the study of "the discipline"
or "the disciplines" on the one hand and such other but somewhat uncertain studies of a nondisciplinary nature on the other hand needs particular
attention. It may be possible to organize some discipline content in the new
configurations that she considers without negative consequences for teaching and learning. Yet many still believe that disciplines such as mathematics
and physics require a uniquely structured or highly sequential approach
that seems threatened by Martin's notion. Others will contend, as Martin
herself has indicated, that all teaching of the disciplines requires an approach that attends to unique characteristics of the disciple in question.
This would likely clash with Martin's suggestion of grouping various disciplines together or teaching them without particular regard to the inner
structure of each discipline.

Although Martin does not explicitly resurrect her proposal regarding
"the discipline," in *Cultural Miseducation* and elsewhere she explores curriculum models consistent with it as she continues to emphasize the superabundance of cultural wealth available. In considering the roles of different
educational agents in her expanded notion of cultural wealth, attention is
given to the organization and distribution of knowledge as among the dif-

ferent agents of education.[64] In *The Schoolhome*, a greater sense is also given of what is meant by the independent grounds to which she refers as a basis for including curriculum content often excluded from the discipline-dominated curriculum. This is done through her emphasis on the importance of the 3Cs as goals for education and her elaboration on the case to be made for greater attention to the issues of gender, race, and the importance of civility as a national aspiration.

However important the place of goals and purposes in determining the general shape and orientation of the curriculum, attending to their implications for practice in relation to teaching, organization, and assessment is clearly important. Yet despite the shortcomings, Martin's main point still stands. There is more to life and learning to live than the academic disciplines and what they provide. If the goals of education or schooling embrace preparation for the broader aspects of living, such as engaging in positive relationships with others, taking action in the cause of tolerance and social justice, acting to preserve the natural environment, and enjoying the arts, she has shown there is good reason to believe that content ranging beyond the academic disciplines ought to be included in the curriculum.

MARTIN'S CRITIQUE OF KNOWLEDGE AS MIRROR

In her critique of the disciplines, Martin pointed to their limitations of scope and reach. While the disciplines may be a storehouse of knowledge and of the skills and dispositions of inquiry, for Martin there is much in the educational needs of the young that they do not address. In "Curriculum and the Mirror of Knowledge," which was first published in 1994, some twenty-five years after "The Disciplines and the Curriculum," Martin turns to additional deficiencies of the disciplines as curriculum content, and in the process she extends a number of the points made in her critique of the academic disciplines and the discipline principle of curriculum selection. She highlights the approach to curriculum adopted by conservative theorists such as William Bennett, Allan Bloom, and E.D. Hirsch. In doing so, she emphasizes the social impact of the curriculum arrangements they favor, arguing that they put a premium on an internally unified curriculum of suspect character over a socially unifying one.

As will be seen in "The Ideal of the Educated Person," Martin's critique of R.S. Peters's ideal of the educated man,[65] Martin argues that the traditional idea of a liberal education, in accordance with which Peters's ideal of the educated man is fashioned, is heavily biased against women because the academic disciplines upon which it is grounded are themselves so biased. With this, Martin moves beyond her epistemological critique and into a gender critique, a tendency that was scarcely detectable if at all in "The Disciplines and the Curriculum." In "Curriculum and the Mirror of Knowledge," strains of the gender critique are also discernible, and they are sup-

plemented by concerns that stress the injustices imposed by traditional
learning upon members of minority groups, the underclasses, and even the
young. In the article by Martin on Peters's ideal, the disciplines are portrayed as decidedly anti-women. In "Curriculum and the Mirror of Knowledge," the principle of curriculum organization found in traditional
curriculum thinking is characterized as essentially pro-male or, more specifically, as a bastion of White European male privilege. In expressing their
concerns about the effects of curriculum fragmentation on the education
of the young to huge audiences, as Martin puts it, the conservative theorists, she argues, have voiced and tapped into the largely unarticulated fear
that the established culture—that of western civilization, "a white man's
culture"—is falling apart.[66] Accordingly, they make an all-out defense of
the principle of curriculum organization that sustains the status quo in
curriculum thinking.

According to the conservative theorists—the elders, as Martin refers to
them, in "Curriculum and the Mirror of Knowledge," the restorationists
as she labels them in "Women, Schools, and Cultural Wealth"[67]—the current curriculum, unlike the curriculum of their youth, is fragmented and
incomplete. As Martin sees it, for Bloom, loss of faith in the possibility of
a unified knowledge will make it impossible to educate the young to become whole human beings. For Hirsch, the curricular fragmentation he
finds us landed with leads to the fragmentation of culture itself. These
appeals to curriculum unity, while self-serving, rest on a shaky foundation,
however, for in Martin's view the very idea of unified knowledge is nothing
but a pipe dream. Philosophers such as Rorty and scholars in diverse fields,
she points out, have raised serious doubts concerning the idea of a unified
knowledge, arguing that knowledge is both inaccurate and incomplete at
the best of times. Speaking the metaphorical language of Rorty, then, both
the mind as mirror of nature and knowledge as reflection in the mirror are
shattered. All that remains is for Martin to demonstrate how this under-
mines the appeal of the elders to their outdated and self-serving principle
of curriculum unity. She begins by arguing that even if knowledge is not
itself unified, it does not mean that the curriculum will inevitably be fragmented.[68]

For Martin, to assume that because knowledge is not unified the curriculum will therefore not be unified either would be once again to fall foul
of the epistemological fallacy.[69] Since it is educational purposes and not
knowledge that are the determinants of what should be in the curriculum,
"if knowledge itself is fragmented, it does not follow that curriculum must
be."[70] Besides, subjects on the curriculum do not have to be connected to
one another in fixed ways, as the logic of mirrors would have us believe.
Cries of distortion arise, she adds, when it is suggested that school subjects
can be seen under different aspects yet they do not gainsay the fact that
subjects as diverse as science, history, mathematics, and social studies could

be organized around such varying themes as world peace and the variety of human culture and experience.

If the status quo in curriculum serves the interests of the elders, as Martin contends, and if it can somehow be intimated that the principle of unified knowledge leaves no choice but to accept the status quo, it would be in the interests of the elders to deflect attention from purposes of education. For Martin this is exactly what the mirror image achieves. It detracts attention from the place of purpose in education and specifically from the fact that curriculum is not preset but entails choices that are guided by human purpose, and it directs attention to curriculum's "inner structure." But an inner-focused curriculum can be remote from and meaningless to students, for a curriculum's internal completeness, connection, and meaning, does not insure its external.[71] There is also an exclusionary character to the one advanced by today's elders: it overlooks women, Blacks, and American Indians.[72]

These issues are played out in the debate surrounding curriculum proliferation in which, according to Martin, today's critics see concession to the laziness and "baser instincts and provincial tastes" of the young, where she sees responsiveness to changing cultural configurations and societal needs. She acknowledges an excess of proliferation. She chooses, however, to assess the suitability of content in contested areas, such as Black history and women's studies, against the experience of all of the nation's inhabitants— rich and poor, Black and White, male and female—rather than just that of the privileged and victorious.[73] But, she reminds us, in considering curriculum proliferation there is also the sheer explosion in knowledge to be reckoned with. Rather than being exclusionary and looking to regain the past, the elders might at least seek some creative ways to contain the expanding mass of discipline knowledge in curriculum arrangements meaningful to the young. If they ever do try, they will need to prepare for another surprise, one which becomes a crucial ingredient in Martin's gender critique of mainstream curriculum theory: growing evidence of biases found in the very disciplines themselves, biases favoring White males over women and Black men.[74]

Upholders of the White man's culture, as Martin puts it, seem to care little for those on the outside. Curriculum offerings may have increased but "the lenses with which schools fit our young are, with few exceptions, still ground by the educated white man to his specifications."[75] This occurs when the issues it addresses are utterly at odds with the sometimes daunting experiences of the underclasses struggling with a curriculum foreign to them, and hence exclusive and heartless. The curriculum of the elders is governed by an integrative principle that is both selective and unseen. But for a country so diverse as the United States, a curriculum that is exclusive may contribute more to social fragmentation and chaos than an inclusive curriculum charged by the elders with creating anarchy.[76]

Not wishing to dash all hope, Martin reminds the reader that rejecting the mirror imagery does not entail a rejection of the relationship between knowledge and the curriculum any more so than does the recognition of the epistemological fallacy. Adopting an epistemological stance surprisingly similar to Hirst's, for Martin, knowledge can still be valued as a "human or social construction rather than a reflection of reality."[77] What is rejected is a causal, one-way influence from knowledge to curriculum and the assumption that all curriculum space belongs to knowledge.

MARTIN'S CRITIQUE OF KNOWLEDGE AS MIRROR CONSIDERED

In the final section of "Curriculum and the Mirror of Knowledge" Martin's epistemological critique merges readily with a gender critique and includes themes of race and class that are subsumed within it. It sees Martin emerge as a postmodernist in providing what Henry Giroux describes as the theoretical and political service of "assisting those deemed as 'Other' to reclaim their own histories and voices."[78] Yet the focus remains primarily upon the issue of the unity or fragmentation of knowledge and its implications for the curriculum. While it does, there is no fundamental analysis of the question of the unity of knowledge, Rorty's position being more or less taken for granted. As for the curriculum position of the elders, only its weaknesses are highlighted; any merits it might contain go unmentioned. The weaknesses highlighted, moreover, apply to its impact on segments of the population, largely the disadvantaged, including girls and women. What is not considered here at all are the merits of traditional learning favored by the elders or the highly pertinent issue of the extent to which the disadvantaged are penalized by underlying social conditions of which education is merely a manifestation and the elders perhaps its unwitting spokesmen.

These comments notwithstanding, issues of this kind are addressed by Martin, although in a broader context when, for example she appeals in *The Schoolhome* to a reinterpretation of the notion of domestic tranquillity as a basis for social as well as educational reform. In "Curriculum and the Mirror of Knowledge," moreover, Martin does raise crucial questions pertaining to the social impact of curriculum arrangements and their responsiveness to the respective needs and interests of the privileged and of the underclasses and women. These are questions that remain, moreover, whether or not one agrees with her views regarding the actual fragmentary and incomplete nature of knowledge. Martin also accomplishes two other important goals in "Curriculum and the Mirror of Knowledge." In the first place, consistent with the overall epistemological critique, she demonstrates the centrality, to her thinking, of the principle that in decision-making about the curriculum, educational goals and purposes ought to determine priorities. This in turn enables her to combat successfully the charge of the elders that a fragmentation of knowledge leads to a fragmentation of curriculum, and through it, a fragmentation of the culture and the denial of the possibility of a proper education of the young.[79] The second goal accomplished by Martin is successfully linking the elders to a model of curriculum organization vulnerable to the charge of being outdated and guilty, by association, of the shortcomings of the discipline principle of curriculum selection and hence vulnerable to her critique of that position too. These shortcomings derive from the insensitivity of the dominant culture toward the experiences of women and minorities and in regard to whom its curriculum outcomes are exclusive.

CONCLUSION

The critique offered in "Curriculum and the Mirror of Knowledge," especially that regarding the injustices imposed by traditional curriculum thinking and practice on women, minorities, and the underclasses, has strong overtones of postmodernist critical theory. It is also resonant of the vigorous debate on general education in the university that raged throughout the later decades of the twentieth century, featuring a sometimes bitter standoff between the elders, as Martin calls them, and those claiming to advocate a more inclusive view of the curriculum. Both Martin's critique and the debate in the academy attest to the gulf that exists between two traditions. On the one hand there are those such as the elders who continue to see the world through fixed notions of knowledge and truth and the preeminence of scientific and disciplined bodies of knowledge, largely the product of the painstaking work of scholars in the various disciplines. By contrast, the postmodernist perspective acknowledges the creative and diverse interpretive perspectives of the young and the competing contributions of alternative, and usually minority, cultural perspectives. As a further consequence, Martin's critique both enjoys and suffers from many of the respective strengths and weaknesses associated with these newer perspectives.[80] There are other aspects of this critique that are more distinctive of her position, however, two of which merit mention.

It is a persistent feature of Martin's epistemological critique of mainstream curriculum thinking ranging from her earliest writings, in which the overt feminist position that she later espoused had yet to appear, to her most recent, that Martin has been an outspoken critic of the academic disciplines, liberal education, and appeals to traditional conceptions of knowledge to support exclusively academic education. As a counterbalance to this, she has made suggestions at various points as to what other forms of knowledge and subject matter should be included in the school curriculum to deal with some of the omissions and objectionable commissions of the academic tradition. She has also made the strong argument, as evident in the three main sources used in this chapter, that one of the reasons for the deficiency of liberal education is the failure to give primacy of consideration to goals and purposes in education rather than accepting the assumption that academic knowledge is the mainstay of the curriculum.[81]

Martin criticizes liberal education, the academic disciplines, and a traditional organization of knowledge in the curriculum on a variety of grounds, including the charges that between them they produce ivory tower people who are incompetent in practical affairs and lacking in emotional development; that they are unresponsive to many of the educational needs of the young; that they denigrate women and the experience of women; and that they facilitate the domination of the underprivileged by powerful elites. This is one of the strengths of her critique. She nonetheless makes it clear in "The Disciplines and the Curriculum," in her critique of Hirst's theory, and in various expressions of her cultural wealth thesis, that the disciplines are to be included in the curriculum. While she is expansive regarding the weaknesses of the academic disciplines, however, little is said of their benefits, or more strikingly, why she favors their retention either individually or collectively. They are taken for granted, ironically, in much the same way that she argues Hirst took for granted the curriculum was to be based on knowledge: they are a given. A similar adverse judgment is offered by Martin against liberal education. Yet she is willing to include it as a basic building block for her new paradigm and is even willing to allow that "initiation of the sort Hirst proposes into the forms of knowledge could be one of its components."[82] So, one is forced to ask, given their very considerable shortcomings as detailed by Martin herself, what can liberal education and the academic disciplines possibly have to redeem themselves, let alone offer toward the education of young boys and girls? Of course it may be the case that, in principle, all of the failings of liberal learning and the academic disciplines could be remedied in some extraordinary way, or even their negative contributions substantially modified. It could also be the case that while the disciplines may not address the needs of the young on a range of issues of importance to them, that between them they provide a sense of context and the intellectual skills for dealing with such matters. Yet nothing is offered by Martin to suggest any such possibilities.

The second aspect of Martin's epistemological critique that merits mention may be viewed more favorably. The old saying that someone is book smart but street foolish captures the fact that the well educated sometimes have pathetic social and practical skills and insensitivities. Martin's epistemological critique of mainstream curriculum theorizing superbly articulates how this may be. Yet as long as one assumes that the curriculum is to be made up exclusively of knowledge, and furthermore of theoretical knowledge drawn from the academic disciplines associated with a liberal education, there can be no reasoned alternative to book knowledge as the

stuff of the curriculum. If this spell is broken, and content other than theoretical knowledge is justified for admission into the curriculum, it becomes
possible to envision a curriculum consisting of a wider range and a greater
diversity of material. This is precisely what Martin achieves by drawing
attention to the epistemological fallacy and insisting that it is goals and
purposes, not knowledge, that are the rightful determinant of curriculum
content. In addition, she shows the potential range of this material as she
elaborates her cultural wealth thesis, arguing that such cultural wealth takes
many valuable forms in addition to the disciplines and so-called high culture.

Once the spell is broken one is enabled to identify the failings of existing
curriculum measures and explore more freely the contribution of various
cultural elements beyond theoretical knowledge. In both "Needed: A New
Paradigm for Liberal Education" and "The Disciplines and the Curriculum," Martin begins this work by pointing out the deficiencies of a curriculum dominated by academic knowledge. The case she presents is
well-detailed when she argues that liberal education ignores education of
the feelings and emotions, education for action, education for commitment
to better forms of social life, and education of the body, leading to incompetent and incomplete human beings. The disciplines are also shown as
failing to address many of the legitimate interests and concerns of the
young, and in "Curriculum and the Mirror of Knowledge," the case is
made that the focus of the traditional curriculum upon internal unity causes
it to overlook community unification and social inclusion.

Having accomplished this, and positing a production model of education
herself, all that remains for Martin before setting out to identify a broader
range of content is to ask, first, what are the goals and purposes of education. To decide this question, Martin argues in "The Disciplines and the
Curriculum," we need to consult the legitimate needs and interests of those
to be educated, largely the young. We also need to consult the legitimate
needs and interests of the community: rich and poor, Black and White, men
and women as is shown in "Curriculum and the Mirror of Knowledge." If
we do so, issues of race, gender, social justice, and connection come into
focus. Combine the goals that emerge from reflecting on such needs and
issues with a broadened view of potential curriculum content suggested by
the cultural wealth thesis, and the way is opened to curriculum content that
may range well beyond academic knowledge. It then remains to be asked,
second, what content from this potentially enormous range is to be selected
for the curriculum, how is it to be justified, and how is it to be handled in
terms of teaching, organization, and assessment, considerations that themselves may also need to be taken into account in the selection and justification processes.

It is not incumbent upon the author of a critique such as Martin's epistemological critique of philosophical thinking in curriculum to provide an

alternative vision. Yet in due course, Martin will attempt to do this when she focuses at greater length on the goals of education in *The Schoolhome*. Neither is the author necessarily required to address issues of curriculum implementation, though this, too, Martin will attempt. On those occasions in the course of her critique where she ventures into such theorizing, shortcomings in her position to which I have drawn attention begin to appear. It remains to be seen when we turn to a fuller consideration of her more positive proposals regarding her vision and its implementation, as presented notably in *The Schoolhome* itself, *Coming of Age in Academe*, and *Cultural Miseducation*, if these inadequacies are successfully dealt with.

This said, the epistemological critique alone makes a powerful contribution to philosophical thinking in curriculum by drawing attention in a new and compelling manner to the shortcomings of traditional perspectives. These shortcomings are rooted in the epistemological fallacy and in the failure to articulate goals. As a consequence, they are manifested in curriculum theories, policies, and practices that lack a clear sense of educational purpose and hence are inadequate themselves to respond to the educational needs of the young and of a changing society.

NOTES

1. Jane Roland Martin, *Changing the Educational Landscape: Philosophy, Women, and Curriculum* (New York: Routledge, 1994) 171. This piece on Hirst was first published as a chapter in *Philosophy and Education*, Eightieth Yearbook of the National Society for the Study of Education, Part I, ed. Jonas F. Soltis (Chicago: University of Chicago Press, 1981) 37–59. For commentary on the chapter, see Decker Walker, "Comments of a Curriculum Specialist on the Eightieth Yearbook," *Educational Theory* 31 (Winter 1981): 23–24; and Foster McMurray, "Animadversions on the Eightieth Yearbook of the NSSE," *Educational Theory* 31 (Winter 1981): 75, 84.

2. Paul H. Hirst, *Knowledge and the Curriculum* (London: Routledge and Kegan Paul, 1974) 30–53. This piece was originally published as "Liberal Education and the Nature of Knowledge," *Philosophical Analysis and Education*, ed. Reginald D. Archambault (London: Routledge and Kegan Paul, 1965) 113–138.

3. Martin, *Changing the Educational Landscape* 19, 133–153; *Readings in the Philosophy of Education: A Study of Curriculum*, ed. Jane Roland Martin (Boston: Allyn and Bacon, 1970) 65–86, where the article was first republished. See also Jane Roland Martin, "Women, Schools, and Cultural Wealth," *Women's Philosophies of Education*, eds. Connie Titone and Karen E. Moloney (Upper Saddle River, NJ: Merrill/Prentice-Hall, 1999) 167–172; Jane Roland Martin, "The Wealth of Cultures and the Problem of Generations," *Philosophy of Education*, ed. Steve Tozer (Urbana, IL: Philosophy of Education Society, 1998) 23–38; and Jane Roland Martin, *Cultural Miseducation: In Search of a Democratic Solution* (Forthcoming from Teachers College Press).

4. Martin, *Changing the Educational Landscape* 214; Richard Rorty, *Philosophy and the Mirror of Nature* (Princeton, NJ: Princeton University Press, 1979).

5. Jerome S. Bruner, *The Process of Education* (New York: Vintage Press, 1960); Harry S. Broudy, B. Othanel Smith, and Joe R. Burnett, *Democracy and Excellence in American Secondary Education: A Study in Curriculum Theory* (Chicago: Rand McNally, 1964); Philip H. Phenix, *Realms of Meaning* (New York: McGraw-Hill, 1964); Joseph J. Schwab, *Science, Curriculum, and Liberal Education: Selected Essays*, eds. Ian Westbury and Neil J. Wilkof (Chicago: University of Chicago Press, 1978).

6. R.S. Peters, *Ethics and Education* (London: George Allen and Unwin, 1966); R.F. Dearden, *The Philosophy of Primary Education* (London: Routledge and Kegan Paul, 1968); P.H. Hirst and R.S. Peters, *The Logic of Education* (London: Routledge and Kegan Paul, 1970); J. White, *Towards a Compulsory Curriculum* (London: Routledge and Kegan Paul, 1973); Paul H. Hirst, *Knowledge and the Curriculum* (London: Routledge and Kegan Paul, 1974); Robin Barrow, *Common Sense and the Curriculum* (London: George Allen and Unwin, 1976).

7. Mortimer J. Adler, *The Paideia Proposal: An Educational Manifesto* (New York: Macmillan, 1982); Ernest L. Boyer, *High School* (New York: Harper and Row, 1983); Allan Bloom, *The Closing of the American Mind* (New York: Simon and Schuster, 1987); E.D. Hirsch, *Cultural Literacy* (New York: Vintage Books, 1988); National Association of Scholars, *The Dissolution of General Education: 1914–1993* (Princeton, NJ: National Association of Scholars, 1996).

8. National Commission on Excellence in Education, *A Nation at Risk* (Washington, DC: U.S. Department of Education, 1983).

9. Hirst's subsequent rejection of his forms of knowledge theory of a liberal education, of course, does nothing to alter its original formulation or the considerable impact it had for over a quarter of a century, and it is this that is the focus of Martin's analysis. See Paul H. Hirst, "Education, Knowledge and Practices," *Beyond Liberal Education*, eds. Robin Barrow and Patricia White (London: Routledge, 1993) 184–199; Terence H. McLaughlin, "Paul H. Hirst," *Fifty Modern Thinkers on Education: From Piaget to the Present*, ed. Joy A. Palmer (London: Routledge, 2001) 196–198.

10. Martin, *Changing the Educational Landscape* 171.

11. Martin, *Changing the Educational Landscape* 172.

12. Martin, *Changing the Educational Landscape* 176.

13. Martin, *Changing the Educational Landscape* 176–177.

14. In considering Martin's response to Hirst on this point, two philosophical principles he espouses that she does not highlight are relevant. The first is his acceptance that the philosophy of education has a limited contribution to make to curriculum decision-making; the second, his acceptance that value judgments of the kind entailed here are beyond the pale. See Hirst, *Knowledge and the Curriculum* 1–2; P.H. Hirst and R.S. Peters, *The Logic of Education* 67; and P.H. Hirst, "The Contribution of Philosophy to the Study of Curriculum," *Changing the Curriculum*, ed. John F. Kerr (London: University of London Press, 1968) 39–62.

15. Martin, *Changing the Educational Landscape* 177.

16. Martin, *Changing the Educational Landscape* 173.

17. Martin, *Changing the Educational Landscape* 173–176.

18. Martin's reluctance to recognize the distinction in many of her writings, and the difficulties to which it gives rise, leads to a fuller discussion of this point in Chapter 3.

19. Martin, *Changing the Educational Landscape* 173–174.

20. Martin, *Changing the Educational Landscape* 175.

21. Martin, *Changing the Educational Landscape* 179.

22. Martin, *Changing the Educational Landscape* 179.

23. Martin, *Changing the Educational Landscape* 180.

24. Martin, *Changing the Educational Landscape* 179–180. For a discussion of differences of interpretation as between Hirst and others and Foucault regarding the interplay of liberal education, personal development, autonomy, and politicization, see also Mark Olssen, *Michel Foucault: Materialism and Education* (Westport, CT: Bergin and Garvey, 1999), especially 165–169.

25. Hirst, *Knowledge and the Curriculum* 96; Hirst, "Education, Knowledge and Practices" 187. See also Israel Scheffler, *The Language of Education* (Springfield, IL: Charles C. Thomas, 1960), 15, where Scheffler characterizes stipulative definitions as ones that "do not purport to reflect the predefinitional usage of the terms they define." He further distinguishes between them and descriptive and programmatic definitions.

26. In this connection, see R.S. Peters, "Ambiguities in Liberal Education and the Problem of Its Content," *Ethics and Educational Policy*, eds. Kenneth A. Strike and Kieran Egan (London: Routledge and Kegan Paul, 1978) 3–21. Unfortunately, Peters does not dwell here upon how knowledge that is considered logically basic might throw light upon the phrase, "knowledge for its own sake."

27. On the nuances of the term "liberal" in association with liberal education, see, for example, Martha C. Nussbaum, *Cultivating Humanity: A Classical Defense of Reform in Liberal Education* (Cambridge, MA: Harvard University Press, 1997) 293–301; Peters, "Ambiguities in Liberal Education," 3–21; Jacques Maritain, "Thomist Views on Education," *Modern Philosophies and Education*, Fifty-fourth Yearbook of the National Society for the Study of Education, Part I, ed. Nelson B. Henry (Chicago: University of Chicago Press, 1955) 77–83; and Martin, *Changing the Educational Landscape* 181–182. For a comprehensive, historical treatment, see Bruce A. Kimball, *Orators and Philosophers: A History of the Idea of Liberal Education* (New York: Teachers College Press, 1986).

28. Martin, *Changing the Educational Landscape* 173. In fact, Martin uses a number of phrases to capture this notion, including "all education deemed valuable," "that education which is valuable," "education deemed valuable," and "the whole of valuable education." See Martin, *Changing the Educational Landscape* 174–175, 180.

29. Hirst, *Knowledge and the Curriculum* 96.

30. Jane Roland Martin, "Transforming Moral Education," *Journal of Moral Education* 16 (October 1987): 207.

31. There are several passages in *The Logic of Education* where the concept of education is identified variously with liberal education as understood by Hirst and general education. See, for example, 19, 25, 66–67. In the original piece on liberal education upon which Martin's analysis is largely based, "Liberal Education and the Nature of Knowledge," Hirst says the outcome of his idea of liberal education is best summed up by Oakeshott when Oakeshott spoke of education as an initiation into the skill and partnership of the intellectual adventure of conversation. In the very paragraph quoted by Hirst, however, Oakeshott uses the word "education" not "liberal education." See Hirst, *Knowledge and the Curriculum* 52.

32. Hirst, *Knowledge and the Curriculum* 30.

33. Harvey Siegel, "Genderized Cognitive Perspective and the Redefinition of Philosophy of Education," *Teachers College Record* 85 (Fall 1983): 100–119.

34. Siegel, "Genderized Cognitive Perspective" 114.

35. Siegel, "Genderized Cognitive Perspective" 114.

36. Martin, *Changing the Educational Landscape* 75.

37. Israel Scheffler, *In Praise of the Cognitive Emotions* (New York: Routledge, 1991) 3–17. For a pertinent consideration of the interplay of emotion and reason in moral judgments, see Kathleen Wallace, "Reconstructing Judgment: Emotion and Moral Judgment," *Hypatia* 8 (Summer 1993): 61–83.

38. R.S. Peters, "The Education of the Emotions," *Education and the Development of Reason*, eds. R.F. Dearden, P.H. Hirst, and R.S. Peters (London: Routledge and Kegan Paul, 1972) 466.

39. Hirst and Peters, *The Logic of Education* 62.

40. In this connection see R.S. Peters, "Reason and Passion," *Education and the Development of Reason*, eds. R.F. Dearden, P.H. Hirst, and R.S. Peters (London: Routledge and Kegan Paul, 1972) 208–229. While Peters appears to accept here that we may reason with passion, he does not similarly assert that reason or understanding is a passion or an emotion. See also R.S. Peters, *Reason and Compassion* (London: Routledge and Kegan Paul, 1973), especially 73–102; R.S. Peters, "Moral Development: A Plea for Pluralism," *Cognitive Development and Epistemology*, ed. Theodore Mischel (New York: Academic Press, 1971) 237–267; R.S. Peters, "Reason and Habit: The Paradox of Moral Education," *Philosophy and Education*, ed. Israel Scheffler (Boston: Allyn and Bacon, 1966) 245–262; R.S. Peters, "Moral Education and the Psychology of Character," *Philosophy and Education*, ed. Israel Scheffler (Boston: Allyn and Bacon, 1966) 263–286; Martin Lipman, "Caring as Thinking," located on the Internet at http://chss.montclair.edu/inquiry/fall95/lipman.html.

41. Hirst, *Knowledge and the Curriculum* 96.

42. Hirst, "Education, Knowledge and Practices" 197.

43. Hirst, "Education, Knowledge and Practices." For a consideration of Hirst's forms of knowledge from a hermeneutical standpoint published in the year before his change of position, which points to the seeds of this change of stance in Hirst's earlier work, see Walter C. Okshevsky, "Epistemological and Hermeneutic Conceptions of the Nature of Understanding: The Cases of Paul H. Hirst and Martin Heidegger," *Educational Theory* 42 (Winter 1992): 5–23. While Martin does not allude to it in her critique of Hirst, or in any part of her epistemological critique for that matter, the praxeological character of hermeneutic conceptions of understanding marks a certain common ground with Martin's own emphasis on know-how and education for action.

44. Martin, *Changing the Educational Landscape* 133–153.

45. Hirst, "Education, Knowledge and Practices" 197.

46. Martin, *Changing the Educational Landscape* 135.

47. Martin, *Changing the Educational Landscape* 133–137. For a consideration of such material that might be considered valuable, see Jane Roland Martin, "There's Too Much to Teach: Cultural Wealth in an Age of Scarcity," *Educational Researcher* 25 (March 1996): 4–10, 16.

48. Martin, *Changing the Educational Landscape* 138–139.

49. Martin, *Changing the Educational Landscape* 139.

50. Martin, *Changing the Educational Landscape* 139.

51. Martin, *Changing the Educational Landscape* 140. Martin herself also recognizes in this early work some such foreshadowing of ideas more fully developed in her later works, notably *The Schoolhome*; see Martin, *Changing the Educational Landscape* 20–21.

52. Martin, *Changing the Educational Landscape* 144.

53. Martin, *Changing the Educational Landscape* 144–145.

54. Martin, *Changing the Educational Landscape* 146–147.

55. Martin presumably thought otherwise but reviewers of *The Schoolhome* and *Changing the Educational Landscape* disagree. See, for example, Benjamin Levin's book review of *Changing the Educational Landscape* in *Journal of Educational Thought* 30 (April 1996): 79–81 and an anonymous and curt review of *The Schoolhome* in *American School Board Journal* 179 (August 1992): 34.

56. Martin's cultural wealth thesis provides further explanation—if not quite complete justification—as to why she wishes to extend the range of curriculum content beyond the academic disciplines; her reference to educational agencies may also be seen as having some implications for pedagogy. See Martin, "The Wealth of Cultures and the Problem of Generations," and Martin, "Women, Schools, and Cultural Wealth."

57. Martin, *Changing the Educational Landscape* 148.

58. Martin, *Changing the Educational Landscape* 150.

59. Martin, *Changing the Educational Landscape* 137–143.

60. Jane Roland Martin, *The Schoolhome: Rethinking Schools for Changing Families* (Cambridge, MA: Harvard University Press, 1992) 94–98, 156–159.

61. See, for example, Martin, *Changing the Educational Landscape* 221, 225; and Martin, "Women, Schools, and Cultural Wealth" 168–175.

62. See Martin, "Women, Schools, and Cultural Wealth," especially 171.

63. Lawrence Stenhouse, *Culture and Education* (London: Thomas Nelson and Sons, 1971), especially 155–167; Lawrence Stenhouse, *An Introduction to Curriculum Research and Development* (London: Heinemann, 1975). In this connection, see also Timothy G. Reagan, Charles W. Case, and John W. Brubacher, *Becoming a Reflective Educator* (Thousand Oaks, CA: Sage Publications, 2000) and J. McKernan, *Curriculum Action Research* (New York: St. Martin's Press, 1991).

64. Martin, *Cultural Miseducation*, especially Part V; and Martin, "The Wealth of Cultures and the Problem of Generations."

65. R.S. Peters, "Education and the Educated Man," in *Education and the Development of Reason*, ed. R.F. Dearden, P.H. Hirst, and R.S. Peters (London: Routledge and Kegan Paul, 1972), 3–18.

66. Martin, *Changing the Educational Landscape* 215.

67. Martin, *Changing the Educational Landscape* 212–227; Martin, "Women, Schools, and Cultural Wealth" 162–165.

68. Martin, *Changing the Educational Landscape* 212–218.

69. Martin, *Changing the Educational Landscape* 215–216.

70. Martin, *Changing the Educational Landscape* 215.

71. Martin, *Changing the Educational Landscape* 219.

72. Martin, *Changing the Educational Landscape* 220.

73. Martin, *Changing the Educational Landscape* 221; Martin, "Women, Schools, and Cultural Wealth" 162–163.

74. Martin, *Changing the Educational Landscape* 222.

75. Martin, *Changing the Educational Landscape* 224.

76. Martin, *Changing the Educational Landscape* 223–226.

77. Martin, *Changing the Educational Landscape* 226.

78. Henry A. Giroux, "Modernism, Postmodernism, and Feminism: Rethinking the Boundaries of Educational Discourse," *Postmodernism, Feminism, and Cultural Politics*, ed. Henry A. Giroux (Albany, NY: State University of New York Press, 1991) 24.

79. It is pertinent to draw attention here to Martin's view of curriculum development as "a genuinely creative human endeavor." See Martin, *Changing the Educational Landscape* 28.

80. For a helpful discussion, see Evan Simpson, "Knowledge in the Postmodern University," *Educational Theory* 50 (Spring 2000): 157–177; James O. Marshall, "Education and the Postmodern World: Rethinking Some Educational Stories," *Educational Theory* 50 (Winter 2000): 117–226. For an introductory overview that focuses on the curriculum implications of the competing perspectives, see Jeannie Oakes and Martin Lipton, *Teaching to Change the World* (Boston: McGraw-Hill, 1999) 108–132.

81. For an argument to the effect that similar assumptions have been made by advocates of liberal education in the university, along with the assumption that "the traditional male Eurocentric curriculum constitutes precisely the knowledge that the universities should transmit to their students," see Ann Diller et al., *The Gender Question in Education: Theory, Pedagogy, and Politics* (Boulder, CO: Westview Press, 1996) 209–211.

82. Martin, *Changing the Educational Landscape* 180–181.

CHAPTER 2

Gender in School and Society

Beginning with her Presidential Address to the Philosophy of Education Society in 1981, entitled "The Ideal of the Educated Person,"[1] Martin extends her critical analysis of educational theory in a direction that hitherto was not commonplace in educational thinking of any kind, including curriculum, namely, its handling of gender. There are two main aspects to this analysis as it grows into a well-developed gender critique, elements of which are already evident in the epistemological critique. The first deals with the treatment of girls and women and their experience in education from school through university. The second is broader in scope, embracing issues highlighted in women's experience, and also found but less celebrated in men's, including their crucial place in the care and nurturing of the young.

When great minds turn their attention to education, what they say about education for the domestic or private sphere, and specifically what they say about the education of women, has been largely overlooked, Martin maintains. Indeed, she holds, to a significant extent discussion of education has been conducted in such a way as to exclude women from its definition. In approaching Martin's gender critique of mainstream educational thought it is therefore helpful to recognize that for her, the exclusion of women from educational thought and practice is a structural problem, not a mere oversight. This exclusion is rooted in a distinction, drawn between what she terms the productive and reproductive processes in society, that is fundamental to her thinking.[2] As she describes them, the productive processes include economic, political, social, and cultural processes such as the production of goods, the exercise of government, and the conduct of military affairs, activities considered to belong to the public world. Most frequently associated with men, they can in fact be undertaken by both men and women. The reproductive processes include caring for and rearing the young, the provision of health care, tending to the needs of family members, and running the household, activities considered as belonging to the private or domestic sphere. These processes are normally associated with women but men can also engage in them and sometimes do.[3]

While Martin does not clearly distinguish in much of her work between education and schooling, understood as a place of institutionalized education, she does write of education as being shaped by the needs of the public world, the world of production, and of the men who people it. The needs of the private world, the world of reproduction, and of the women who inhabit it, she maintains, somehow do not enter into the picture. Yet the dispositions and knowledge needed to carry out the reproductive processes are not innate and do not develop naturally, according to Martin. If they are not natural to women, neither are they beyond the reach of men. Both men and women can and need to engage in them; both men and women need education to engage in them.[4] In today's world of women increasingly working outside of the home, such education of men as well as women is necessary for equalizing relations between men and women. Such education may also have salutary effects in a world of seemingly increasing violence toward girls and women and disrespect for minorities, the poor, the downtrodden, and even nature itself.

If we are ever to reach the point of educating both men and women for the roles of both the public and the private worlds, it will be necessary to understand how education is viewed in each. Martin's analysis attempts to highlight just this.

WOMEN'S EDUCATION IN A MAN'S WORLD

Their writings on education, their work in the rearing of children, and all that has been written about these notwithstanding, "the status of women in the subject matter of philosophy of education has not yet been studied," Martin wrote in her essay, "Excluding Women from the Educational Realm."[5] This is so because education, like politics, is defined in relation to the productive processes in society, and the status of women is "a-educational."[6] That is, according to Martin, what women have to contribute on the issue is predefined out of the issue. This is why in standard works the role of women has not been grasped.

Some have gone to extraordinary lengths to exclude women from the educational domain, according to Martin. Rousseau went so far as to argue that it was women's nature that made them unfit for education. Others have compounded the problem by sweeping under the carpet what major figures such as Plato and Rousseau have had to say on the subject. Even when tied to the productive processes by Plato, the treatment of the education of women in his writings is largely lost to view.[7] Contemporary philosophers of education sometimes do no better than earlier ones. Peters, for example, as was seen already, finds no place for "rearing" in the serious discussion of education. In fact, Martin writes, analytic philosophy of education "excludes the teaching, the training and the socialization of children for which women throughout history have had prime responsibility."[8] Hirst follows Peters by defining out of the curriculum of a liberal education, content related to the reproductive processes, once again excluding the activities and experience of women from the educational realm. As with the curriculum, so too with teaching, for by defining teaching after the intellectualist model of Socrates, philosophers have once again excluded from the realm of education the "teaching" activities of women in rearing children, because these are often not "intellectual" but more like modeling, coaxing, and showing. The net result of these multiple exclusions, Martin concludes, is that educational thought keeps women's ideals, experience and contributions outside the domain. In addition, it keeps "the body of knowledge, the network of skills, and the various sets of tasks, duties, and traits that the culture associates with the institution of home and family and with the 'reproductive processes' of society that are housed therein" outside of the school curriculum![9] When the educational realm makes women invisible, moreover, "philosophy of education cannot provide an adequate answer to the question of what constitutes an educated person." Yet, for Martin, so long as the decision as to what falls within the educational realm is based upon the distinction between production and reproduction, the remedy for the narrow intellectualization of Peters is unavailable.[10]

Gender Bias in Plato and Rousseau

The exclusion of women from educational thought has been exacerbated by historians of education, Martin contends. In the case of Plato, for example, proposals presented by him in Book 5 of *The Republic* regarding the education of women and their roles have been rejected, she maintains, because they contradict and challenge the western tradition on a range of touchy issues. Accepting elements of the widely accepted interpretation of Plato,[11] in her view of Plato we are born with different natures and talents from one another. Our role in society and our education will be determined by these differences, of which there are mainly three. Women as well as men are endowed by nature with the capacity to become artisans, warriors or auxiliaries or, because of special qualities of intellect, guardians or philosopher kings. Sex plays no part in determining our nature, and therefore none in determining our role in society or our education. Women will receive the same education as men, depending only on their nature or talents. According to Martin, Plato largely ignored the reproductive processes in society, confining attention mostly to the productive ones; yet he did not assume that engaging in the reproductive processes belonged by nature to women. He may have located the reproductive processes in the ontological basement, but unlike many that came after him he did not locate women there.[12]

Notwithstanding those views of Plato that cast women in a favorable light and relieve them of some requirements placed upon them by Western cultural beliefs rather than nature, in the final analysis, according to Martin, even Plato was unable to provide for equal treatment for women, in education or in society. He allows for "role opportunity" for males and females, for example, but not for "role occupancy." This is because, for gender reasons and to the extent that there is differential socialization for boys and girls in Plato's just state, his educational model is more suited to males than to females.[13] Plato's identity postulate "extends a male-based pedagogy and subject matter to women, making it difficult for women to achieve equal role occupancy and all but impossible for them to be perceived and treated as equals of men." The curriculum Plato provides, accordingly, favors males and denigrates females. The identity postulate ensures this by requiring the same education for all, not an equal (and equally suitable) education for all. Martin's concern is "that identical education is not in every instance equal education."[14]

What Martin sees as Plato's production model of education is consistent with all of this, yet it raises the issue of equal respect and equal treatment for men and women. Identical education may not be equal because it can lead to trait genderization in which women are penalized for possessing traits such as rationality and autonomy that in a man are considered admirable and valued. So also, as the traits attributed to the guardians are considered masculine, females would have to acquire such traits to be considered guardians. Yet they would be derided for possessing them. So females will receive different and unequal treatment and respect for possessing the same traits and receiving the same education as males.[15]

In Plato, gender was a determinant neither of one's nature nor one's education, yet Plato is criticized by Martin for offering the same education to males and females. One reason for this criticism, presumably, is because of the impact of trait genderization. A second reason is because, for Martin, different people learn differently, not because of different natures but because of differences in upbringing and experiences,[16] suggesting to her that the education of boys and girls ought to be different to some extent. In turning to Rousseau where one's nature and, accordingly, one's education is to be determined by gender, one might therefore expect to find a different education for men and women, and one of which Martin may be ready to approve at least in some respects. Martin may be glad to learn that Sophie's education is different from Emile's; she is dismayed to discover that it is also unequal. Through his constant reiteration of his growth model of education, according to which one's education is to be determined by nothing other than one's nature, Rousseau would have us believe that such a different education is tied to women's different nature. In having us so believe, Rousseau is misleading us, says Martin, and historians in large numbers have joined in the deception.[17]

Historians of educational thought, Martin writes, "have implicitly defined their subject matter as the education of male human beings, rather than the education of all human beings."[18] In so doing they have downplayed, if not entirely disregarded, Rousseau's differential treatment of the education of Emile and Sophie—and Emile's dependency on Sophie—as much as Plato's inconvenient views on the education of women. They have also allowed to go unchallenged Rousseau's differential treatment as being grounded in nature and a growth model of education. Martin takes up the challenge and offers a reinterpretation. She argues that Rousseau's educational ideas are basically functional in character, employing a production model of education just as Plato's did and, contrary to the general view perpetuated by historians of education, not based on a growth model. Both Emile and Sophie are, in fact, educated for what Rousseau sees as their particular male and female roles in society, even though this entails severe constraints on their natural growth. The role envisaged for Emile is that of family patriarch and citizen; the role for Sophie is that of pleasing and subservient wife and mother. The education of each will be different based upon their roles as much as, if not more than, their different natures. The place of manipulation allowed by Rousseau in the education of Emile Martin sees as further evidence that a nature or a growth model is abandoned by Rousseau.[19]

For Martin, Rousseau's education proposals for Sophie cannot be explained by his theory of following nature—the model of growth and autonomy. Clearly, according to Martin, Rousseau would have both men and women function within gender boundaries. By nature men and women are different, he conveys, so their education will be different; it will fit the nature of each and, as with Plato, will bring potential to fruition. But nature needs an assist. Accordingly, only those traits that Rousseau wants to develop will be promoted, and he even shows fear lest other unsuitable ones might emerge. It is societal and political forces or values, according to Martin, that shape Rousseau's image of male and female education, not, as he insinuates, a growth principle. This is the whole point of his production model of education. Both males and females are to be educated—formed or produced—for two very different societal roles even though in both cases this may involve the inhibiting of natural tendencies at odds with the declared wishes of Rousseau. Thus, Martin holds, whether one agrees or not with the education or with the social roles Rousseau assigns to males and females, either for his own time or any other, this education and these roles are not rooted in their different natures as Rousseau alleges, but in culturally rooted gender biases.[20]

For Martin it is important to establish that the education and roles set for Emile and Sophie respectively are not rooted in their different natures but in culturally rooted gender biases. This being so, Rousseau cannot appeal to nature to sanction the kind of "female-as-unenlightened-but-manipulative subservient" role for Sophie and "male-as-ivory-tower citizen" for Emile. Because of the unequal relations and different qualities that Emile and Sophie possess, moreover, their marriage is likely to fail and with it the base building block of Rousseau's state, a happy family unit, which is needed to nurture the good citizen. Finally, since a feeling of community is necessary for Rousseau's state, only the qualities of caring and nurturing that Sophie—and not Emile—possesses can bring this about.[21]

Gender Bias in Peters

None have worked harder in Martin's own time in refining the notion of the ivory tower person than Hirst and Peters, and Martin has no doubts this person is a man. In Martin's view, Peters's concept of the educated man[22] represented widely held thinking in the field on a number of fundamental gender-related issues in education that were in need of serious scrutiny.[23] The first objective of her response to Peters, accordingly, is to challenge the adequacy of the traditional ideal of the "educated man," as propounded by Peters and others, by examining its suitability for the education of both boys and girls. Martin is less concerned with the gender-biased language employed by Peters than with the gender-biased content of his ideal, namely, its bias in favor of males and against females, a theme elaborated upon in later works, notably *Reclaiming a Conversation* and *The Schoolhome*. The second objective is more positive in orientation, namely, to fashion a gender-sensitive—as distinct from a merely gender-neutral—ideal of education and to indicate some of its qualities. The male-based ideal, she will argue, does harm to boys and men as well as girls and women, the harm it does to men being intimately tied up with the injustice it does to women.

According to Martin, Peters and others conceive an educated person as viewing things in a certain way, resulting from a study of the disciplines. From the standpoint of the ideal of an educated person, however, the disciplines are in several respects seriously flawed, because they contain a thoroughly male cognitive perspective. They have a male image of women and they focus on the public world and its productive societal processes, as opposed to the private world and the reproductive processes. "In sum, the intellectual disciplines into which a person must be 'initiated' to become an educated person *exclude* women and their works, *construct* the female to the male image of her and *deny* the truly feminine qualities she does possess."[24] One may add that school subjects likely exhibit similar tendencies.[25]

According to Martin, the masculinity of Peters's model of the educated person does not derive only from the content of the academic disciplines: the traits attributed to the educated person are male as opposed to female. And so even though the ideal of the educated person may be attained by women, as was the case with Plato's guardians, it is genderized in favor of males. A woman will possess the traits of an educated person at her peril. For Martin, therefore, "Peters's ideal puts women in a double bind. To be educated they must give up their own way of experiencing and looking at the world, thus alienating themselves from themselves. To be unalienated they must remain uneducated."[26] Such a view she sees as just another example of our willingness to impose male models on females. Not only are women devalued as a consequence, but males are likewise deprived of an education in the reproductive processes of society. Males are damaged because the masculine ideal creates people lacking in emotions and feelings, the drawbacks of which Martin sets out in her critique of Hirst's theory of a liberal education.[27]

For Martin, Peters's concept of the educated man is also yet another example of viewing education in terms of production. The educated man of Peters, Martin argues, no less than Plato's guardians or Rousseau's Emile, "is designed to fill a role in society which has traditionally been considered to be male."[28] His educated man, accordingly, is not equipped to carry out roles associated with the reproductive processes in society traditionally considered to be women's. Even if many today see schools as neglecting academic education, as was seen already, for Martin, people need to be educated in—to learn—the reproductive roles, such as how to be a parent, roles not intuitively known. By excluding such education, "there is an unwarranted negative value judgment about the tasks and activities, the traits and dispositions which are associated with them."[29] The inhabitants of the educational realm, by which Martin appears to mean those in the public world who control education, are actually insensitive to its biases, she maintains. They will tell you that in the less civilized domain of the home, the main commodity is socialization, not education, and child rearing activities are so instinctual, effortless, and lacking in purpose they do not constitute teaching.[30] This is why Peters could deny that rearing was part of education. But for Martin, an adequate ideal of the educated person must do more than give the reproductive processes their due. We must avoid the trap of assigning males and females to different processes and at the same time ignoring one of the processes. We must also recognize the power of the hidden curriculum to convey bias.[31]

Martin's Critique of Plato, Rousseau, and Peters Considered

Martin's discussion of Plato, Rousseau, and Peters highlights the issue of gender in education. It is this aspect of her work that has attracted most attention and generated the greatest commentary.[32] Chief among the issues that have been debated and to which attention is given here are the notion of male cognitive perspective, the production or functional model of education that Martin attributes to all three philosophers, equality of educational provision for boys and girls, and the interrelations between liberal and professional education. I shall begin by considering the question of male cognitive perspective.

Male Cognitive Perspective

Martin's notion of male cognitive perspective, a modification of Peters's own concept of cognitive perspective, attracted immediate criticism following her critical appraisal of Peters's concept of the educated man. In her critique of Hirst's theory of a liberal education, Martin argued that the understandings and skills acquired in a liberal education are of limited value in the workplace and everyday living. In her critique of Peters's concept of the educated man she brings this criticism a step further and argues that the understandings and skills acquired in the course of a liberal education are positively harmful and prejudicial when it comes to the education of girls and women. This is so, she maintains, not least, as we have just seen, because the disciplines upon which it is based reflect a thoroughly male cognitive perspective, forcing women to give up their own way of looking at the world, thus alienating themselves from themselves. Both Mc-Clellan and Siegel take issue with Martin on the question of male cognitive perspective,[33] while proclaiming their agreement with the broad sentiments found in the feminist point of view she advances.

For McClellan the notion of male cognitive perspective is wholly untenable, "cognitive perspective" itself being a metaphorical expression. According to McClellan, it follows from Martin that once you experience a liberal education you come away with a male cognitive perspective. But this, he acknowledges, seems to overlook the fact that some come away as conservatives and others as liberals, that there is no necessary common or distinguishing element. In its second sense, cognitive perspective for Mc-Clellan can refer to an abstract feature or property of subject matter, something in the curriculum. But what property, McClellan inquires? Perhaps that of ignoring the experiences and lives of women. But why does, say mathematics, ignore the lives of women? He adds that it is conceptually absurd to suggest, as Martin does, that it is because mathematics has a male cognitive perspective. "The curriculum ignores and misrepresents the truth of many things because the dominant ideas in society are those of the dominant class, the dominant sex, the dominant race," McClellan continues. "It is not an abstract property like a cognitive perspective, male or female, that determines what biases will be found in a society's curriculum for its young, but rather the material relations of power, wealth, and ownership sustained among different segments of that society."[34]

In a broadly based critique of her analysis of contemporary analytic philosophy of education, Siegel extends the analysis of 'male cognitive perspective' and its implications for Martin's position. He rejects Martin's charge that Peters's ideal corresponds with our cultural stereotype of a male, as Martin describes it, when, he points out, "Peters explicitly demands, for example, that moral education include the development of empathy and compassion" and he contends that Martin is wrong in her claim that the disciplines embrace a male cognitive perspective. Martin, he says, is also incorrect in "blaming" Peters for trait genderization: we err, he writes, "if we find fault with Peters's ideal on the grounds that it leads to the self-alienation of women, for the fault lies not with the ideal, but with erroneous and damaging genderized societal evaluations. Peters's ideal looks bad here only because it encourages women to have traits—good traits—that society mistakenly regards as traits that are bad for women to have."[35] Martin is wrong, Siegel further suggests, when she writes that the intellectual disciplines into which a person must be initiated to become an educated person "*exclude* women and their works, *construct* the female to the male image of her and *deny* the truly feminine qualities she does possess." Siegel retorts, "Can this be said of disciplines such as physics or mathematics, which do not treat of women—or men—at all?"[36]

Siegel argues that Martin is wrong in two ways in her claim that philosophy of education, because it has excluded women both as subjects and as objects of educational thought, suffers from a bad case of male cognitive perspective. She is wrong, he asserts, on the exclusion of women thinkers (women as subjects) because the criteria for considering them to be philosophers of education are not set forth by Martin. Similarly on the issue of women as objects, he contends, she fails to say what is philosophically significant about women's lives which is germane to philosophy of education and that requires it to be specifically treated.[37]

Siegel strongly criticizes Martin's two objections to the rationality theory of teaching because it demeans the work of women as child rearing people by excluding childrearing activities from the realm of teaching. According to Siegel, Martin fails to show that child rearing activities are teaching activities, overlooks the fact that the rationality theory of teaching does not value only teaching, and has no difficulty in putting a value on other forms of child rearing activities. Siegel adds that Martin is confused in thinking that the rationality theory of teaching denies that learning can take place without teaching, adding that she sadly muddies the waters of technical analysis of teaching to which, in his view, Scheffler and Green contributed so much.[38]

Siegel next argues that Martin is caught in a dilemma of arguing that there is a male cognitive perspective as distinct from a female while she herself assumes a male cognitive perspective (i.e., rationality and objectivity), in the process. Siegel further sides with McClellan in thinking that the concept "cognitive perspective" is untenable and slippery. He also argues that Martin badly misconstrues Peters's position on the relations between reason and the emotions, on the role of the emotions in education, and on the relationship between thought and action.[39]

In Chapter 1, I dealt with Siegel's criticisms of Martin on the role of the emotions in Peters. Several of the additional objections raised here by Siegel can be dealt with together. His criticism of Martin on the specific issue of blaming Peters for trait genderization is apt and one which Martin fails to refute when she later acknowledges the criticism.[40] On Martin's charge of the exclusion of women both as subjects and as objects of educational thought, Siegel is also correct in pointing out the weakness of Martin's argument. This does not mean, however, that Martin's position is incorrect, merely her arguments in support of it. Siegel's criticism of Martin's objections to the rationality theory of teaching are well-taken only to a point, for it remains an open question if child rearing can be summarily excluded from the domain of education and whether the rationality theory of teaching covers all cases of teaching. To exclude child rearing certainly does not square with everyday understandings of child rearing as part of education of the young and the fault may lie in Martin's failure to demonstrate that Peters holds a too-narrow concept of education. Perhaps she also needs to challenge the rationality theory of teaching as unduly narrow. This need not be done to the point of including indoctrination and brainwashing, for example, but sufficiently to accommodate aspects of child rearing activities that are pedagogical in character yet lack criteria demanded in the rationality theory.[41]

Siegel's position, and that of McClellan with whom he sides on the question of male cognitive perspective, is quite problematic, for the issue is not as clear-cut as both writers make out. Siegel, for example, agrees with McClellan that the idea of male cognitive perspective is untenable, yet he writes of it in terms of rationality and objectivity.[42] But the problem runs deeper than this. In defense of his charge that Martin is wrong when she writes that the intellectual disciplines into which a person must be initiated to become an educated person "*exclude* women and their works, *construct* the female to the male image of her and *deny* the truly feminine qualities she does possess," Siegel comes up with little more than an exclamation mark. Leaving aside completely subject areas such as literature and social studies, he merely asks if this can actually be said of disciplines such as physics or mathematics, which do not treat of either men or women.[43] Aside from the fact that it may need to be shown and not merely assumed that mathematics and physics do not exclude women's experience, the real crux of the Siegel and McClellan positions is that they perceive of male cognitive perspective in a limited way. While it may be true that there is no such entity as male mathematics or female mathematics, this is altogether different from saying that the discipline of mathematics has excluded women. While it may appear conceptually absurd for Martin to say that mathematics ignores the lives of women because mathematics has a male cognitive perspective, it is not necessarily absurd. While it may sound contradictory for Martin to claim that women can adopt a male cognitive perspective, or use a male cognitive perspective to argue against a particular position, it is not necessarily contradictory. While one might not be able to claim that an abstract property such as a male cognitive perspective has the force of economic power, this is not to say that the concept has no philosophical or educational value. The reason why none of these charges by Siegel and McClellan necessarily holds up is because of the role of experience in how we come to know and understand.

No one will deny that men and women have different experiences, some based in nature, such as in childbearing, others in culture, such as in treating men as breadwinners and women as caregivers. Whatever the basis, they lead to different ways of viewing the world, of interpreting differently what is seen and heard, of responding differently, of using knowledge— even the same knowledge—differently. Crucially, they lead to different inquiries, interests, and questions. With men historically dominating the world of knowledge creation, at least insofar as the disciplines are concerned, it comes as no surprise that this world was shaped by the interests and questions of men more so than of women. As the authors of *Women's Ways of Knowing* put it, "women, paddling in the bywaters of the culture, have had little to do with positing the questions or designing the agendas of the disciplines."[44] When the time came to teach the knowledge gained through the disciplines, it was men's knowledge that was taught since little else had been recognized to be formulated in accordance with the requirements of an academic discipline, adhering to strict and objective criteria of evidence and proof they demanded. The fact that it was men's interests that dictated the shape of the disciplines does not mean that women could not learn them nor, given the time and opportunity, have contributed to them in the first place; after all women, too, are intelligent creatures. It does mean, however, that women's interests were excluded whether the knowledge creation was in algebra or geometry, in physics or biology, in politics or psychology. Imagine how differently theology would have evolved as a discipline in the Catholic tradition, for example, if women were included among the clergy; and imagine how differently still if men and women priests were married. How differently might geometry have turned out if it was born of the needs of lace making and kitchen design rather than farming and land measurement? How differently would philosophy itself have turned out if more women had practiced it? As none other than Peters himself reminds us, "Hare once claimed that, if moral philosophers addressed themselves to the question 'How shall I bring up my children?,' many of the dark corners in ethics might thereby be illuminated." Sounds as though he's pining for these very women philosophers![45]

The academic disciplines followed certain directions as a function of the topics that men's experiences brought men to inquire about. Martin chooses to label this a male cognitive perspective without at the same time claiming that it is characterized by a uniquely male way of thinking about their experiences and interests. It would be less rather than more surprising, moreover, if this perspective should have come about under the influence of what McClellan calls "the material relations of power, wealth, and ownership sustained among different segments of . . . society."[46] Given the origins of the academic disciplines, it would be less surprising, too, if women were to find the content and approach of the disciplines less pertinent to their lives, less compelling, and even less fulfilling than men do. Yet, whether such influences as the relations of power, wealth, and ownership that McClellan talks about were decisive or not, they do nothing to change the underlying phenomenon that the academic disciplines were shaped more by the interests and experiences of men than of women.

Understood in this way, Martin's claim, even if overstated, makes perfect sense: the intellectual disciplines into which a person must be initiated to become an educated person excluded women and their works, constructed the female to the male image of her, and denied the truly feminine qualities she does possess. In fairness to McClellan and Siegel, however, the term "male cognitive perspective" is vague and open to different interpretations. Nonetheless, at least under the interpretation of male cognitive perspective offered here, Martin's charge of bias against girls and women in the academic disciplines, and consequently in liberal education, still stands. That, in the final analysis, is the main point at issue.

The Production Model of Education

Martin's treatment of the idea of a production model of education, which she attributes to Peters in addition to Plato and Rousseau, also attracted immediate attention following the presentation of her critique of Peters. It may be open to more serious criticism than her notion of male cognitive perspective. In order to examine this, it will be helpful to begin by looking at the interplay between production and education in Plato.

It is understandable that Martin should characterize Plato's plan of education as conforming to a production or functional model of education, as it does contain the key elements of such a model. As commonly understood, the philosopher king has a crucial role to play in governing the state, and Plato envisaged a certain form of education to prepare him or her for this purpose. More crudely stated, Plato designed a form of education to

create a product that could function in such a capacity. This form of education was made up of four main parts. The first part was compulsory
for all citizens, its purpose being to educate for citizenship and for carrying
out a variety of basic additional functions required of the working class. It
was also envisioned as a means of social and political enculturation. While
no particular form of work or job preparation was entailed, such education
was expected to provide the artisan with the kind of general knowledge
and skills that would be helpful in fulfilling his or her economic role in
society. To that extent it enabled the artisan to reach his or her full or
natural potential, whatever that might be—within certain culturally accepted boundaries as regards growth in knowledge and understanding—
along with forming or producing him or her as a law abiding and patriotic
citizen. Much the same holds true for the second part of education, that
which was fashioned for the purpose of producing the auxiliaries. This also
may be viewed as conforming to a production model, one that enabled
those naturally endowed with the potential to become fighting men and
women in defense of the state to achieve the fulfillment of their nature as
well as to serve the state.

The situation is somewhat different in regard to the third part of education, that first of two parts reserved for those destined to undertake positions of political leadership and who were naturally gifted with a superior
intelligence to engage in it, be they men or women. Viewed in itself, this
third part of education had as its goal nothing more nor less than the
promotion of knowledge and understanding, with a view to the student
grasping the everlasting truths and immutable values and first principles
governing the universe, including the just society. Its outcome or product
was the philosopher who, unlike others, was endowed by nature with a
capacity for such knowledge and understanding. Being exposed to the
higher studies—those on the upper half of the divided line of knowledge,
notably dialectic—merely enhanced the future philosopher's tendency to
achieve his or her full intellectual potential. To the extent that his or her
learning was uninhibited, as a philosopher's should be, one may consider
it to contain elements of a naturalistic model. It may even be considered
liberal in the sense of being free—albeit within the kinds of knowledge
boundaries permitted by Plato—and freeing or liberating.

With the philosopher entering the fourth and final part of education,
that is, the apprenticeship in political leadership, in which he or she is to
be formed for the particular role of governing in the just state, the production model of education reemerges. The free or uninhibited pursuit of
knowledge—the liberal nature of the education—is once more eliminated,
giving way to a professional education insofar as the focus turns to acquiring the particular knowledge, habits, and practical skills required of
the politician or leader. These include conducting the affairs of the state,
making laws, leading the people; in a word, governing. When Plato's own

pupil, Aristotle, later employed the concept of liberal knowledge, he would surely have considered that Plato's studies in the upper half of the divided line of knowledge fit well his characterization of the pursuit of liberal knowledge. The kind of knowledge needed for the limited tasks of governance, however important, Aristotle would likely have considered a non-liberal or "vulgar" form of knowledge, and the kind of education associated with it would have been considered a professional as distinct from a liberal education.

To carry this line of reasoning further, one might question the usefulness of arguing that any model of education is a production model of education as distinct from a naturalistic one. Perhaps some forms of education might be labeled "naturalistic" to the degree that they are committed to furthering knowledge and understanding through free and undirected inquiry. But education is a cultural phenomenon, not a natural one, one that we shape in accordance with certain value and knowledge preferences. For the most part, therefore, saying that a particular model is a production model is little more than a tautology; to the extent that they aim to lead the young to live by certain standards and ideals, all models are to a greater or lesser degree production models. To talk of goals and purpose in education, as Martin does with effect in many of her writings,[47] for example, is to be committed to a production model. To have no goals might not rule out the possibility of learning but it does rule out the possibility of education understood as a goals-oriented enterprise.

Whether it is useful or not to characterize his model of education as a production model, there are several reasons to draw out the distinction between liberal and professional education in Plato. In the first place, it bears out the criticism leveled at Martin in the previous chapter against her argument that Hirst's idea of a liberal education produced only the ivory tower person. Liberal education on its own may do that but liberal education almost never was conceived as existing within a vacuum. To view it as existing in this way—as when Martin is at pains to point out that her critique of liberal education is directed toward liberal education understood strictly as a theory[48]—is essentially to construct a straw man. In Plato's case, liberal education is set within the context of the other three parts of education to which I have alluded, all of which were required in the education of the philosopher king. Whatever one may wish to say of Hirst's idealized person, the philosopher king was by no means merely an ivory tower person. Neither was Newman's celebrated idealization, the gentleman, for whom a liberal education was experienced within the context of a strong moral and religious formation.

If one accepts Martin's critique of liberal education as a concept standing alone, her ivory tower criticism stands strong. Thus, if the only education the philosopher king were to receive was the third part in Plato's scheme as I have outlined it, the philosopher king could be characterized as an ivory tower person, to use Martin's term. Significantly, that is how Martin describes the student of a liberal education in her critique of Hirst's theory of a liberal education. The guardian, as she talks of the philosopher king and other members of the leadership class in Plato, is bereft of feelings and emotion. Given the position she developed in her critique of Hirst's theory of a liberal education, she could easily have added that Plato's philosopher king would also be lacking in a commitment to pursuing justice for the just state.

But this is to be selective at a crucial point.[49] Martin's failure to recognize it notwithstanding, the philosopher king was to be educated in all four parts of Plato's educational program, only one of which, the third, consisted of what might reasonably be characterized as liberal education. One of the key elements of basic education, that is, the first part required of all citizens from age five through sixteen approximately, was education in love of country and a life of morally acceptable behavior. Hence the sanctioning of censorship and the promotion of desirable knowledge, attitudes, values, feelings, emotions, and modes of behavior dedicated to the well-being of the state. In the second part, to which the philosopher as well as the auxiliaries were exposed, there was a military preparation to serve in defense of the state. And in the fourth and final part there was the preparation of the philosopher to become king, a just ruler in a just state.

This point of disagreement with Martin goes to the heart of her argument about the male gender-bias she sees pervading mainstream educational thought and practice. Of the five major figures—Plato, Rousseau, Mary Wollstonecraft, Catharine Beecher, and Charlotte Perkins Gilman—considered in *Reclaiming a Conversation*, only Rousseau is excused from the criticism of failing to recognize the importance of the 3Cs because of the traits of nurturance he attributed to Sophie. However true it may be of Wollstonecraft, Beecher, and Gilman, it is not true of Plato, and of varying historical ideals of liberal education, that they did not allow for a broader education in feelings and emotions.[50] Philip H. Phenix, a notably strict adherent to the discipline principle of curriculum selection, for example, insisted on the inclusion of what he termed "personal knowledge" in the curriculum, even though he recognized that "for the most part, personal knowledge is not developed through formal instruction." He also recognized the centrality of caring in personal relations and understanding, and that personal knowledge may be aided by formal studies.[51] This being so, it would not be unreasonable to find the free pursuit of knowledge one associates with a liberal education providing some education even in matters of the private world of home and family as distinct from the public world. In "Women, Schools, and Cultural Wealth," Martin writes that "mindless imitation is, however, the easiest path for someone to follow who has not been trained to bring intelligence to bear on living. In the worst of cases, then, an education for spectatorship consigns students to the nasty, brutish, and short life that the philosopher Thomas Hobbes long ago attributed to the state of nature." This may be true but Plato and other advocates of liberal education did not fail to incorporate training "to bring intelligence to bear on living." Perhaps some, such as Hirst, did fail, but not all. Martin is selective and wrong when she writes as if all did. To that extent her gender critique of liberal education is off target.[52]

As a basis for her gender critique of mainstream educational thought, Martin herself sometimes overlooks, and at other times strips it, of those very elements she criticizes it for not possessing. These include education in attitudes and feelings, in action and behavior, and in caring and commitment to a cause. She downplays, too, the likelihood of someone of a liberal education applying reflection and critical thought to matters of home and family life. This being so, it exposes a serious weakness in what was a powerful plank sustaining her general gender critique in education, namely, that Plato and others had overlooked the 3Cs. For this reason, too, the weight of the argument in *Reclaiming a Conversation* is jeopardized. Viewed in the way just set out, Plato's educational theory already contains some of those key elements of education in feelings, care, and commitment to the welfare of others that Martin found wanting in his position, and for which she searched in other portrayals of women's education in *Reclaiming a Conversation*. To education in the feelings and emotion Plato added, moreover, an education for action that Martin found lacking in Hirst's ivory tower person but which she overlooks in Plato's philosopher king. To say this, of course, is not to say that Plato attended to the full range of dispositions involved in the 3Cs and family living as Martin delineates them, and she is correct in pointing out that the emphasis in Plato was on preparation for service in the public world.[53] Yet in the account given of domesticity as the reproductive process of homemaking in *The School-home*, she considers domesticity to be integrally related to citizenship. In fact, to the extent that domestic activities are to be engaged in as a matter of citizenship, domesticity is portrayed as being subservient to citizenship.[54] This leads one to wonder if one standard of citizenship formation—in which there is no connection between citizenship and domesticity and the 3Cs—is to be applied to Plato and another more congenial one in which citizenship embraces both domesticity and the 3Cs is applied to Martin herself.

The interpretation just presented challenges Martin's persistent and selective criticisms of gender bias in the historical ideal of a liberal education while at the same time accepting several of her more specific charges. Moving from the historical to the contemporary setting, Martin's critique also overlooks aspects of schooling today by similarly stripping it of social, structural, and non-academic curricular elements associated with it both as a matter of practice as well as policy. These come in various forms, including the positive "hidden" curriculum elements built into schools (e.g., counseling, homeroom, parent-teacher liaisons, sporting activities) and universities (e.g., residence halls, religious and youth organizations, student unions, and the Y) and the attention given to activities in these and other nonliberal education pursuits by admissions criteria in universities, businesses, and other employers of liberal education graduates. In a word, even in schools and institutions committed to the primacy of liberal education, the formal curriculum does not exist in a vacuum. Advocates of liberal education normally proceed on that understanding and often even make it explicit. The goals of public schooling, too, acknowledge that there is more to education than the formal academic curriculum.[55] Even if they may not go so far as to include all the additional elements that Martin hopes for or fall short in other ways, there is a commitment to programs in character education and community service. To fail to recognize all of this and then to proceed to criticize accordingly—even if the focus is on the theory of a liberal education as Martin points out—is to suspend reality. One does not need to go this far to concur with Martin that education in the 3Cs and education for action is still seriously neglected in theory and practice or that there is gender bias in the curriculum.

MEN'S EDUCATION IN A WOMAN'S WORLD

According to Martin, the writings of educational thinkers such as Plato, Rousseau, and Peters; the interpretations put upon them by historians of education; and the impact of concepts such as liberal education, have significantly shaped the discourse on education, and in the process imposed male perceptions upon the way girls and women as well as boys and men have been educated. As is evident in *Reclaiming a Conversation*, women have sought to express different educational values, shaped by their different experience, and their views of education have not been nearly so influential as men's. Relegated to and therefore concerned more with the values of the private world of the home, Martin argues, they have highlighted values of nurturance, care of the young and the elderly, connection and community; to use Martin's word, domesticity. Such values do not fare so well, however, in school or society.

Domesticity Repressed

According to Martin, the forces arrayed against domesticity within our culture are strong. They jeopardize the new goal of education in the 3Cs that she wants to assign to the school. Caring for and nurturing the young to be civic minded and concerned for others, for example, was a matter for which Sophie rather than Emile was fitted by nature according to Rousseau. Yet Sophie was also deprived of doing so because of Rousseau's insistence that her young son be removed from her influence at an early age and formed by a tutor in the image of the father figure, Emile. In *Emile*, however, autonomy, rationality, and lack of intimacy are emphasized; concern for others, a trait required of the citizen that could only have been nurtured in her sons by Sophie in the family setting, are forfeited. Such nurturing is but one example of how, in Martin's contention, the reproductive processes can contribute not only to betterment of the individual but also of the public world.[56]

A source from which Martin draws greater inspiration in support of her proposal to pass on to schools the work of education for domesticity and family living is Montessori and her work with the poor children of the San Lorenzo Quarter of Rome. According to Martin, the work of Montessori and her espousal of domesticity was given a harsh reception in the United States when it first appeared early in the twentieth century. Held up as a model for social and personal education by many child advocates today, Montessori's work was roundly criticized and, due to his influence, ultimately banished by William Heard Kilpatrick, a leading critic who, in Martin's account, failed to understand its significance. Focusing on the methodological aspects of Montessori's work, Martin suggests, Kilpatrick failed to appreciate its deeper significance in relation to education for domesticity. Dewey too, Martin believes, failed to grasp the significance of Montessori's insights regarding the crucial importance of domesticity and the changing nature of the home and their implications for the future of home, school, society, and their interrelations at the dawn of the twentieth century.[57] When she thinks of Kilpatrick's resistance to Montessori, she understands the oversight, Martin writes in *The Schoolhome*. Then reflecting fondly on her own schooldays and the sometimes unloving actions and relationships she found there, she remembers that through the years, her school had tried to develop the strong sense of community that Kilpatrick and Dewey extolled. Yet, she continues, their theories did not deal with a concept of school as a domestic environment, one that was permeated by a family affection influencing the activities of the classroom as well as behavior generally in the school.[58]

This caring dimension of schooling, which reputedly existed in Dewey's own laboratory school at the University of Chicago, he somehow overlooked in his theorizing, according to Martin. When the industrial revolution forced fathers out of the home, and with them the economic work that once existed there, Dewey argued that the school should respond in a manner appropriate to such social change, she writes. What Dewey overlooked in arguing that the occupations of the home should therefore be transplanted to the school, according to Martin, was that the home was not merely a place of mothers and fathers working but of loving, caring, and connecting too.[59] As a consequence, he failed to locate this dimension in the new school. When Montessori did attempt to do just that, both Dewey and Kilpatrick failed to grasp its significance. It was, in Martin's words, a case of domesticity repressed. If Dewey had seen the need to locate affection and domesticity in the school, Martin believes, the kind of self-discipline he advocated in schoolwork, but which teachers had difficulty bringing about in their students in practice, would surely have evolved. It would have found support in an atmosphere of caring and mutual support among students that a loving environment brings with it, as it did in Montessori's Casa dei Bambini and other such school settings.[60] Thus, to his own question, "what radical change in school suffices when home has been transformed?" Dewey, repressing the domestic aspects of the earlier American home, could not see, as Montessori was proclaiming, that the answer lay in domesticity.[61] Had Montessori's critics understood her domestic metaphor and its implications, Martin continues, they would have been forced to reconsider their assumptions about the relationship between the home and the school and recognize the important contribution of the home to the maintenance of culture.[62]

Resistance to domesticity did not begin and end with Kilpatrick, of course. Nor is it confined to heartless schools, according to Martin; it goes to all corners of our culture. Escape from home, and the domesticity associated with it, is a deeply rooted theme in American literature. The American literary classics depict home as a place to escape from. They have kept its positive contribution a well-guarded secret and they have taught us "to forget what it is necessary to remember."[63] For educators, Martin adds provocatively, the flight from the home is necessary in order to teach the knowledge, skills, and attitudes of the public world;[64] in literature it is a flight from responsibility.[65] "The dream of escape encoded in our literary canon is not just a figment of the American imagination, however," Martin writes. It is enacted daily by husbands and fathers who abandon wives and children and by runaway adolescents who fall prey to the streets, drugs, crime, prostitution, and AIDS.[66]

Disregard for home and domesticity also characterizes the public debate on education, according to Martin, citing as supporting evidence the many reports of recent decades on the subject.[67] In these reports, she notes, the preoccupation is with preparing children for the world beyond the home. Many homes no longer provide preparation for family life, yet these reports and their authors never understand that because homes have been transformed, schools might also have to change. Even though she phrases it differently from place to place, there is no ambivalence on Martin's part as to how much of the role of education for family living the school should take over. Indicating that the schools cannot do everything, in places she talks of a sharing of the work with the family.[68] At other times she speaks of the school as "a moral equivalent of home" and at still other times as a "surrogate home" in which children of all ages and both sexes "engage in the domestic activities that ground their everyday lives there—the planning, cooking, and serving of meals or the cleaning, maintaining, and repairing of the physical plant," reminiscent of the activities of those children of Montessori in the San Lorenzo Quarter of Rome.[69] Elsewhere she more clearly indicates that the full education role, one extending beyond mere academics, should be taken over by the school. Referring to the authors of the aforementioned reports, Martin adds that the idea that schools "should take over its partner's responsibility" to prepare the young to live in homes and families "was the furthest thing from their minds."[70] She continues that, in a stunning reversal of how school is perceived in relation to home, instead they view the very intimacy and informality of the home that made it an effective partner as an obstacle to schooling for the outer world.[71]

The banishment of domesticity and of the study of women's issues is rampant in the academy, too, a point on which Martin elaborates in *Coming of Age in Academe*. According to Martin, the gendered character and values of the university and the double standard it employs are seen in the low status assigned to women's studies in the curriculum and various research agenda. It is seen in the academy's negative attitude toward nursing, education, and home economics, subjects tainted because of their association with women and the home.[72] The curriculum advocated by conservative theorists, the elders, in both schools and universities provides no relief from this uneven treatment, for it is governed by an integrative principle that is both selective and unseen, according to Martin. It keeps out the viewpoints and lives of women and minorities, a dangerous exclusion in today's society. "Calling curricular inclusiveness 'anarchy,' " she writes, the elders "try to ban the very subject matter that would enable us to acknowledge the differences of sex, race, class, ethnicity, religion without having them make a difference to such questions as who is qualified to govern, be educated, practice the professions."[73] Elders, such as Hirsch and Bloom, who wish to promote the unifying potential of a "core curriculum," may be well intentioned, she says, but their efforts will fail if the core is not inclusive.[74] Where it is inclusive, all are enriched, just as all in the community were enriched in Martha's Vineyard through the use of sign language.

In *The Gender Question in Education*, Diller et al. speak of what they term a "multiplicity of axes of privilege and oppression" such as gender, race, and class. In all, they identify fourteen such axes, each with the potential for domination.[75] Similarly, Martin wishes to broaden the canvass beyond gender, for the language of domesticity, of care, concern, connection, and inclusion is not confined to gender. And so, she writes in *The Schoolhome*, there must also be sensitivity to all salient dimensions of children's lives, including race, class, ethnicity, religion, physical abilities, and sexual orientation.[76] She elaborates in part by referring to the experience of Richard Rodriguez. In his autobiography, *Hunger of Memory*, published in 1982, Rodriguez recounts the pain, loss, and sense of alienation he attributes to his education as it increasingly isolated him from the world of his childhood, family, and parents and removed him from them. For Martin, his loss and pain is unnecessary and is a result of a split between reason and emotion that is built into the traditional idea of a liberal education, and of which she was critical in the work of Hirst and Peters. Such education seeks not the development of mind as a whole, but of rational mind. In Plato's terms, it seeks inner harmony at the expense of outward connection. Not only is there no room for education for action; neither is there any for other-regarding feelings and emotions.[77] Relating this to Rodriguez, becoming educated did not have to move him from intimacy to isolation: "his journey of isolation is a function of a definition of education, a particular ideal of the educated person, and a particular definition of excellence—all of which can be rejected. Becoming educated can be a journey of integration, not alienation. . . . Loss, pain, isolation: It is a tragedy that these should be the results of becoming educated, the consequences of excellence."[78] Harshness might be considered a desirable—even necessary—quality by William James and others, but Martin is clearly of an opposing view. By giving the reproductive processes their due, she maintains, by providing care and concern, by joining reason and emotion, thought and action, we can avoid this tragedy.[79]

We have a tendency, Martin argues, to see the 3Cs as being in conflict with the purpose of education, even seeing them as a barrier to preparation for membership of the public world, which we see as the main purpose of schooling—hence our willingness to have the school dispense with domesticity. We make preparation for entry to the public world—a world of our creation—the work of education, whereas we assume that there is no need for preparation for living in the private world of the home, a natural institution.[80] For Martin the evidence suggests otherwise: domestic violence is rampant, men being the major perpetrators and women and girls the major victims of assault and abuse.[81] In fact, the highest level of sexual abuse is perpetrated by family members; and so, she continues, it is folly to think that being a member of a family is learned naturally.[82] Children also live in a violent world in school, another site for misogynist messages. Citing gender research by Best that uncovers a scorn that boys have for girls and women, Martin concludes that boys need training in the 3Cs, educators must include caring in the curriculum for both boys and girls, and men must be educated to respect women. Otherwise we will be torn apart.[83] But, she reminds us, the reports on education in America in the 1980s to which she has already referred, and that emphasized standards and excellence, blithely ignored the 3Cs and the relationship between school and home. We can ill afford to deny the educative role of the home as we have, however, she maintains.[84] As it is, we already "reap the consequences of one sex's doubting the other's qualifications for membership in the human race."[85]

Even though women have made great gains in society, for Martin, do-

mesticity is still considered to be the role of the woman, and the continued
tracking of women into the caring professions is troubling, in part because
these fields are low-status and low-paying. Even more important, "it is a
dangerous policy to divide up society's work between the sexes in such a
way that the 3Cs of care, concern, and connection continue to be women's
responsibility when what is so desperately needed is that they become
women's and men's."[86] One of the lessons to be learned from the replica-
tion within the public world of the gendered division of labor that used to
span Virginia Woolf's two worlds "is that society has a crying need for the
occupations and practices that tradition placed in women's charge. Another
is that without a concerted effort to change the cultural assumption that
girls and women are caregivers by nature and that boys and men are not,
either women will do the major portion of society's so-called caring work
or it will not be done."[87]

The exclusion of domesticity from the curriculum sends a message of
devaluation. While some educational theorists do not, many readily forget
or underestimate the vital and unique contribution of the domestic sphere
of society and of the women who inhabit it, in Martin's view. Pestalozzi,
the Swiss educational practitioner and theorist of the late eighteenth and
early nineteenth centuries, seemed aware of it. The contribution of domesticity is emphasized in the work of Itard and Séguin in providing for the
education in basic social norms of the "Wild Boy" of Aveyron. Montessori's scrutiny of their work was surely a factor, Martin believes, in having
her recognize, in a way Dewey did not, the critical educational role of the
home. For others, however, domesticity does not rise to the level of education, even basic education.[88] Since man's resistance to domesticity is taking its toll on society, Martin claims that society will benefit if we bring
domesticity into the schools for boys and girls in the form of a subject such
as family studies.

Today's preoccupation with the so-called basics, instead of the plight of
mothers and children caught between the private world of home and the
public world of work, fits Freud's neurosis theory of displacement-
substitute, according to Martin.[89] Collective amnesia about domesticity
puts a stranglehold on educational thought, causing us to discount the term
"basic education." Fearful of things domestic, we are unable to solve the
problem of educating a generation of children left behind each morning.[90]
We need a transformation of the American schoolhouse, according to Martin, one that is premised on the remembrance of domesticity. The view is
expressed by William James, for example, that absent harshness and manly
challenge, culture will not attain the highs. This fear of femininity is un-
founded given the achievements of women, Martin maintains. Yet the mistaken belief lies at the bottom of a fierce resistance to domesticity as an
ideal of the nation, or the idea of nation as home, threatening the full
realization of the domestic tranquillity to which appeal is made in the Pre-

amble to the U.S. Constitution. Invoking Freudian theory, and her own speculations, Martin argues that the resistance to femininity is based on the reduction of women to part of brute nature and the acceptance, at least in western culture, that nature is less than human.[91]

Overstating the Case for Repression

Martin's concerns about the dismissive attitude toward domesticity, the values and activities associated with it in many facets of our culture, and its association with women, undeniably has a good deal of truth to it. The so-called manly virtues are commonly held in high esteem and those associated with women, the "weaker sex," often dismissed in a paternalistic manner. Martin draws support too from critical pedagogy where it has long been held that the structural characteristics of formal institutions of education tend to reinforce the positions of privilege enjoyed by dominant groups in society,[92] a stance consistent with her characterization of the curriculum organization favored by the elders.

The impersonalizing power of bureaucracy, moreover, leads even schools to be insensitive to the plight of individuals and unsuited to promoting and reflecting values of care and connection. Bureaucratic institutions, whether guided by goals of caring or harshness, promote values of an increasingly bureaucratized world of work. These include competition, lack of a sense of community, authoritarianism, uniformity, and a disregard for the personal feelings and aspirations of individuals. An ethos of preparation for the world of work leads schools to replicate those bureaucratic values in place of those traditionally associated with home and family. Even in regard to the subjects of the formal curriculum, public policy has long shown its preference for subjects associated with the world of economic growth and competition, such as science and mathematics, rather than those associated with personal values and feelings, such as the arts and humanities.[93]

Turning to the issue of gender relations more specifically, the findings of Best, to which Martin makes reference regarding the hostility shown toward females by males even in schools, find support elsewhere as well.[94] This suggests that Martin is correct when she diagnoses schools as sites of misogyny, where primacy of place may be given to the value of brute force over that of care and sensitivity to others. Whether our reason for omitting attention to education for living is, as Martin maintains, that we assume that family education is learned in the home, or whether we do for other reasons, the outcome may be much the same.

For these reasons the criticisms of domesticity repressed laid out by Martin are in many respects not only compelling but call for an appropriate response from the world of education. If, for whatever reason, we fail as a society to promote the 3Cs, such neglect bodes ill for all of us. At the same time, care is needed to ensure that Martin's criticisms are more rather than less accurate and that the full picture regarding the place and regard for domesticity in our culture is grasped. This is not always the case, for Martin's account sometimes shows a lack of balance and an unwillingness to consider all aspects of an issue. Martin's reluctance to listen carefully to Dewey, who also saw the school "as for the time being, a home, and not simply a place to go to learn certain things," one which is based on a view which implied such "*interest* in others as will secure responsiveness to their real needs—consideration, delicacy, etc.,"[95] is a case in point. The need to consider whether the evidence favoring the school taking over the educational role of the home is as strong as she believes it to be is another; the need to do justice to all images of home in the wider culture and its importance in our lives is yet another.

Contrary to Martin's claims, Dewey stresses the connection between home and school and sees the home as the source of values to be perpetuated and developed in the school. He also sees the school as a place to continue to grow in household activities rooted in the home: activities related to food, shelter, clothing and the like. In fact, he sees the central role of the school as one of leading the child to develop a sense of community and social service, in which respect for and service to others are guiding principles. To say that for Dewey domesticity was left out of the school, furthermore, is to slight the fact that domesticity remained in the home. Fathers may have left the home and brought their work with them into the public domain but mothers stayed at home and the home remained the center of domesticity. It is also to overlook the fact that for Dewey the values of the home should be those of the school. In "My Pedagogic Creed," Dewey wrote that "the school life should grow gradually out of the home life; that it should take up and continue the activities with which the child is already familiar in the home." He continues a little later, "a home is the form of social life in which the child has been nurtured and in connection with which he has had his moral training. It is the business of the school to deepen and extend his sense of the values bound up in his home life."[96] As long as domesticity was among those values it was a value of the school. But beyond this, Dewey also wanted many of the domestic activities of the home to take place in the school as well. Dewey actually identifies a wide range of learnings that bear a striking resemblance to the kinds of domestic activities that Martin envisages those students in *The Schoolhome* engaging in. Thus, in "Plan of Organization of the University Primary School," a work unpublished in Dewey's own lifetime, having said of the school that it is not something apart in the child's life but a home, an institution that "is intermediate between the family and other larger social organizations," he continues a little later in the same vein: "As the family is the institution with which the child is familiar, the school life must be connected as far as possible with the home life. The child should be led to consider, and to get some practical hold of, the activities which center

in the family—for example, shelter, the house itself and its structure; clothing, and its construction; food, and its preparation; as well as to deepen
and widen the ethical spirit of mutual service."[97] In what may be taken as
an appendix, Dewey provides lists giving examples of those household activities of which the child should get a practical hold.[98] Dewey, no less than
Martin, wished these to be built into the young child's experience in school.
It comes as no surprise to the reader, therefore, that having spoken of the
many potential learning opportunities that may be found in *"the ideal
home"* in *The School and Society*, Dewey goes on to say that "if we organize and generalize all of this, we have *'the ideal school'* [italics
added]."[99]

   This, clearly, is not the Dewey of which Martin speaks but even if, for
the sake of argument, one grants Martin's claim that Dewey showed little
interest in domesticity as an educational goal, her broader point is still open
to debate. Martin's criticism of Dewey and others such as Kilpatrick is not
merely that they do not perceive the crucial role of domesticity, as Montessori does, but that they furthermore fail to locate such education for
domesticity in the school. Since she is convinced by the work of Montessori,
and of Itard and Séguin, that this education can be achieved in schools,
Dewey and others she feels should be similarly convinced. This is an especially tall order given Martin's own declaration of the unsuitability of
schools and how horrible their record has been in this regard. How, it must
be asked, can she now suddenly have faith in schools to do what schools
as well as homes increasingly fail to do, namely, educate for family living
or the 3Cs? Is the evidence brought by Montessori and Itard and Séguin
this compelling? Perhaps *The Schoolhome* will hold the answer.

   Martin's charge that Dewey overlooked domesticity, when he clearly advocated forms of domestic education that are essentially identical to many
of those advocated by Martin herself, raises a related matter, namely, the
fact that Martin's own concept of domesticity is less than definitive. One
can distinguish between at least two distinct versions of the idea, a narrow
and a broad. In its narrow sense, as found for example in that passage in
The Schoolhome where she is detailing the kinds of domestic tasks she sees
the students performing, from diapering infants and washing the dishes to
repair-work and groundskeeping, domesticity is defined in terms of the
largely routine and somewhat mechanical, if social, activities of housekeeping.[100] It is this characterization of domesticity that is akin to the one held
by Dewey but which she denies in his case amounts to domesticity. Yet in
elaborating the broader sense of domesticity, she also seems to tacitly recognize it: in its broader sense, domesticity is conceived in *The Schoolhome*
as "a fusion of the love Montessori built into her idea of school and the
social activity that Dewey built into his."[101] Here the 3Cs and an atmosphere of nurturing are emphasized as they are in "Women, Schools, and
Cultural Wealth," and added to the skill-based activities of housekeeping.

What, it may be asked, are the social activities of Dewey that she refers to? Are these not the domestic activities of cooking and household maintenance that when advocated by Martin amount to an expression of domesticity in its narrower sense but when advocated by Dewey are considered to fall short of this mark? It would appear so.

It could perhaps be objected by Martin that, unlike her, Dewey wanted to lead the young beyond or away from home and family, that he had no real interest in home other than it being a starting point for further growth of the individual. Yet growth of the individual for Dewey meant growth as a member of the social group, a cooperative and civil society, where there was respect for all. It was to approximate a state of domestic peace and tranquillity, you might say, and rather than leading away from home or family, may be seen as extending family, which after all is Martin's goal too. Since it is only with domesticity understood in the broader sense that Martin's accusation against Dewey holds water, if at all, it suggests that for her the broader sense is the more important and more fundamental meaning that she has in mind. It is from domesticity understood in the broader sense, moreover, that much of the force of Martin's work derives. Yet both uses are prevalent throughout her writings.

There is a further and perhaps more important aspect of Dewey's position from which Martin detracts attention: in suggesting that it is the role of the school to build upon the values children bring from the home, in "My Pedagogic Creed," Dewey appears to assume a universality of home values. Given the great variety and outright conflict among different configurations of home values that exist today, such a belief is naïve. To expect schools to act supportively of all values rather than acknowledging and attempting to deal as may be seen fit with the range of conflicting values that do exist, is to mislead. The values that some homes wittingly or unwittingly promote—values such as abuse, violence, and neglect—may well be open to question, and any reliance such as Dewey's upon the home to teach the "right" values may be misplaced. If this is so, it raises the question of what needs to be done educationally to deal with this difficulty. It also raises the question of which values of home and family living should be taught.

Asking what needs to be done educationally embraces more than schools, a point that Martin often overlooks in *The Schoolhome* in her willingness to assign so many tasks of education and socialization to the school. Options are actually considered by Martin herself in "Women, Schools, and Cultural Wealth" and at greater length in *Cultural Miseducation*, where she recognizes the possibility of excess in *The Schoolhome*. For now it is sufficient to say on this point that Martin's own conceptualization of the schoolhome as the educational provider almost without limit is in need of correction. But if it is, so also is her position in relation to which home values are to be taught by the school. She conveys the impression that we all know what the good home is, yet she is reluctant to spell it out. This may be because she also wants to recognize different models of the good home. In the process she raises more questions than she solves when she pursues this latter option, as we shall see presently.

Turning to Martin's portrayal of home in literature, flight from home has been hailed in literature for sure. But so have the virtues of home life and family living. A short list of such writings includes *Little House on the Prairie, Johnny Appleseed, Where the Red Fern Grows*, to which may be added a wide range of children's literature. Turning a little further afield, *Pride and Prejudice* and *King Lear* come to mind, and where has a longing for home ever been captured more powerfully than in *A Christmas Carol* when we hear the young Scrooge in the presence of the Ghost of Christmas Past cry out, "home, home, home, home is like heaven"? Movies and TV programs in a similar tradition include, *The Wizard of Oz*, where Dorothy repeatedly exclaims, "There's no place like home," *It's a Wonderful Life, Miracle on 34th Street, The Brady Bunch*, and *Little House on the Prairie*. Flight from home as a sociocultural phenomenon is a reality, of course, but so also is the longing for home as borne out by people in large numbers actually living in homes and even returning to home having been away. It is also reflected in such popular songs as "God Bless America," "Home on the Range," "I'll Be Home for Christmas," and "There's No Place Like Home for the Holidays."

Martin is also unduly dismissive of the positive perceptions of the role of the school in relation to home in our culture, as when she claims that no one was listening when John Goodlad and Sarah Lawrence Lightfoot were stressing that "the schoolhouse must be a kind of home."[102] Already we have seen Dewey speak of the school in terms of home and Martin surely knows full well the principle, long revered, that schools act in loco parentis. In universities and colleges, too, the role of the residence hall or, in English universities, the college, follows an established role in this regard. Newman saw the college as a home away from home, a place of emotional, moral, and religious grounding while students were undergoing the rigors of a liberal education.[103] Even the very term "homecoming" tells a tale, one in which, for example, the alma mater—itself a motherly image—is seen as home.

Martin is erroneous, too, in saying that recent reports on education neglect the home, even if she is correct that the emphasis has been on standards, academics, assessment and results, and economic competition. A notable feature of the public debate on education in the United States in recent years, even as political bipartisanship came under severe pressure in educational policy matters, was the attention given to the goals of education. These included improving educational and nutritional programs for young children, attending to the recreational needs of youth, and promoting positive relations between parents and schools. Such goals were actually included in *Goals 2000*, the landmark education bill signed into law in 1994. Activities in support of these and other goals advanced by *Goals 2000* included provisions for partnerships between schools and parents. The same is true of the commitment in *Goals 2000* that all children enter school ready to learn, based in part upon satisfactory nutritional and health care provisions.[104] School breakfasts also bespeak awareness on the part of governments and schools about the changing circumstances of homes. And while some object to these and to programs in sex education and "sex intervention" programs such as condom availability in school, they do at the least give the lie to accusations that governments and schools show no interest in such family life matters.

In his State of the Union Address on January 27, 2000, President Clinton went a step further, making two specifically pro-family commitments: he emphasized the twin aspirations that all families succeed at home and that there be support for the work of families through health care and education support.[105] Nor were these lone rhetorical outbursts. His personal failings aside, they were consistent with his administration's general policies of support for education, health care, people from minority populations in general, and the less well-off. Republicans for their part have not wished to be outdone in making their claims to favor family values. In his Inaugural Address, President George W. Bush himself emphasized to an unusual degree the notion of nation as a caring family to which everyone belongs, affirming "a new commitment to live out our nation's promise through civility, courage, compassion and character."[106] It may be countered that these are but ploys to curry favor and that politically inspired measures to bring about improvement in such areas as health care and medical insurance may not be as satisfactory or as heartily embraced as one would wish. Yet the debate has been joined. It may be politically motivated in whole or in part, but to overlook or deny it entirely in this context as Martin does is quite another matter altogether.

Domesticity for All

Before concluding her Presidential Address to the Philosophy of Education Society in 1981, Martin suggested that philosophy of education may be enriched as a field if it were to follow a broader agenda, one that includes issues such as the reproductive processes and a range of practical matters. The following year, in "Excluding Women from the Educational Realm," she returned to this theme. The remedy for the narrow intellectualism contained in Peters's conception of the educated person, she now wrote, is unavailable as long as the criterion for what falls within the educational realm "mirrors the distinction between the productive and reproductive processes of society."[107] Since such criteria are determined, or in Martin's view ought to be determined, by the purposes sought after by educators, it is a cause of concern to her that criteria pertaining to the reproductive processes in society seem never to occur to them. She elaborated further on what she sees as the relevant criteria in "The Radical Future of Gender Enrichment." Drawing attention once more to the centrality of goals in education, Martin writes,[108]

> It has been said that "the stated goals of education in modern democratic societies remain constant: the development of each person as (a) a worker, (b) a citizen, and (c) an individual" (Waks and Roy 1987, p. 24). A case for adding (d) a keeper of the cultural heritage can be made, but the list with this emendation seems correct. To be sure, the four goals are not given equal time in every discussion of education. Still, together they represent the full range of what education is expected to do. That these expectations fail to take account of a basic function of education in a modern or postmodern society, namely (e), the development of each person as a member of a home and family, escapes everyone's notice.

In her critique of Hirst's theory of a liberal education, claiming that education ought to be concerned with the development of a person—and not just a mind—Martin had argued that Hirst's theory was incomplete.[109] It needed to be supplemented in a number of ways, she argued, such as through initiation into various skills of making and doing, by allowing room for feelings to flourish, and a commitment to moral action.[110] To these she now adds (e), the development of students as members of a family. Now the focus is also different. In the article on Hirst, Martin was dealing with the conceptual issue of what constituted a suitable form of education. Here she is dealing with how such an idea can be realized in a changed world, in which women in large numbers work in the public domain yet still do the work of the home as well. Some can afford to withdraw from work in the public world but others cannot, and for some women the burden of working in both worlds is becoming unbearable.[111] And so, as a consequence of women joining men in working outside the home, homes generally are no longer in a position to teach children about family. The question comes up, then: where does the responsibility to do so lie?

In answering this question, Martin follows the lead of Dewey when he argued that change in the home and society must be accompanied by corresponding change in the school: schools can afford no longer to shirk the responsibility to deal with the issue. Living in a different age, she sees herself as going beyond Dewey, and concludes that teaching children about family must be done in the schools if we are to fill the "domestic vacuum" caused by the removal of work from the home that requires both parents to leave the home. Changing homes are not up to teaching about family.[112] She recognizes that the odds against success are enormous, not just because schools have traditionally focused upon education for the public domain, but because they are permeated with male dominated values, to the detriment of females, males themselves, and domesticity. Martin is quite blunt about it: from kindergarten through graduate school, education is gender-related, and the traits acquired in education that are most highly valued in society are genderized in favor of men and to the disadvantage of women. If we are ever to promote education that integrates reason and emotion, as does education in domesticity, she maintains, the challenge will be huge, and we need to change our value hierarchy, especially since men will need to acquire traits now genderized in favor of women.

In today's world this is a double negative for men. Not only will they feel abnormal for acquiring traits normally associated with females, Martin holds, but these traits are also seen as having little or no value, a humiliation that women are spared when they have to acquire traits genderized in favor of males.[113] Today's pro-male, pro-productive value structure is reflected not only in our ideal of the educated person but also in the curriculum. Priority is given to male experience in school subjects, as was already argued by Martin in her analysis of Peters's idea of the educated man and of the disciplines as curriculum content. It recurs in "Becoming Educated: A Journey of Alienation or Integration?" in which she examines the potentially alienating effects of education itself. Likewise, *Coming of Age in Academe* provides an extended exposé of her view that even in the academy the most invidious distinctions take place involving the subjects traditionally associated with women, such as nursing, home economics, and education.[114]

Tackling this problem of pro-male bias in schooling calls for a redefinition of the educated person, and the traits generally associated with women in our minds—notably the 3Cs—need to be included in any such redefinition, Martin asserts.[115] Such thinking needs to be reflected in the curriculum by an integration of the productive and reproductive processes and values rather than by splitting them apart, for "the general problem to be solved is that of uniting thought and action, reason and emotions, self and other. This was the problem Dewey addressed, but his failure to understand the workings of gender made it impossible for him to solve it."[116] As long as women remain invisible in the educational realm, moreover, Martin adds, we cannot adequately answer the question of what constitutes an educated person.[117] When the academy discriminates against women, and the study of women's issues and domesticity, it simply bears out this point.

Understating the Prospects for Domesticity

If one grants as Martin does that there is more to life than the academic disciplines and the public world of work, the inclusion of goal (e), the development of each person as a member of a home and family among the goals of education, makes good sense. Almost everyone lives in homes and families and the values of care, concern, and connection associated with them even have applicability well beyond the boundaries of home. That one needs education to acquire the knowledge and skills associated with these values also appears evident and lends further weight to Martin's argument for their inclusion in the education of all. It is, of course, a separate matter whether such a goal should be established for schooling, a point easily overlooked because of Martin's general failure to distinguish more clearly between education and schooling in her writings prior to those dealing with her cultural wealth thesis, notably *Cultural Miseducation*.

Martin's argument for assigning goal (e) to schools, in part, is that with both parents working outside the home it has become a necessity. That the landscape of education in both schools and homes has been utterly transformed by the fact that both parents now commonly work outside the home is beyond dispute. Martin is correct in concluding that the implications for education, and especially family life education, are considerable, and call for a reassessment of how we attend to them. She is correct also in arguing that both boys and girls should be educated for family life and the 3Cs in general, and throughout her various writings she makes a powerful case to this effect. One of the difficulties associated with this argument, of course, is the one to which she has just pointed, namely, the difficulty of educating males in the attitudes and skills of domesticity normally associated with females. The conclusion to which she is led in regard to the concept of the educated person is also persuasive, namely, that if we are ever to stand a chance of success in this broad enterprise, we need a redefinition of the educated person. Here, too, Martin has begun to provide such a redefinition, beginning as early as her responses to the ideas of Hirst and Peters and developing them especially in *The Schoolhome*, "The Radical Future of Gender Enrichment," and "Women, Schools, and Cultural Wealth." Central to this redefinition is a concept of education that joins thought and action, reason and emotion. Martin and others have made a strong case that the lives and experiences of girls and women have been overlooked in education while those of men have been emphasized and that this may have led to unequal and even harmful education for females. Granted the priority given to men's experience in education, it is ironic, therefore, that Martin may also be right in suggesting that only by giving due recognition to the lives and experiences of girls and women may we ever be in a position to develop such a holistic concept of education.

In arguing as she has along these lines, however, Martin has inadvertently exacerbated rather than eased the task of finding a solution to the very considerable problem she articulates so well. Once again it is because of a tendency to become selective and lose balance in the analysis. In this instance it has led her to highlight the obstacles and impediments while losing sight of all those rich sources of tackling the problem that lie before our very eyes. These are to be found in the history and literature of educational thought and in present-day professional practice. They provide a substantial, if hitherto underrated, foundation upon which to begin to fashion a solution, a building block to which contemporary feminist theory and women's advocates such as Martin have much to add.

As Martin's treatment highlights those features of our culture, be they in literature, education, or patterns of social behavior, in which domesticity is downplayed or rejected, she conceals potential sources of support for her very own ideals of mutual affection and domesticity in that minorstream tradition of educational thought to which she greatly contributes herself.[118] Such sources include the writings of Rousseau, which Martin does recognize, where the emphasis is upon education in feeling and emotions, physical dexterity and practical skill, and self-reliance. They include the educational ideas of Herbert Spencer, who decried the lack of attention given to education for the tasks of everyday living, including those of parenting. They include the pioneering work of Catharine Beecher in the field of home economics, work with which Martin herself is more than familiar, and which further highlights the domestic dimension in education. They include the balanced and carefully crafted appeals of Horace Mann for a system of public education that pays attention to education for what Martin terms the reproductive processes as well as the productive processes in society. This is clearly manifest as his keen awareness of the values of personal health and interpersonal and community relations, for example. A similar strain is found, if less emphasized and less well-justified, in *Cardinal Principles of Secondary Education*, in the attention given to education for health and worthy home membership for boys and girls. Such thinking is put on a more solid footing in the work of Florence Stratemeyer and her colleagues, where many such matters are dealt with more systematically and comprehensively.[119] Advances both in theory and practice in the cluster of student services sometimes labeled pastoral care, including health education, sex education, the varied work of school counseling, and cooperation between schools and social workers, also testify to a greater attention to education for domesticity than Martin is willing to recognize in schools and such agencies today. It is true that among them, all of these advances and supportive points of view may not ensure that sufficient attention is given to domesticity. There undoubtedly is still a way to go to combat a mentality that, for example, excludes domesticity from such recognized, if faulty, measures of educational achievement as SAT tests. This is to say nothing of the crucial omission of goal (e), the development of each person as a member of a home and family, from Martin's list of the commonly stated goals of schooling pursued in our society today.

Failure to recognize the advances that have been made may blind one to the possibilities that they hold out for greater successes down the road and serve to further a self-fulfilling prophesy that all is nearly lost. It may also lead one to overlook the likelihood that the forces of violence and anti-domesticity that pervade our society, and that operate for profit almost without conscience or control through our systems of mass communication, will still be at work. They will not simply cease to exist once the task of family life education, as Martin suggests, is passed on to the school. Despite concrete physical evidence of the ill effects of smoking, fighting the tobacco lobby has been long and tortuous. Imagine the struggle, fully recognized by Martin herself in *Cultural Miseducation*, to conquer the purveyors of media violence and abuse where psychological evidence and argumentation may be all that there is to go on. Thus the question arises, what is to be done to counter these forces of media influence which families today struggle often in vain to resist, and what difference will it make whether family-life education takes place within the home or the school if they remain untouched? Martin's answer in *Cultural Miseducation* and elsewhere is in turning the spotlight of public opinion upon them so that by legitimizing them as educational agencies they would henceforth be held accountable for what they transmit, as other educational agencies are. Whether this is true or not, as Giroux has drawn to our attention, it still leaves unchecked the impact of the many and insidious media and other powerful influences in our culture that take particular aim at our youth.[120]

One especially important example of Martin's failure to recognize advances in line with her wishes for connection, care, and concern is her response to the call of the elders for a common curriculum, which she dismisses as a call for sameness for all, combined with a lack of inclusiveness. The sameness that Martin speaks of may be seen as a byproduct of the kind of curriculum that Hirsch, for example, advocated in much the same way as it would be a byproduct of Hirst's curriculum or that proposed by Adler.[121] But while these theorists advocate varying forms of a common curriculum for all, they do not do so just to achieve sameness, at least in the sense of "identical student product." Indeed, Adler is confident that the individuality of students will lead to different responses in each.[122] The intent is to promote a common knowledge and set of understandings, among other goals. This common knowledge and understandings are seen as promoting communication among peoples, surely a desideratum in any community wishing to stay together, as was argued in regard to the community of scholars in C.P. Snow's celebrated *The Two Cultures*.[123] Accordingly, for Martin to cast the issue as one of sameness, lack of inclusiveness, and even domination is to do an injustice to the elders. To be sure, she is correct in arguing that student abilities, interests, aptitudes, and backgrounds need to be taken into account, and likewise that the content of the curriculum ought to reflect such differences so well articulated by Martin herself, by allowing for a rich and diverse range of cultural experiences to be included. But for Martin to portray the issue of sameness as exclusively an attempt at exclusion or the shaping of a uniform kind of student outcome regardless of the cultural and socioeconomic background of students is misguided. It is to dismiss possibilities for unification of people from different social and economic backgrounds that may come from understanding and discussion of at least a core of common curriculum content. As a consequence, it dismisses the potential for unification that a unified curriculum may bring with it in much the same way as does her inclination in *Cultural Miseducation* to drop the idea of a common curriculum for all,[124] and it insinuates a false dichotomy between internal integration and outward connection. Rather than furthering the cause of social connection, arguing against commonality in the curriculum runs the risk once again of overlooking possibilities for achieving these goals wherever they exist.

For Martin to cast the issue as one of sameness, moreover, is to play with slogans. To add that the sameness being promoted is dismissive of women and women's interests is not only to attach the gender issue to a lame cause. It is also to overlook the fact that a curriculum that entails substantial commonality for all is essentially what Martin herself advocates when she calls for a gender-sensitive education. While she is far from committed on the question of a common curriculum in *Cultural Miseducation*, in *The Schoolhome*, where she dismisses the importance of commonality based upon bits and bodies of knowledge, she still rejoices in the thought of a commonality based on attitudes, skills, and values.[125] The commonality of curriculum for both boys and girls that Martin once appeared to favor required some differentiation for boys and girls. She was never explicit on what the differences should be but intimated that they would be minor if crucial. Given her interest in a gender-sensitive model of education, however, it now becomes imperative for her to spell out more fully than she has how this ideal can be sustained in the absence of a curriculum that is at least partially common for all students.

Moving beyond the issue of gender equality to that of cultural equality, Martin's treatment of the case of Rodriguez, to which she assigns considerable importance, illustrates a certain cultural insensitivity on Martin's own part. Few will question the veracity of the account given by Rodriguez of the pain and loss he suffered through his academic education, notwithstanding the fact that he does value these successes and claims himself that the loss of identity was worth the other accomplishment. It is, nonetheless, the response of just one student. There are others similar to Rodriguez whose response to the kind of education he received might not include the feelings of alienation he experienced. It might be welcomed instead as a source of great connection to new worlds never dreamt of before, of new friends made, and of a heightened sense of family and family pride and connection. One cannot ignore individual cases of pain, of course; neither does pointing out counter examples mean that one is insensitive to the kind of loss and pain of which Martin and Rodriguez speak. Yet Martin's use of the Rodriguez case poses as many difficulties for her desire to give over to the school the task of education for domesticity as it resolves. It leads one to ask, for example, would the school attended by Rodriguez—be it day school, boarding school, or college—have eased the pain he felt—or that of other students in his place—and heightened his connection to family and its cultural roots if it embraced the stance adopted by Martin when she writes in "The Radical Future of Gender Enrichment" that she is "not presupposing any particular type of home and family." Then she continues, "lesbian families, interracial families, stepfamilies, single parent ones: whatever the type, education is needed for life therein."[126]

While the stance adopted by Martin in regard to the different kinds of families she identifies may be admirable for its inclusiveness, it nonetheless betrays a certain insensitivity to those whose cultural roots and moral and religious beliefs, for example, may differ from Martin's. Even allowing for the respect of persons and families of different lifestyles, the question arises as to who decides how a public school is to proceed in such matters, for one may respect others without accepting or agreeing with their lifestyle. Do the parents, for whom the circumstances of a particular single parent family may be the determining factor in judging its acceptability as a lifestyle on moral grounds, decide? Or, as in the case of Rodriguez's academic education, does the school decide such matters? If the school is the one to decide, what would be its stance on the moral and cultural issues raised, and consequences that arise for any young Rodriguez, given his particular family and moral beliefs? More specific aspects of these broader questions, and the controversy that surrounds them, arise in schools across the country every day. The question that arises in regard to the distribution of condoms in school, and whether parents or schools decide, is a case in point. If the school makes that decision instead of parents, what does it do to the goal of heightened parental involvement in the family-life education of their children and the furtherance of their family values? And what about the question of religious formation: are public schools to proceed as if it is not an issue at all, that it is one area where parental neglect need not be addressed in school? Or, conversely, would this neglect be the one case where the schools should provide a religious education?[127]

One thing we may be sure of: if the school takes over the educational work of the home, questions such as those just raised are inescapable. Yet these are but a preview of the difficulties that Martin is now running into. Martin's reluctance throughout to indicate particular values by which the school curriculum is to be shaped, though she does indicate some, also creates difficulties for her position. Here, for example, in discussing the home, she maintains that she is not presupposing any particular type of home or family. As she puts it, "whatever the type, education is needed for life therein." Notwithstanding the criteria of loving environment, sexual equality, and nonviolence that she lays down for an acceptable family, given what she has argued all along about the importance of education for living in the home and family, to suggest now that the type of family does not matter is less than helpful. If the type of family does not matter, what is the point of her entire thesis? The particular types of family and home that she identifies might not pose problems but what about those she does not give examples of, types that may or may not abide by the criteria of acceptability she delineates: uneducated, drunken and disorderly, drug-infested, incompetent? It is equally unhelpful to say that whatever the type of family or home, "education is needed for life therein." It surely is. But what matters is the type of education to be offered, the goals by which it is to be shaped, and the values of home to which it is committed. When politicians say they favor family values, the question on everyone's lips is: which family values? Having emphasized that "Montessori did not model her school on just any home,"[128] Martin herself now balks and suddenly finds she is in awkward disagreement.[129]

CONCLUSION

However tentatively Martin addresses the question of the home values to be promoted, it must be recognized that in even raising this question she is taking a bold stand. Many hold vehemently and as a matter of principle that the school has no business dictating the values of the home. Martin does not dwell upon such potential criticisms. For her the evidence of abuse and violence which she finds pervasive in contemporary society, the enormous impediment to providing adequately for education in domesticity presented by large-scale evacuation of working women as well as men from the home, and the benefits which she believes derived from the intervention of Montessori in the rearing and education of poor children in the San Lorenzo Quarter of Rome, all make the case for her stand. As a result, perhaps she over-generalizes that family living or the proper rearing of the young has been ignored in the home just because it is now neglected in some or even many homes. Perhaps she overlooks too that to require a greater role for the school may serve to remove all responsibility or sense of obligation from neglectful parents to attend to the rearing and education of their children.

Yet there can be little doubt that in highlighting the importance of domesticity, of the values of caring for others, showing concern for others, and connecting with others—not merely as a matter of principle but in action—Martin is pinpointing a critical issue for our twenty-first century society. One thing is for sure: there are serious difficulties of practice as well as principle raised here. As Martin herself points out, not only theorists of liberal education but schools themselves tend to focus on theoretical education not practical, giving support to those who have argued that schools simply are not well-suited to providing many forms of moral or practical education. Even by Martin's own admission, moreover, schools are themselves serious perpetrators of abuse, especially toward girls and women. She has also made it clear that at least in some respects schools have even come to adopt an anti-home agenda.

Even those who favor supplementing the academic role of the school will recognize that her stance raises serious questions for Martin herself. It remains to be seen when we turn to her proposals for a gender-sensitive education, and her treatment of what she has termed the new problem of curriculum, if she herself can provide fuller direction in answering them.

NOTES

1. Jane Roland Martin, *Changing the Educational Landscape: Philosophy, Women, and Curriculum* (New York: Routledge, 1994) 70–87. This essay was Martin's Presidential Address to the Philosophy of Education Society in 1981 and was originally published as "The Ideal of the Educated Person," *Educational Theory* 31 (Spring 1981): 97–109.

2. In her later work, Martin prefers to use the phrase "public world of work, politics, and the professions" in place of "productive processes of society." See Martin, *Changing the Educational Landscape* 13–14 and Jane Roland Martin, "Women, Schools, and Cultural Wealth," *Women's Philosophies of Education*, eds. Connie Titone and Karen E. Moloney (Upper Saddle River, NJ: Merrill/Prentice-Hall, 1999) 155.

3. Martin, *Changing the Educational Landscape* 13, 79, 116.

4. Martin, *Changing the Educational Landscape* 79–80, 209; Jane Roland Martin, *Reclaiming a Conversation: The Ideal of the Educated Woman* (New Haven, CT: Yale University Press, 1985) 194–195.

5. Martin, *Changing the Educational Landscape* 36.

6. Martin, *Changing the Educational Landscape* 38.

7. Martin, *Changing the Educational Landscape* 35–52; especially 36–39. See also Jane Roland Martin, "Bringing Women into Educational Thought," *Educational Theory* 34 (Fall 1984): 341–345.

8. Martin, *Changing the Educational Landscape*, 41; and Martin, "Women, Schools, and Cultural Wealth" 157.

9. See Martin, *Changing the Educational Landscape* 42–45, where Martin bolsters her argument by reference to what she considers different kinds of teaching engaged in by Gertrude in Pestalozzi's *Leonard and Gertrude*. See Johann Heinrich Pestalozzi, *Leonard and Gertrude*, trans. Eva Channing (Boston: D.C. Heath, 1891). See also Martin, "Women, Schools, and Cultural Wealth" 151–152.

10. Martin, *Changing the Educational Landscape* 47–48. See also Carol Gilligan, *In a Different Voice* (Cambridge, MA: Harvard University Press, 1982) for a consideration of the case of psychology.

11. See Robin Barrow, *Plato and Education* (London: Routledge and Kegan Paul, 1976) and any of a number of treatments of Plato's educational thought, such as Gerald L. Gutek, *Historical and Philosophical Foundations of Education* (Upper Saddle River, NJ: Prentice-Hall, 2001) 9–26; Edward J. Power, *A Legacy of Learn-*

ing (Albany, NY: State University of New York Press, 1991) 29–37; and Henry J. Perkinson, *Since Socrates* (New York: Longman, 1980) 14–30. See also, of course, Plato, *The Republic*, trans. Benjamin Jowett (New York: Airmont, 1968).

12. Martin, *Reclaiming a Conversation* 12–17

13. Martin, *Reclaiming a Conversation* 17–23.

14. Martin, *Reclaiming a Conversation* 26.

15. Martin, *Reclaiming a Conversation* 26–34. Martin's reference to the experience of Rosalind Franklin, 31–34, is especially helpful.

16. Martin, *Reclaiming a Conversation*, especially 19–20; and Martin, "Bringing Women into Educational Thought" 341–343.

17. Martin, *Changing the Educational Landscape* 53–69; and Martin, *Reclaiming a Conversation* 38–69.

18. Martin, *Changing the Educational Landscape* 66.

19. Martin, *Changing the Educational Landscape* 61–66; and Martin, *Reclaiming a Conversation* 38–43, 47.

20. Martin, *Reclaiming a Conversation* 38–53.

21. Further, by removing the young boy from his own mother—a Sophie mother-figure—at a young age, he was deprived of such learnings. Thus the education of the citizen is impossible, since the crucial input of the Sophie mother-figure is ignored. Martin also elaborates in different ways on how the ideal state, or a general will, cannot be achieved either, because of the manipulative powers over Emile that Rousseau gives to Sophie and her lack of capacity to recognize the general will. See Martin, *Reclaiming a Conversation* 53–69.

22. See especially R.S. Peters, "Education and the Educated Man," *Education and the Development of Reason*, eds. R.F. Dearden, P.H. Hirst, and R.S. Peters (London: Routledge and Kegan Paul, 1972) 3–18. See also Jane Roland Martin, "Transforming Moral Education," *Journal of Moral Education* 16 (October 1987): 204–213.

23. Martin is not alone in characterizing Peters's concept of the educated man as representing a dominant viewpoint. See also Eleanor Kallman-Roemer, "Harm and the Ideal of the Educated Person: Response to Jane Roland Martin," *Educational Theory* 31 (Spring 1981): 117.

24. Martin, *Changing the Educational Landscape* 74.

25. See, for example, *Gender In/forms Curriculum*, eds. Jane Gaskell and John Willinsky (New York: Teachers College Press, 1995).

26. Martin, *Changing the Educational Landscape* 77.

27. Martin, *Changing the Educational Landscape* 170–186.

28. Martin, *Changing the Educational Landscape* 79.

29. Martin, *Changing the Educational Landscape* 80.

30. Jane Roland Martin, *The Schoolhome: Rethinking Schools for Changing Families* (Cambridge, MA: Harvard University Press, 1992) 140.

31. Martin, *The Schoolhome* 80–81. See also Martin, *Changing the Educational Landscape* 154–169.

32. See, for example, James McClellan, "Response to Jane Martin," *Educational Theory* 31 (Spring 1981): 111–114; Kallman-Roemer, "Harm and the Ideal of the Educated Person" 115–124; Harvey Siegel, "Genderized Cognitive Perspectives and the Redefinition of Philosophy of Education," *Teachers College Record* 85 (Fall 1983): 100–119; J.C. Walker and M.A. O'Loughlin, "The Ideal of the Educated

Woman: Jane Roland Martin on Education and Gender," *Educational Theory* 34 (Fall 1984): 327–340; and Hilary E. Davis, "Docile Bodies and Disembodied Minds," *Educational Theory* 46 (Fall 1996): 525–543.

33. In the light of Martin's insistence on women and their views on education being excluded from the educational realm, it is noteworthy that the kind of objections to the notion of cognitive perspective, whether male or otherwise, raised by both McClellan and Siegel have not been similarly addressed to Peters's, from whose original usage Martin adapts it. See, for example, *Beyond Liberal Education*, eds. Robin Barrow and Patricia White (London: Routledge, 1993).

34. McClellan, "Response to Jane Martin" 113.

35. Siegel, "Genderized Cognitive Perspectives" 102–105. For Martin's own interpretation of Siegel's criticism here, and a response to critics of her analyses of Hirst and Peters and her approach to doing philosophy of education, see Martin, *Changing the Educational Landscape* 7–8.

36. Siegel, "Genderized Cognitive Perspectives" 106.

37. Siegel, "Genderized Cognitive Perspectives" 107–108. Martin's assessment of Siegel's criticisms can be found in Martin, *Changing the Educational Landscape*, 11.

38. Siegel, "Genderized Cognitive Perspectives" 111.

39. Siegel, "Genderized Cognitive Perspectives" 112–114.

40. See Martin, *Changing the Educational Landscape* 7. For a helpful discussion of difficulties that arise and a possible solution when the one person is placed in a situation in which conflicting gender expectations arise, see the discussion of educational criticism and nurturance in Ann Diller et al., *The Gender Question in Education: Theory, Pedagogy, and Politics* (Boulder, CO: Westview Press, 1996), 135–143.

41. In this connection, see Martin, *Changing the Educational Landscape* 43–45. See also Harvey Siegel, "Israel Scheffler," *Fifty Modern Thinkers on Education: From Piaget to the Present*, ed. Joy A. Palmer (London: Routledge, 2001) 146–147.

42. See McClellan, "Response to Jane Martin" 113; and Siegel, "Genderized Cognitive Perspectives" 112.

43. Siegel, "Genderized Cognitive Perspectives" 106. See also Ursula A. Kelly, " 'The Feminist Trespass': Gender, Literature, and Curriculum," *Gender In/forms Curriculum*, 96–108; and Jane Bernard-Powers, "Out of the Cameos and Into the Conversation: Gender, Social Studies, and Curriculum Transformation," *Gender In/forms Curriculum* 191–208. Of particular interest here is the fact that when female-friendly content is introduced, the performance of females tends to improve; see especially 198–199.

44. Mary Field Belenky et al., *Women's Ways of Knowing* (New York: Basic Books, 1986) 198.

45. Peters, "Education and the Educated Man" 15.

46. McClellan, "Response to Jane Martin" 113.

47. See, for example, Martin, *Changing the Educational Landscape* 133–153, 170–186, and 212–227.

48. Martin, *Changing the Educational Landscape* 175. In this connection, see Lionel Elvin, *The Place of Commonsense in Educational Thought* (London: Allen and Unwin, 1977) 52–53.

49. A specific example of such selectivity is found in Martin, *Reclaiming a Con-*

versation 190, where Martin writes, "Yet Plato designs for his guardians an education of heads, not hands. (Presumably the artisans of the Just State will serve as their hands.)" She overlooks that part of Plato's educational design where the future guardian had the same education as the artisan; to the extent this included an education of the hands for the artisan, it did likewise for the guardian. See Jane Roland Martin, "Redefining the Educated Person: Rethinking the Significance of Gender," *Educational Researcher* 15 (June/July 1986): 7; and Jane Roland Martin, "Reforming Teacher Education, Rethinking Liberal Education," *Teachers College Record* 88 (Spring 1987): 406, where she retains the same position.

50. See Bruce A. Kimball, *Orators and Philosophers: A History of the Idea of Liberal Education* (New York: Teachers College Press, 1986).

51. Philip H. Phenix, *Realms of Meaning* (New York: McGraw-Hill, 1964), especially 196; see also 193–211.

52. Martin, "Women, Schools, and Cultural Wealth" 163; Phenix, *Realms of Meaning* 196.

53. This emphasis is highlighted in Jane Roland Martin, "Home and Family," *Philosophy of Education: An Encyclopedia*, ed. J.J. Chambliss (New York: Garland, 1996) 275.

54. Martin, *The Schoolhome* 157–159.

55. See, for example, *Connecticut's Common Core of Learning* (Hartford, CT: Connecticut State Board of Education, 1999), especially 1–8 and 21–28.

56. Martin, *Reclaiming a Conversation* 58–61; Martin, *Changing the Educational Landscape* 205, 206.

57. See Martin, *The Schoolhome* 123–135.

58. Martin, *The Schoolhome* 132–133.

59. Martin, *The Schoolhome* 126. See also Martin, "Home and Family" 276–277.

60. Martin, *The Schoolhome* 120–135.

61. Martin, *The Schoolhome* 123–127; see also 127–135.

62. Martin, *The Schoolhome* 140–141.

63. Martin, *The Schoolhome* 149.

64. Martin, *The Schoolhome* 136.

65. Martin, *The Schoolhome* 141–149.

66. Martin, *The Schoolhome* 148.

67. Martin, *The Schoolhome* 121–122; Martin, "Women, Schools, and Cultural Wealth" 158, 161.

68. See, for example, Martin, "Women, Schools, and Cultural Wealth" 159–162; Jane Roland Martin, "There's Too Much to Teach: Cultural Wealth in an Age of Scarcity," *Educational Researcher* 25.2 (1996): 9–10; Martin, *The Schoolhome* 153–154; and Martin, *Changing the Educational Landscape* 232–233.

69. Martin, "Women, Schools, and Cultural Wealth" 164, 159–164; Martin, *The Schoolhome* 46.

70. Martin, *The Schoolhome* 137.

71. Martin, *The Schoolhome* 137.

72. Jane Roland Martin, *Coming of Age in Academe: Rekindling Women's Hopes and Reforming the Academy* (New York: Routledge, 2000) 53.

73. Martin, *Changing the Educational Landscape* 225. See also Martin, *The Schoolhome* 67.

74. Martin, *The Schoolhome* 51–52, 69–70.

75. Diller et al., *The Gender Question in Education* 105–122.

76. Martin, *The Schoolhome* 118. See also Martin, "Women, Schools, and Cultural Wealth" 166–167.

77. Martin, *Changing the Educational Landscape* 202.

78. Martin, *Changing the Educational Landscape* 210–211.

79. Martin, *The Schoolhome* 127–135; Martin, *Changing the Educational Landscape* 211.

80. Martin, *Coming of Age in Academe* 48–49.

81. While there is good reason to believe that domestic violence may be the most widespread form of violence experienced by women, there is not the same level of agreement that men are the major perpetrators of violence as between men and women, although the levels of severity may differ. For a consideration of opposing viewpoints, see Mary Roth Walsh, ed., *Women, Men, and Gender* (New Haven: Yale University Press, 1997) 207–209; Murray A. Straus, "Physical Assaults by Women Partners: A Major Social Problem," *Women, Men, and Gender* 210–221; and Demie Kurz, "Physical Assaults by Male Partners: A Major Social Problem," *Women, Men, and Gender* 222–231.

82. The same point is made in Linda Peterat, "Family Studies: Transforming Curriculum, Transforming Families," *Gender In/forms Curriculum* 176. Insofar as education for family living includes and implies learning to care, however, it should be noted that there appears to be a difference of sorts between Martin and Nel Noddings on this point. Noddings argues for the existence of natural caring which is spontaneous as distinct from ethical caring which involves reflection. See Nel Noddings, *Philosophy of Education* (Boulder, CO: Westview Press, 1995) 186–187.

83. Martin, *The Schoolhome* 98–104; Martin, *Changing the Educational Landscape* 232, 235–238. Research by Stein indicates that even when sexual harassment takes place in school it is often overlooked by the authorities, sending the wrong messages to both offenders and victims. See Nan Stein, "Sexual Harassment in School: The Public Performance of Gendered Violence," *Harvard Educational Review* 65 (Summer 1995): 145–162. For a Foucaultian interpretation in which such behavior may be seen as the exercise in power by students, see Ann Middleton, *Disciplining Sexuality: Foucault, Life Histories, and Education* (New York: Teachers College Press, 1998).

84. Martin, *Changing the Educational Landscape* 235–238; Martin, *The Schoolhome* 120–127.

85. Martin, *The Schoolhome* 104.

86. Martin, *Coming of Age in Academe* 56–57.

87. Martin, *Coming of Age in Academe* 61.

88. Martin, *The Schoolhome* 24–31, 135; Martin, *Changing the Educational Landscape* 71–73.

89. Martin, *The Schoolhome* 159.

90. Martin, *The Schoolhome* 160.

91. Martin, *The Schoolhome* 17–19, 153–160, 192–197; Martin, *Changing the Educational Landscape* 232–233. In *The Schoolhome* 153–154, Martin makes clear that the kinds of domesticity that the schools cannot provide for is buying the groceries, tending the children and doing the housework, for example. This would imply that all facets of the educational task could be taken over by the school.

92. See, for example, James McLaren, *Life in Schools* (White Plains, NY: Longmans, 1994).

93. A short list of such policy positions includes *A Nation at Risk*, which was published in 1983, *The Education Reform Act* of 1988 in England; President George H.W. Bush's Address to the Governors at the Education Summit in 1989; and *Goals 2000*, signed into law in 1994.

94. See Stein, "Sexual Harassment in School: The Public Performance of Gendered Violence."

95. John Dewey, "Plan of Organization of the University Primary School," *The Early Works, 1885–1898*, 5 vols. (Carbondale, IL: Southern Illinois University Press, 1972) 5: 224–225.

96. John Dewey, "My Pedagogic Creed," *The Early Works* 87. Note that Dewey writes the school should "continue with" not "ignore" and that he says "deepen and extend" not "abandon" the activities and values of the home.

97. Dewey, "Plan of Organization" 224–225.

98. Dewey, "Plan of Organization" 232–243.

99. John Dewey, *The School and Society* (Chicago: University of Chicago Press) 35.

100. Martin, *The Schoolhome* 157–159.

101. Martin, *The Schoolhome* 121.

102. Lightfoot quoted in Martin, *The Schoolhome* 121.

103. See D.G. Mulcahy, "Personal Influence, Discipline and Liberal Education in Cardinal Newman's Idea of a University," *Internationale Cardinal Newman Studien*, Elfte Folge. Achter Newman-Congress Freiburg, eds. H. Fries, W. Becker and G. Biemer (Heroldsberg: Glock und Lutz, 1980) 150–158.

104. *Goals 2000: Educate America Act* (PL 103–227) 31 March 1994. See, for example, Title I of this Act.

105. William Jefferson Clinton, "State of the Union Address," 27 Jan. 2000.

106. George W. Bush, "Inaugural Address," 20 January 2001.

107. Martin, *Changing the Educational Landscape* 48.

108. Martin, *Changing the Educational Landscape* 231.

109. Martin, *Changing the Educational Landscape* 170–186.

110. Martin, *Changing the Educational Landscape* 180–181.

111. Martin, *The Schoolhome* 150–153.

112. Martin, *Changing the Educational Landscape* 232–233.

113. Martin, *Reclaiming a Conversation* 195–196.

114. Martin, *Coming of Age in Academe* 47–55.

115. Martin, *Changing the Educational Landscape* 208–210.

116. Martin, *Changing the Educational Landscape* 211.

117. Martin, *Changing the Educational Landscape* 47.

118. Martin does draw attention to conceptions of school as a home away from home but only to stress that such conceptions are largely ignored when they do crop up. See Martin, *The Schoolhome* 121.

119. Herbert Spencer, *Education: Intellectual, Moral, and Physical* (Totowa, NJ: Littlefield Adams, 1969), especially 21–96; Catharine Beecher, *A Treatise on Domestic Economy* (New York: Schocken Books, 1977); Horace Mann, *Annual Reports on Education* (Boston: Horace B. Fuller, 1868), especially "Report for 1847" 559–639; and "Report for 1848" 640–758; The National Education Asso-

ciation, *Cardinal Principles of Secondary Education* (Washington, DC: Government Printing Office, 1918); 11–16; Florence Stratemeyer et al., *Developing a Curriculum for Modern Living* (New York: Bureau of Publications, Teachers College, Columbia University, 1957), especially 146–332; Martin, *Reclaiming a Conversation* 103–138

120. See Henry A. Giroux, "Doing Cultural Studies: Youth and the Challenge of Pedagogy," *After the Disciplines: The Emergence of Cultural Studies*, ed. Michael Peters (Westport, CT: Bergin and Garvey, 1999) 229–265; and Henry A. Giroux, *Channel Surfing: Race Talk and the Destruction of Today's Youth* (New York: St. Martin's Press, 1999).

121. E.D. Hirsch, *Cultural Literacy: What Every American Needs to Know* (New York: Vintage Books, 1988); Paul H. Hirst, *Knowledge and the Curriculum* (London: Routledge and Kegan Paul, 1974) 30–53; and Mortimer J. Adler, *The Paideia Proposal: An Educational Manifesto* (New York: Macmillan, 1982).

122. Adler, *The Paideia Proposal*, 41–45.

123. C.P. Snow, *The Two Cultures: And a Second Look* (Cambridge: Cambridge University Press, 1965).

124. Martin makes it quite clear that she does not believe a common curriculum for all is any guarantee of social unity, a point that is considered more fully in Chapter 4. See Jane Roland Martin, "The New Problem of Curriculum," *Synthese* 94 (1993): 85–104.

125. Martin, *The Schoolhome* 84.

126. Martin, *Changing the Educational Landscape* 231.

127. In this connection, see Robert L. Cord, "Church-State Separation and the Public Schools: A Re-evaluation," *Educational Leadership* 44 (May 1987): 26–32. For Cord, the case on legal grounds for a constitutional ban on religion in schools is far from convincing.

128. Martin, *Changing the Educational Landscape* 91.

129. For a helpful consideration of "family values" and its evolving interpretations, see, for example, Gill Jagger and Caroline Wright, eds., "Introduction," *Changing Family Values* (London: Routledge, 1999) 1–16.

CHAPTER 3

Women and Education: Ideals, Realities, and Ambiguities

The general neglect of women's education and women's experience in education to which gender bias has led is not an uninterrupted neglect. Even if they were not always listened to, great minds of the past did sometimes turn their attention to women's education and in the case of women writers especially, to the significance of women's experience for women's education. What they had to say is an important formative influence in the development of Martin's educational thought as she considers the ramifications of giving the place of women and gender in education the attention she believes they deserve, and then seeks to fill in the general void in educational thought occasioned by their neglect.[1] In this chapter, accordingly, attention shifts first to Martin's study of the historical ideal of women's education, its distinguishing characteristics, and how it shaped Martin's own thinking. Attention is next given to Martin's study and her ringing critique of how women's education and women themselves are treated in the university today. Lastly, attention turns to the ambiguities that arise in Martin's thought as it is extended to embrace a wider range of issues, including her notions of reproduction and education.

THE IDEAL OF THE EDUCATED WOMAN

In *Reclaiming a Conversation*, Martin looked to prominent women educational writers of the past whose voices had been overlooked to learn what they had to say about the education of women. Before examining the educational ideas of these women, Martin studied closely the ideas of both

Plato and Rousseau, who had given considerable attention to that question in their own influential writings on education.

According to Martin, it will be recalled, Plato did not consider gender differences important in determining the kind of education a person should receive, and so he recommended the same education for women as for men. But, she argues, the form of education envisaged by Plato was more suited to men than women—having been designed primarily for carrying out the duties of the public world, man's domain. A form of education that on the surface seemed equal for all actually put women at a number of disadvantages; it also put women's experience and women's issues—and the study of them—at a disadvantage because it largely ignored them. The ideal to be attained by Plato as commonly understood, after all, was the philosopher king, not the philosopher queen.

Insofar as women were considered by Plato to be every bit as fit as men to be educated, he sought to make no distinction in education or in the workplace between men and women. According to Martin, however, he did make a huge distinction between the work of the public domain and that of the private, essentially recognizing one and not the other. A serious consequence of the neglect of education for the private world of home and family, in Martin's view, was his failure to provide for education of the feelings and emotions, a position of Martin's that I have questioned. Such education, Martin maintains, is nonetheless essential to carrying out many of the functions of the public world, not least the governmental.

Although he greatly admired Plato's writings on education, the views of Rousseau on these questions were radically different from Plato's. In Rousseau's view, according to Martin, the natures of men and women were very different and consequently their education was to be different. Martin has said that in some instances the same education for men and women may not be a good idea but the differential education for boys and girls proposed by Rousseau does not pass muster for her either. If Plato's proposals for the same education for men and women falls short of the ideal form of education for girls—in part because it is the same—and Rousseau's proposals for different education for boys and for girls also fall short—notwithstanding the fact that it is not the same—the question arises what conception of education for girls will fit the bill. Already Martin has intimated that there are circumstances in which the same education for boys and girls is not always the best solution, and that a somewhat different form of education for each may be necessary if one is to pursue the same educational goals for boys and girls.[2] In her treatment of the ideal of the educated person as previously considered, however, Martin did not elaborate on this point. She does explore these questions more fully in the course of her careful analysis of the educational thought of three leading women writers on women's education, namely, Mary Wollstonecraft, Catharine Beecher, and Charlotte Perkins Gilman, to which much of *Reclaiming a Conversation* is given over.

Wollstonecraft

According to Martin, Wollstonecraft's "*A Vindication of the Rights of Woman* represents one long rejection of Rousseau's definition of Sophie's nature, the education he would give her, and the person he would have her become."[3] To deprive Sophie of her rational nature, or undercut it by education or in any other way, is to undermine her potential, to deprive her of the possibility of being moral and immortal, and to prevent her from being even a good mother. There is for Wollstonecraft, in other words, an inconsistency in Rousseau between what he wishes Sophie to become and how he wants her to be educated for that role. According to Martin, Wollstonecraft also rejects as misguided Rousseau's conception of the "wife-mother role," its qualities of gentleness, docility, and spaniel-like affection making Sophie nothing but the man's toy.[4]

Martin sees Wollstonecraft setting herself a threefold task in *A Vindication*: "to rebut the presumption that women are not rational but are slaves to their passions; to show that if the rights of man are extended to females, women's domestic duties will not suffer; and to propose an education and upbringing for females that will sufficiently develop their ability to reason independently so that they will clearly deserve the same political rights as men."[5] Martin is satisfied that Wollstonecraft accomplishes the first two tasks well. She accomplishes the first by arguing that the female's "irrationality" is no more than a social construction and forcing those who disagree to disprove it. If female "irrationality" is a social construction, there is no way of knowing if women are irrational by nature or by upbringing. Accordingly, she recommends an education similar to that of men, in which there is an emphasis upon rational development, and the outcome of which can be evaluated in due course. As Martin sees it, by so reasoning, Wollstonecraft succeeded in putting the opponents of her views on the defensive, requiring them to show rather than assume that women cannot be rational.[6]

Being cut from the same enlightenment cloth as John Locke and Thomas Jefferson, in which reason forms the basis of morality and political action, "Wollstonecraft accomplishes her second task by incorporating the characteristics the Enlightenment associated with the good citizen into her redefinition of the wife-mother role. Rationality and personal autonomy in the sense of self-government: these are the traits thought to be required for citizenship, and these are the traits she attributes to good mothers and successful wives."[7] But to attain these traits, and thereby to become a good wife and mother, Martin continues, she needs an education wider in scope than Rousseau allows Sophie, one which enables her to become a citizen of the world as well as a good wife and mother. Then will she be fitted to become a good wife and mother, that is, once she lives in the public sphere as citizen as well as in the home? As Martin puts it, "by redefining the wife-mother role, she makes the performance of women's domestic duties and even domestic tranquility [sic] dependent on the extension of the rights of man to woman and also a natural consequence of it."[8]

The fact that women have the capacity to be rational does not lead Wollstonecraft to conclude that they attain it naturally. On the contrary, for Martin, Wollstonecraft believes it requires an appropriate education, one that for Wollstonecraft ought to be akin to that envisioned by Rousseau for Emile rather than Sophie. Yet there would be significant differences. In content this education will be intellectual but in pedagogy it will not be like Emile's. The young girls will mix with boys and girls of their age and not be isolated as Emile was. In content it will be traditional and largely "bookish." As with Plato, while including physical education, it will focus on the rational. Such a focus, according to Martin, would be anathema to Rousseau.[9]

Turning to the third of the three tasks that Wollstonecraft set herself in A Vindication, namely, her proposal for the education and upbringing of females, Martin has serious reservations concerning the portrayal of the educated woman that emerges. Wollstonecraft's idealization of the educated woman she names "Emily" because Rousseau's idealization is her model; Emily's education, accordingly, is to be like that of a man, Emile. Martin also compares Emily to Elinor, as opposed to Marianne in Jane Austen's Sense and Sensibility, because the emotions, senses, and feelings are governed by reason; they do not overwhelm. Wollstonecraft's ideal of the educated woman is of one full of reason but lacking passion and feeling. For Martin it is, accordingly, erroneous. Wollstonecraft, she writes, has forced herself into the false dilemma of picking either a Sophie or an Emily. To put it in the literary terms that Martin does, she forced herself into choosing between an Elinor or a Marianne when the possibility of a more balanced or centrist position also existed in the form of an Ann Elliot of Austen's Persuasion; for example: "Elinor's problem—and Emily's, too—is not that in being responsible for running the domestic sphere her life will be dominated by feelings and emotion but that by fulfilling Wollstonecraft's rationalistic redefinition of the wife-mother role feeling and emotion will be entirely suppressed."[10]

As with Plato and Rousseau, according to Martin, Wollstonecraft, too, adopts a production model of education. Unlike Plato's guardians, however, Wollstonecraft's Emily is to occupy two roles in society: those of citizen and wife-mother. Accepting that the nurturing capacities do not emerge naturally even in women, it would follow that education for both roles would be necessary. The problem is that Emily's education, being based on that of Emile and being the same as for men, will fit her for only the one role, that of citizen. This is the heart of Martin's criticism of Woll-stonecraft's ideal of the educated woman, the consequences of which she considers perilous, especially for children. Given Wollstonecraft's beliefs surrounding this matter, and given in particular her belief that women have primary responsibility for child rearing, "her theory of female education must include education for mothering."[11]

In Martin's view, Wollstonecraft's rationalism has a number of positive and highly beneficial aspects. It enables her to claim the rights of men for women, bringing them into the domain of citizenship, and it demonstrates in a way that neither Plato nor Rousseau did the compatibility of the roles of citizen and wife-mother. Despite its shortcomings when it comes to fash-ioning a vision of women's education, Wollstonecraft's rationalism, more-over, also serves to illuminate intelligence and a certain stability of character as aspects of mothering often overlooked today, along with the place of reason and self-control in the educative aspects of mothering. Fi-nally, Wollstonecraft's rationalism "inspires her to claim for women the academic education historically reserved for men and, like Plato, to rec-ommend a system of coeducation."[12]

Yet, according to Martin, this very rationalism does not allow Wollstone-craft to envision a form of education that is suitable for women, lacking as it does the virtues of Sophie that are necessary to carrying out the re-productive processes. Wollstonecraft "presents us with an ideal of female education that gives pride of place to traits traditionally associated with males at the expense of others traditionally associated with females." As a function of its gendered origins, it is one-sided, lacking the emotional con-tent necessary for the reproductive processes her role of mother requires of her. And, presumably because Plato's female guardians will not marry or engage in child rearing, in the final analysis, Martin concludes, a society "that does not abolish the institutions of private marriage, home, family, and child rearing cannot afford to take as its model the education Plato devised for his guardian class."[13]

Beecher

Having identified the complexities of the role of mother, Wollstonecraft, in Martin's view, creates a vision of female education that fails to provide for the education of mothers. Even if she is fitted by reason to carrying out the tasks of running her household and raising her children, it is doubtful that Emily's education will give her the knowledge and skill necessary to carry out the job. Beecher doubts that it will, and she turns her attention directly to the question of what form of education is necessary for this very purpose. As she does, she also illuminates for Martin a feature of the in-terrelations between men and women that is a persistent theme in Martin's own thought: the dependency of men on women.[14] For all of this, her vision of the educated woman—Sarah, as Martin labels her—will still fall short in Martin's view. Granted, it does focus on the mothering aspect that Wollstonecraft neglects, and pays close attention to the many specialized tasks of running a home and raising children well, such as cooking, sewing, child rearing and caring for the sick. No mere itemization of tasks to be undertaken and how, it also elaborates on the notion of autonomous homemaker, wife, and mother, new in the American setting. Yet, for Martin, its definition of homemaker, wife, and mother is itself deficient. This is because it fails to recognize the profound importance of the 3Cs of care, concern, and connection for a true vision.[15]

Emphasizing the homemaker character of Sarah, Beecher abandons Wollstonecraft's aspiration to the dual roles of wife-mother and citizen for her idealized woman in favor of the single role of wife-mother. This being so, it is almost to be expected that for Beecher women are subordinate to men in society. The realm of the female may be in the home and not in the state but Beecher also acknowledges her rationality. Accordingly she will be educated for domestic affairs, not to participate in the affairs of the state as a citizen. As Martin puts it, "Beecher's philosophy of female education, like Rousseau's, is a mirror image of Plato's. Whereas Plato is able to design an education in ruling for females because he has detached them from family and children, Beecher is able to design a domestic education for her daughters because she has detached them from the responsibilities and duties of citizenship."[16]

Sarah will be pious, pure, submissive and domestic, and she will be mother, daughter, sister, wife, and woman. Yet it would be incorrect to conclude that these features support her political subjection or confinement to the home. It is true, of course, wives must obey their husbands and both inside and outside of marriage women are subordinate to men. While this is required in the interests of efficiency, it is also part of Beecher's political philosophy that women have certain protections: women's interests are entrusted to men and are not to be sacrificed to men's own interests. Women also have choices and responsibilities. As members of communities, and as wives, mothers, and homemakers, they must also be capable of acting on their own. To carry out their responsibilities well requires judgment, skill, and intellectual achievement and, therefore, education, and Beecher's views on education clarify the character of the kind of person she wishes to create.

According to Martin, for Beecher "female education constitutes a preparation for carrying out the domestic role."[17] Accordingly, Sarah will be well educated in "domestic economy." To this will be added physical education and a liberal education. The latter has an important educational transfer value. The objective of this general education is critical thinking, therefore, not the amassing of information, and is required by arduous domestic duties and the study of domestic economy. Critical thinking will also enable Sarah to add rational self-control to the virtues of piety, purity, submissiveness, and domesticity honored in visions of women prevalent in her own day.[18]

Why the study of domestic economy, a subject that scarcely existed at the time, so much so that it was to a large degree created by Beecher herself?[19] In the first place, it is useful and it might not be learned otherwise. Domestic economy in Beecher's view was not reducible to simple skill training, however. Domestic skills would have been acquired by a young girl during long hours of apprenticeship with her mother. The formal study of domestic economy included much more. In addition to the principles of domestic practice, Beecher's course in domestic economy included knowledge from many subjects including anatomy, architecture, botany, chemistry, child development, and moral philosophy. An understanding of the theoretical and practical elements was considered necessary for Sarah to carry out her domestic duties. If she knew only the background theoretical knowledge upon which the principles were based, she would not know what to do. If she understood only the principles of action, she would not know how to apply them properly. The formal study of domestic economy then, in Martin's words, is designed to build upon that apprenticeship of the young girl to her mother "by providing her with a set of rules or principles of action to guide domestic practice and, more important, with a grasp of the theoretical knowledge upon which those principles rest." This would equip Sarah to carry out the complex wife-mother role successfully. It would also enable her to take charge of the home and therefore make a contribution to the society and the nation—even if she is subject to her husband.[20]

Making wives subordinate to their husbands and at the same time in control in the domestic sphere raises some tricky questions for Beecher. The answer to whatever apparent riddles arise lies in "her claim for the overriding social significance of the educative function of women."[21] Education, after all, is the most responsible of all duties, and it is committed to the care of women. As Martin puts it, "For Beecher, the educational function of women provides an essential grounding for her claim to sex equality, if not actual superiority." Given this, not surprisingly Martin adds that if a perception of mothers as educators is not original with Beecher, "she is the one who elaborates women's educative function and derives the strongest possible implications from it."[22] One of the implications to which Martin makes reference is the perception of educators as professionals, with Beecher's definition of domestic economy supporting the idea of women making professional judgments in the manner that doctors and architects would. Martin also appears to agree with Burstyn's observation that Beecher was staking out women's sphere of influence to be a profession as men were theirs.[23]

For Beecher, education is *the* moving force in society. A professional by virtue of her study of domestic economy, and an educated being herself, crucial to her educational role is the education she gives her sons and daughters to be moral citizens—for the well-being of the state. This is the educational role of the mother, born not of mere skill, but reason, under-standing, and character. This conscious joining together of reason and do-mesticity in Beecher is for Martin a breakthrough. It shows that theoretical learning, associated with men, and domestic activity, associated with women, do not stand worlds apart, and that women's roles also call for educated reason. For Beecher, civil society is constituted of both the do-mestic and the public spheres, and there should be education for the roles required by each. It also shows that—perhaps for men as well as women—liberal education needs to be supplemented by a form of practical as well as theoretical education aimed at preparation for the reproductive proc-esses, one akin to that body of knowledge once defined by Beecher and referred to by her as domestic economy.[24]

Despite her important practical and theoretical contributions to the ed-ucation of girls and women, Beecher ultimately falls short in at least one crucial respect in Martin's eyes. For all her emphasis on moral, liberal, and professional education, in the end she fails to provide for education in the 3Cs, largely it would seem, because as a nation we have not cultivated them. In the final analysis, Sarah's liberal and professional education, and the moral education she receives at home, do not make adequate provision for the development of the "kindly feelings" and "sympathetic emotions" that Beecher herself says Sarah must have in order to be a good wife and mother. As was true of Wollstonecraft who also emphasized the educative role of the mother, because of the lack of attention to the "gentler feelings" in Sarah, for Martin, Beecher is also guilty of the "fallacy of false dilemma" and a too heavy reliance on reason.[25]

Given the difficulty, in Martin's view, that the excessive attention to reason over the gentler feelings has presented for both Wollstonecraft and Beecher in their efforts to fashion a suitable concept of the educated woman, the question arises, as McMillan suggests, if we should change our attitude to reason itself? If such a change now appears fanciful given the claims for the education of women's reason that have been presented, Gil-man's focus requires no less imagination as it invites us to depart from the reality of a gendered world.[26]

Gilman

Even before she begins her examination of Gilman's *Herland*, Martin acknowledges the limitations arising from its illusory philosophy originat-ing in its single-sex society. Herland is instructive in Martin's view, how-ever, for the attention and status this society assigns to education, the role of mothers and educators therein, and its approach to and conception of child rearing and education. A crucial question that arises following the failure of Wollstonecraft and Beecher to do so is whether Gilman makes adequate and appropriate provision for the 3Cs in her educational ideal.

In summary, for Gilman, child rearing and education of the young is deemed the most valuable role and so is reserved for specialists only. Education forms a seamless web of experience, with no separation of school from the world. Education includes a wide range of knowledge and physical activity, and mother-love is Herland's overarching cultural and educational ideal. The Herland Dream, moreover, is "neither the accumulation of private wealth nor an increase in the gross national product; rather, it is the growth and development of children."[27] Reason is "at all times harnessed to the practical goal of making the best kind of people."[28] Hence too, the educational emphasis on "far-reaching judgment and a strong, well-used will."[29] By contrast with Wollstonecraft, however, for Gilman the nurturant capacities traditionally associated with women come first, "fundamental elements of an improved social order."[30] Not surprisingly, to be a good mother in Herland is to be a good citizen and vice versa.[31]

According to Martin, the identity Gilman sees in women's interests and the state's, to which she brings a particular image of family relationships, makes her utopian vision very special. This, of course, as we shall see, resonates with Martin's own appeal in *The Schoolhome* for a reinterpretation of the domestic tranquillity clause in which the values of domesticity, namely, care, concern, and connection will be to the fore. Moreover, not only does Gilman see the state as family but, for Martin, she also includes the very family members that Plato, Dewey, and other social philosophers who invoke the family ignore: "mothers and daughters, particularly mothers." Since he sees the traditional family as a necessary breeding ground in love and respect for the state, Rousseau would criticize Gilman's extinction of private family. While this criticism may be correct as applied by Rousseau against Plato, Martin argues that it does not hold up against Gilman because she builds in mother-love and "large family" love missing in Plato. For Gilman, the world is family in a way that for Rousseau only the immediate family was; and in a way that for Martin, too, perhaps under the influence of Gilman, can be instilled through her invocation of a revised interpretation of the domestic tranquillity clause.[32]

The next question that Martin raises has two parts. Firstly, how do we resolve the issue of whether child rearing is to be reserved for an elite, as in Gilman, or for the masses, as in Beecher? Secondly, should specialist knowledge—call it home economics or family studies—be required for all who are involved in child rearing? As to the second part of this question, Gilman agrees with Beecher that all those entrusted with the rearing and education of children should have the kind of specialist knowledge that Beecher enshrined in domestic economy. As to the first part, we have seen, of course, that she does not accept Beecher's assumption that all women should be entrusted with the education of the young. But there is at least one alternative answer to the question that neither Beecher nor Gilman considered, one that Martin herself pursues in due course: males sharing with females the reproductive processes in society. Martin does not believe that those educational theorists she examined in *Reclaiming a Conversation* have said all that needs to be said on this issue and it is evident from their work, she concludes, that we ourselves "must consider both what would constitute a proper preparation for performing those processes, and to whom such preparation should be extended."[33] As can be seen, this is a task from which Martin does not shy away.

Women's Education and Gender-Sensitive Education

According to Martin, at least one crucial element is lacking in the ideal of the educated woman as it has been variously treated by the writers she considers, namely, adequate attention to the 3Cs, to education for carrying out the reproductive processes in society, and to how to combine the rational and emotional elements that she clearly considers essential to the ideal of the educated woman. This, of course, does not blind her to the fact that it is also lacking in idealizations of the education of men. So important are these omissions that it leads Martin to conclude in *Reclaiming a Conversation* that the educational ideal to which primary attention ought now to be given is not the ideal of the educated woman or of the educated man but of a gender-sensitive ideal. The fact that it is to this gender-sensitive ideal that Martin turns does not mean that pursuing the ideal of the educated woman is a wasted effort or needs no further attention.[34] On the contrary, much has been learned in exploring this ideal, such as the arguments made respectively for high quality intellectual education and for high quality education for domesticity for women.

Does Martin's consideration of the ideal of the educated woman give way to an ideal of gender-sensitive education because Martin is unhappy with the ideal of women's education as she finds it in the authors she has examined in *Reclaiming a Conversation*, as we know she is with the ideal of the educated man as portrayed by Peters? It is clear that there are aspects of the ideal of the educated woman as set forth by Wollestonecraft with which she is satisfied, such as the emphasis on the intellectual formation of women. We can see, too, that she values the emphasis in Beecher on education for domesticity, believing that Beecher has made a most important contribution to the ideal of the educated woman in mapping out that dimension. Yet, for Martin, education for emotional formation—the 3Cs— necessary to carry out the nurturing responsibilities normally associated with mothering and therefore related to education for domesticity, understood in the broader sense that Martin uses it, is sadly lacking not only in Wollestonecraft but also in Beecher. While Martin pays little attention to the place of intellectual education in the ideal set forth by Gilman, it does appear from her recognition of the crucial role of mother-love, the over-arching educational and cultural ideal in *Herland* as she explains it, that Martin recognizes that at least Gilman's ideal embraces this crucial caring and associated aspects of the ideal of the educated woman.

As portrayed by Martin, there appear to be three crucial elements in the ideal of the educated woman: intellectual formation, emotional formation (including formation in the 3Cs), and education for domesticity in the nar-rower sense of housekeeping. It would appear from Martin's account that she does not find all three elements in any of the portrayals examined in *Reclaiming a Conservation*, including those by the three woman authors. Taken together, however, it would appear that all three elements have been identified among these authors and it merely remains for someone else to present an appropriate formulation by combining them all in the one ide-alization of the educated woman. For her part, Martin backs off of such an undertaking.

Unprompted by any debate over the matter in the five authors considered in *Reclaiming a Conversation*, Martin turns instead to a new question en-tirely: why not include men along with women among those entrusted with the education and care of the young? Martin clearly believes that men should be so entrusted, and this leads her to forego a concluding review of the ideal of the educated woman where one would normally expect to find it, namely, the final chapter of *Reclaiming a Conversation*. In its place Martin lays out an entirely new ideal. It is an ideal that holds out the prospect of answering a question that none of the thinkers she had written about considered. For her the dominating question becomes this: how can we educate both men and women for carrying out the reproductive pro-cesses in society, for living well in the private world? Enter the ideal of a gender-sensitive education. Enter, too, Martin with a new and likely highly rewarding line of inquiry for philosophical research in education. Martin may have jumped to this question based on views of her own rather than those of the authors she had been considering as she explored the ideal of the educated woman. Whatever the explanation for getting to this point, the topic she now plans to pursue is of the greatest significance for edu-cation, for men and women, and for children, as Martin herself has ex-plained in "Bringing Women into Educational Thought."[35]

This may be an unlikely outcome to the investigation of the ideal of the educated woman so skillfully portrayed in *Reclaiming a Conversation*, al-though Martin had already indicated her interest in the idea of a gender-sensitive education some years previously in her critique of Peters's concept of the educated man. Not only did the idea not arise in the conversation among the participants she was now examining, the idea in principle was even anathema to Gilman. Other elements that are more compatible with Gilman's philosophy do later surface in Martin's own thinking as she pursues the ideal of a gender-sensitive education, especially the idea of nation as family and its implications for peace and tranquillity.

Before leaving this matter, there is one further aspect of Martin's treatment that needs attention, namely, her failure to fully recognize what those writers who were studied by her have contributed to the place of the 3Cs in education. Of those examined, only Rousseau is credited with recognizing this aspect as he does in the education of Sophie; yet it is difficult to see how this element is lacking in Gilman. For all her stress on the importance of practical education and education for action, Martin also fails to recognize the attention given to the role of apprenticeship in the educational writers she considers in *Reclaiming a Conversation*. I have already drawn attention to this omission and its consequences for her argument in relation to Plato's plan for the formation of the philosopher king. A similar question arises here out of Martin's assessment that Beecher fails to provide for the 3Cs. Martin acknowledges that Beecher does provide in her theory for the young Sarah to spend long hours apprenticed to her mother during which she would learn the domestic skills. For Martin to hold now that Beecher omits the 3Cs, therefore, she must have concluded that Sarah's mother also omitted them during this same apprenticeship. Since it is in such settings that education in the 3Cs commonly takes place, one surely has to allow for this likelihood in Beecher's case also.

THE REALITY OF THE UNIVERSITY WOMAN

The fact that the ideal of the educated woman is no longer the overriding educational ideal for Martin does not mean that there are not pressing issues unique to the education of women that are considered a source of concern by her. There are: above all else, there are those that, in the absence of gender-sensitive education, tend to penalize women rather than men. So urgent are some of these that they have recently become the focus of renewed attention by Martin in *Coming of Age in Academe*.

The Academy, God Help Us

Vigorous and insightful as is her analysis of the work of other educational theorists, Martin is relentless in her critique of the academy, especially as it bears upon the experience of women: the membership, the mechanisms, the mores, and the values of the world of scholarship. Many of the central themes already enunciated by Martin recur here. Chief among them are the distinction she draws between the productive and reproductive processes in society and the favor shown toward the productive in our institutions of education; the generally more positive cultural response to matters pertaining to the experience and interests of men compared to the experience and interests of women; the serious limitations of liberal learning in relation to dealing with the everyday problems of living and the conduct of a good and just society; and the chronic neglect and outright rejection of the values of domesticity and its associated values of care, concern, and connection both in society at large and in our homes and schools. One of the goals—and achievements—of *Coming of Age in Academe* is to seek out, expose, and call to task these disturbing qualities and tendencies in the world of higher learning. What, we may ask then, does Martin's analysis of the academy contribute to our understanding of the education of women beyond what we have learned already; and what does it contribute to the improvement of women's experience generally within the university—and without?

The fundamental basis for Martin's new contribution is her characterization of the thoroughly gendered nature of the academy. Until this is rectified, she maintains, there is not much hope for the improvement of women's higher education, women's experience in the academy, or even the education of men and the betterment of society in general. In Martin's opinion, the genderization that is rampant in the academy is strongly pro-male. This is grounded in several biases and perhaps most fundamentally in the separation that takes place in all institutions of education, including the university, as between the productive and reproductive processes in society. The productive processes are the assumed focus of the university and hence the promotion of men's studies and experience, and the neglect of women's and that of the private sphere. It is this that leads to the devaluation of women's experience and concerns and those of the private sphere, the exclusion of women's experience from both the subjects and the texts of the university and, most notably, from liberal education itself.[36]

That this gender-based exclusion comes at a heavy cost for women and the children who fall under their care can be seen readily enough, Martin believes; less visible are its untoward consequences for men and society at large. These include a failure to round out the harsher side of men's nature through education in the emotions, the feelings, and the caring tendencies. They also include the brain drain set in motion that incapacitates all graduates of a liberal education in dealing with the serious practical activities of everyday living, not least the promotion of the common good, the establishment of a just society, and addressing the evils of racism, sexism, poverty, war, and environmental destruction. For, as was already expounded by Martin in her critique of Hirst's theory of a liberal education, in its preoccupation with theory, liberal education, from the time of Plato up to Hirst, provides an incomplete education.

This exclusion of the practical, the emotional, and the experience, concerns, and contributions of women is accompanied by other forms of gender bias in the operational aspects and ethos of the academy, making what, for Martin, is a veritable education-gender system. Comparing the experience of women in the academy to the experience of the immigrant, Martin

sees them being kept outside the promised land under whatever pretext
that works.[37] An example is the chilly classroom climate in which fellow
students and faculty alike belittle and demean young women even to the
point of intimidation and harassment.[38] To these may be added the relative
absence of female role models in the form of women professors. But female
students are not the only women that face discrimination in the academy.
Female faculty members fare no better when it comes to gender. In addition, Martin writes, to the double standards they face in the matters of
promotion and recognition for professional achievement, they face strategies of containment and tokenism that are designed to keep their numbers to a minimum and their impact muted. To these are added such
strategies as the escapist mode of communication required by the academy
that has the same effect, namely, aerial distance, esotericism, and practice-
independent theory.[39]

First among Martin's contributions to promoting women's education and
improving the experience of women within the academy is this analysis:
when we contemplate the higher education of women today, we are forced
to view it as an education-gender system; to pretend otherwise would be
sheer folly. To recognize it as such is not to accept it, however. Rather, it
is time for a revolution. It may take time to achieve what is necessary, as
it did for women to gain admission to the university.[40] Yet in addition to
the complicity to maintain the education-gender system in which women
are implicated, however unintentionally, the response of women themselves, and even of feminist scholars, in dealing with the challenge before
them has not always been enlightened. A prime illustration is women's
neglect of the subject of education itself and the issues it raises for women.
A manifestation in itself of women departing from the study of traditional
women's subjects—whether in the fear of refeminization or for other reasons—neglecting the study of educational issues is a particularly unfortu-
nate omission from the women's agenda.[41] Not all women are expected to
engage the issue, but the failure to do so in general has the effect of blinding
women to the persistence of those very educational conditions that maintain them in their position of disadvantage, according to Martin. In particular it blinds them to the scarcely diminished, gendered character of
the academy. Ironically, and perhaps most seriously, it blinds them too
to the refeminization feared by so many. This is perpetuated daily through
the selection anew of women into traditional women's areas and men into
men's and otherwise having women do men's bidding; it is accompanied
by the de facto gender-tracking that occurs even with the spread of coeducation.[42] How can women achieve a better future, Martin asks, if they do
not study the problem? It is no surprise, then, that many women dream
small dreams when they have no vision, for to go without a vision "is to
accept existing educational structures and assumptions unquestioningly.

But these structures and assumptions are the educational correlates of an outdated gender ideology."[43]

Whether large vision or small dream, what might the future hold? Central to any educational vision, in Martin's view, will be the study of women and women's experience. There are two interrelated aspects to such study: a curriculum one and a research one.[44] One addresses the inclusion of the study of women in undergraduate and graduate programs; the second addresses the advancement of knowledge through research. One of Martin's own important contributions treats of the curricular aspect of the issue, namely, her characterization of the traditional academic disciplines and traditional forms of liberal education as being biased in favor of men and prejudicial against the study of women and women's issues. This view emphasizes that in excluding the study of women's experience from education not only are important skills, attitudes, and understandings crucial for the conduct of both public and private life, ones traditionally associated with women, excluded. So, too, in Martin's opinion, are those pertaining to the reproductive processes that are fundamental to civilization itself. Thus, not only do we need to inject the study of "women's experience" into the university curriculum; we need to broaden the curriculum beyond mere theory to include its practical underpinnings and implications. We need to do it for the proper education of women and for the better education of men if we are to prevent the brain drain occasioned by an impoverished version of liberal education. We need to do it if we are ever to have a world inhabited by people committed to and possessing the knowledge, attitudes, and skills necessary to promote a just society.[45]

Even women scholars who mean well can hurt the cause of women's education, Nussbaum being a case in point, singled out by Martin. Overlooking many of Martin's criticisms of the traditional theory of a liberal education and her characterization of the gendered nature of educational institutions set forth above, Nussbaum presents what Martin herself views as an ill-considered and too-traditional ideal. Responding to the oversights in Nussbaum, Martin writes, "I do not see how an idea of liberal education as cultivation for *the functions of life generally* can be put into practice if that [education-gender] system is not dismantled. Nussbaum's discussion illustrates the problem. She ignores the cultivation of human beings for living in families. . . . Yet what good is it to teach young people to debate the structure of families and the future of children intelligently without also cultivating their abilities to participate wisely and well in these practices?"[46]

In other ways, too, Martin maintains, women, and feminist scholars in particular, have often been a hindrance to progress. Factionalism, competition, strife, and pettiness have led to the dismissal of important bodies of work on women's experience and to an unhealthy narrowing and consequent loss of creativity in the research agenda on women's issues. Depriving undergraduates and aspiring women's scholars of rich sources of understanding, it has left them to their own resources to reinvent the wheel.[47] Seeing strength in complementarity, and seeking to harness the insights of all perspectives, Martin calls on all feminists for an end to hostilities among adversaries and for a more eclectic approach. She also calls on women scholars in general to return to the study of women's issues across a wide range of disciplines and to reject the gender-biased grant apparatus that seeks to lure them away from these studies and the many misguided charges of refeminization leveled at such work. Thus, in Martin's view, the introduction of both stand-alone women's studies programs and integrationist approaches across the college curriculum are to be welcomed.[48]

It is important that the study of women's experience and women's issues be brought into the curriculum; it is important, too, that female professors be brought into the classroom as role models for women undergraduates and graduates alike. The absence of such models, Martin says, not only sends messages of devaluation but hinders the perception that women can fill such roles and that female students can aspire to become professors and researchers themselves. Beyond such modeling there is room and promise for the improvement of women's experience and its standing in the academy in other forms of activity, too, many of them small-scale but with the power to be effective nonetheless. In addition to classroom teaching, women can come together to help young students and even colleagues address many of the gender-related issues that hinder such improvement of women's experiences in the university and the improvement of women's education. In all, Martin identifies about a half dozen of these kinds of activity that can be undertaken even in existing circumstances. They include the merging of the traditional culture of the academy with one in which women's experience and interests are equally valued. She likens this to intermarriage rather than assimilation in which the host group changes little if any. Other activities she identifies include feminists reconnecting with one another, the transformation of the academy's underlying system of beliefs, the establishment of progressive research institutes devoted to women's studies, and the setting-up of a *fika*, a meeting-place in, say, a department, where women faculty and students share common concerns, experiences, agendas.[49]

Finally, achieving a woman-friendly academy, one rid of its gender system, in which women will become full-fledged members, will require concerted political action. Resistance may help but positive action will be necessary too. That's how the vote for women and other rights were won.[50] If all turns out well, it is Martin's hope that one day "the very idea of an academy that welcomes feminist scholarship, a genuine co-professoriate, a true co-curriculum, and women-friendly classrooms will be taken for granted and the scorn and derision these now occasion will finally be laid to rest."[51]

Martin's Critique of the Academy Considered

Martin's criticisms of the gender system she calls the academy, which leads her elsewhere in *Coming of Age in Academe* to make proposals for reform, is unyielding and it goes right to the very foundations—the values and modus operandi as she puts it—of the academic world of research and teaching. The object of this criticism is undoubtedly the gender biases she detects, but the critique raises questions not only about these biases but about the very legitimacy of the academy's search for truth and its dissemination.

Martin's argument about the brain drain to which liberal education leads and the failure of Nussbaum's proposals to take account of it is a revisiting of her critique of Hirst's theory of a liberal education and of the academic disciplines as curriculum content applied to the university. It remains in many respects a telling argument. Her critique of factionalism among feminist theorists and the harassment and double standards which females at all levels in the university experience ring true, too, even if recourse to the kind of anecdotal evidence Martin draws upon could also be used to show otherwise. Similarly, Martin's urgings that the struggle for women's rights in the university must not only continue, but be guided by greater attention among women themselves to the issue of education, is pertinent and provides a promising basis from which to set forth and sustain the kind of reform endeavor she proposes.

The reliance upon anecdote rather than hard data to which I just alluded spills over to Martin's claim that women themselves neglect the question of education as a topic. Leaving this aside—for one could contest the empirical claim—let's consider Martin's concern about the neglect of education by feminist scholars on its merits. Martin identifies three compelling reasons why indifference to the education issue is poor policy for women. Firstly, she suggests, it prevents women from comprehending and ultimately transforming the context and conditions in which they pursue their scholarly investigations. Secondly, it prevents women from fulfilling their dreams, for to do without a theory of education suited to the changed social conditions to which they aspire is to accept existing educational structures and assumptions unquestioningly, structures and assumptions that "are the educational correlates of an outdated gender ideology." It renders the education-gender system invisible and fosters the illusion that such social reform can be achieved without fundamental educational reform. It also "perpetuates the myth that whatever changes in education feminist scholars might think necessary can be accomplished by simply inserting what is wanted into the existing systems. Above all, the education gap hides from us the fact that because our education system is thoroughly gendered, in order to effect the desired changes in society, the system itself must be dismantled." Thirdly, it causes women to act irresponsibly toward their students and themselves when knowing, for example, that both educational theory and practice are genderized, they pretend otherwise or ignore the fact that the worst fear of feminist scholars—women's refeminization—is already being enacted. If the academy is ever to cast off its gendered character, it will not do so without a concerted attack upon this gendered nature itself, along with a concerted effort to envision new possibilities for higher education. Unless women scholars engage in the education issue once more, such developments are unlikely to occur, for "education is implicated in both the fact of our refeminization and the prospect of turning the tide. This means that we have got to close the education gap in the feminist text. Otherwise, even if feminist scholars undertake the desperately needed project of discovering how to undo the refeminization, their proposals for action will almost certainly be wanting."[52]

The case Martin makes about the need for feminists to have an educational theory to guide any serious effort to reform the social conditions and structures that penalize women and to be intellectually involved in the question of education irrespective of their academic specialty is apt. It is supported by the approach of the great social reform theorists such as Plato and Rousseau, for whom education was a central aspect of their overall social and political philosophies. Martin's arguments for dismantling a thoroughly gendered education system highlight the importance of having such a guiding theory. They also raise the fundamental question of what is to be put in the place of the academy following the revolution, which in turn raises the question of what educational future for women Martin herself envisages, and how well she articulates and justifies it. Before turning to examine these questions, however, a basic aspect of Martin's critique of the academy merits some consideration.

It is possible to analyze the academy in terms of gender, as Martin has done, and to see an imbalance in terms of the justices and injustices dealt to those on different sides of the gender divide. Given the fact that the academy has historically been dominated by males, it is hardly surprising if it has been shaped in the interests of men, even to the point of this becoming reflected in the structures, the entire modus operandi, the purposes, and even the very ethos of the academy. It would be incorrect to say that no change has taken place over time, however, or to hold that the academy has not come to respond to the interests and needs of female members. Even though Martin does not deny this, she is nonetheless insistent that progress has been so slight that there is a need to dismantle the existing institution and to start all over again in a spirit of reform.[53]

Dismantling and reform may well be necessary; if they are, the grounds on which they are conducted need to be got right. This raises the question of the analysis of the existing institution, in particular the question of the adequacy of Martin's gender analysis as the basis—and in Martin's argument, the sole basis—for dismantling and reform. This, in turn, brings us to the question of the role and purposes of the academy in contemporary life, whether it has a continuing legitimacy and, if so, the extent to which it meets the needs of our contemporary society. While the gender analysis may contribute to our understanding and even the reform of the academy, it is, of course, just one perspective. Other perspectives and interpretations may cast different lights, reveal different imbalances, expose quite different strengths and weaknesses, justices and injustices, and unmet needs, purposes, and possibilities. They may also reveal many of the same features of the educational landscape that Martin's analysis of gender draws to our attention.[54] It is not my purpose here to consider what all of these may be. There are several issues that arise from Martin's gender analysis, however, that hold out the possibility of alternative interpretations that hold even greater promise than the one offered by Martin; and they remain consistent with the thrust of her own thinking, especially as elaborated in her School-home thesis.

Even though she recognizes their limitations,[55] Martin has relied upon the following dichotomies in the course of her analysis: male/female, production/reproduction, and public/private, with male most closely associated with production and the public world, and female with reproduction and the private world or family sphere.[56] A possible alternative analysis to which I wish to draw attention here is based on the public/private dichotomy but rejects the imputation of male to the public and female to private worlds. One may analyze the academy as an institution oriented primarily to the *public world* and the preparation of students for the public world as distinct from the *world of men*. By their very nature, the universities from which the academy largely draws its lifeblood are public places as distinct from private ones such as homes. By that I mean its members, both students and faculty, are not drawn from any particular family or home. Many are strangers to one another. The structures, goals, and modus operandi of the university over time have become formalized in a way that is not true of homes. Faculty and even many students receive an income for the services they render to the university; not so in the private home or family. In fact, many universities are even called public universities, their goals, purposes and modus operandi being shaped at least in part by the community, be it state or city. In addition to the membership, goals, and modus operandi, the programs offered by the university are usually shaped, as Martin has argued, to prepare students for participation in the public world as distinct from the private world of the home.

Up until the twentieth century, more males than females attended university, in part because men were dominant in the public world. As women gained entrance to the university, as they did other public places, including government, business, and industry, some adapted more readily than others to its public ethos. It is true that many suffered, and still do, from trait genderization of the kind Martin discusses. One could argue, however, that the traits in question—following bureaucratic procedures and schedules, impersonal relations with colleagues in a hierarchical workplace, objective assessment of evidence and decision-making, and being assertive and competing for public honors—are less male traits than traits associated with the public world. True, women may still have been penalized disproportionately over men, not because they were men-like but because they were "public-like," and women were commonly expected to behave "home-like." It was this very expectation, for example, that made possible the often harsh if hilarious depiction of Prime Minister Margaret Thatcher as Chairman and Chief Executive Officer clad in business suit and tie in *Spitting Image*, the popular British television satire.

The point of such an alternative analysis of the academy is not to argue that women are not penalized over men, and that the academy is not biased in favor of men. It is, rather, to say that there are possible analyses other than a gender analysis of the kind Martin presents that could account for, or at least throw helpful light upon, these biases. If there is to be a dismantling of the academy and its various institutions, and if whole-scale reform is to take place, we need to be circumspect in the analyses on which we base such thoroughgoing change, lest we do more harm than good. We also need to consider the implications for the home and for carrying out the caring and nurturing activities associated with it. Martin talks in terms of those activities associated with the home as falling to women, and she wants men to become involved. As long as these activities are perceived as women's, they may never be taken on by men; but men, like women, are quite happy to live and work in homes as well as in public places, and quite happy and competent even by Martin's admission to exercise the 3Cs in both. This raises the possibility of seeing the caring and nurturing activities not in terms of women's work needing to be shared by men but the work of the home needing to be shared by the public world. Interestingly, this brings us directly to Martin's own compelling call for a reinterpretation of the domestic tranquillity clause of the Constitution in which the entire nation is seen as home. It also brings us to her proposal that the school take on some roles of the home. To conceptualize and seek the resolution of the issues in gender terms detracts, then, from the potential of resolving the difficulties associated with them in terms of the public world, in terms of domestic tranquillity as Martin portrays it, and in terms of the school, itself a public place. Yet the school is precisely where Martin wants many of the difficulties with which she is concerned to be resolved. If Martin is correct or, put a little differently, if it takes a village to rear a child, then the issue may be less one of getting men involved and more one of getting the village or the public world involved. This, after all, is precisely the reason Martin wants to shift the caring of children, or at least some of it, from the home to the school—that is, from private to the public world.

Even though this alternative analysis is derived from Martin's own view of the interaction between the private and public worlds and her wish to bring education for the private world of the home into the public world of the school, for her the academy remains characterized primarily as a highly gendered institution. To recognize its thoroughly gendered character is not to accept it as inevitable, however; hence her call for reform. To accept it as inevitable would be to give up the struggle for the proper education of women, to consign them forever to the contradictions inherent in the lives of educated women today, and to accept the denigration of those women who make their careers within the academy. For there is no prospect whatever of reclaiming a suitable education for women without first eliminating the gendered nature of the academy and dismantling the apparatus that keeps it in place. Assimilation alone will not bring about the desired outcome.[57] That is to say, there is no prospect for reform without a direct challenge to the status quo: it is time to take action for change, radical change.

Martin may be right in holding that there is no prospect for reform without a challenge to the status quo. Without dismissing the improvements in women's education and the treatment of women that Martin seeks, focusing on gender exclusively without paying adequate attention to other facets of the complex issue is no guarantee either that there will be progress. These include a comprehensive alternative vision of the academy and a philosophy of women's education. In addition to filling out such a picture, other aspects of the analysis need attention too. To focus on the gender character of the academy without acknowledging the changes that have taken place since more women have become members is not to look at the full picture. In fact, some of the very injustices Martin treats, such as harassment of female students and faculty members, are ones that occur because there is now major participation by women in the academy. The cultural dimensions of male/female relations in the university, and the wide-ranging nature of the social and cultural change in which we find ourselves today, also need to be taken into account. Most importantly, since at least some of the injustices found in the academy are caused by moving from one social era to another, and hence are rooted in the broader society, care needs to be taken that the ideals associated with the "new" era to which Martin aspires, including its implications for schools and families, are actually for the better. While proof is an elusive property in arguments of this kind, we do at the very least need something beyond mere preference. We need a detailing of how and to what extent society and the individuals who make it up—women as well as men—are going to be at least no worse off than now.

In *Reclaiming a Conversation* and *Coming of Age in Academe*, Martin explores the question of what is a proper education for women and how it is handled in the university. Her treatment of the evolution of the historical ideal women's education shows deep understanding, and the ideal of a gender-sensitive education that she conceives is original and well-articulated. While her critique of higher education is well-focused and forceful, her alternative vision of the academy, to which we are to turn once the dismantling of the one we now have has been completed, is weak and lacks strong theoretical support. It prompts the question, why?

REFORM, REPRODUCTION, AND AMBIGUITY

Reform

The final chapter in *Coming of Age in Academe*, in which many of Martin's direct proposals for reform are set forth, is called "Actions Great and Small." It is a less-than-fitting title, for in the end, no great proposals for action emerge. In a review of *Coming of Age in Academe*, Thayer-Bacon recognizes the positive contribution of its critique of current conditions for feminist scholars and the treatment of the containment of women in academia. Thayer-Bacon also speaks of the critique as unduly negative in its characterization of the impact of the women's movement in higher education, failing to recognize concrete progress where it has been made. Thayer-Bacon's most serious concern relates to Martin's vision for the future, however, as she raises questions about the extent to which Martin connected with the felt needs of younger women today, possibly falling foul of her very own accusations of aerial distance.[58]

In all, there are four main areas of reform recommended by Martin in *Coming of Age in Academe*: curriculum, research, political action, and new social arrangements. The proposals for curriculum and women's research which focus on women's experience are the most deeply rooted in Martin's analysis, providing them with a source of support and rationale. The proposals for different kinds of social arrangements in the form of meetings of women faculty and students turn out to be largely strategic in character. While there are suggestions of activism in the call for political action, they are muted and a far stretch from the kind of revolutionary thrust intimated when the critique was in the full flow.[59] Despite what feminist pedagogy itself offers on the subject, and her own criticisms, Martin has little or nothing to say even about how feminist pedagogy might impact on the university classroom.[60] Stated in terms of her own analysis of the work of Patricia Mann when dealing with the idea of a research institute, Martin's ideas lack the backing of a conceptual or theoretical model needed both to sustain whatever proposals are presented and to provide a comprehensive vision while keeping one's feet on the ground.[61]

It was talk of revolution and overthrow of existing institutions that led me earlier to caution that such talk made it imperative to formulate replacement alternatives, which of necessity would need to offer a very different vision of the academy. To talk on the one hand of overthrow and revolution, yet in the final analysis to come up with proposals that themselves presume the continuance of the very institution to be abolished, is already an indication of a failed prescription. Yet this is largely where Martin finds herself, and it could hardly have been otherwise, for in *Coming of Age in Academe* the focus is upon existing structures and the modus operandi. Nowhere in her critique and discussion of the academy does she resort to the kind of emphasis on first principles that characterized her charge of epistemological fallacy against mainstream curriculum theory or her suggestion in "The Radical Future of Gender Enrichment" that existing goals of schooling needed to be amended by the addition of an important new goal. This goal, namely goal (e), the preparation for membership of a family, was then taken both as a source of direction and justification for an expanded role for the school, one that included an emphasis on the 3Cs. Put differently, preoccupied with the gender character of the academy as she finds it, nowhere does Martin contemplate in a fundamental way the role of the academy in society. Having chided Hirst and others for putting content before purpose in education, Martin herself fails to focus adequately upon what her analysis of gender means for the goals and purposes, and even the modus operandi, of a reformed academy after the manner, for example, of Kathleen Weiler when she considers some pedagogical applications of Freire's work from a feminist perspective.[62]

The closest Martin comes to doing this is in restating her view that the traditional theory of a liberal education is impoverished by its preoccupation with theory at the expense of practice, the key criticism she makes of Nussbaum's position. A similar criticism of Hirst's position led Martin ultimately to a full-blown examination of its implications for schooling in *The Schoolhome* and elsewhere. Fundamental to that examination was the analysis of the notion of peace and tranquillity found in the Constitution and the goal of preparing students for membership of a family. Had Martin attempted a corresponding analysis suited to the university setting, it could have served as a basis for a set of broadly conceived prescriptions not only for changing its modus operandi but shaping its programs and sustaining its moral and educational authority. If she had done so, she might have arrived at a theoretical model, a vision, and a source of justification; she might also have laid the basis for a coherent and broadly conceived revolutionary way of dealing with the gender biases in the academy that she articulates so forcefully. Martin's addition of goal (e) to those generally accepted for the conduct of public schooling threw open the possibility of revolutionary change in schooling, and yet it did not necessitate a complete overthrow of existing institutions. If what is good for the goose is good for the gander, a similar additive theoretical stance could have been taken in relation to the academy. Martin's approach is actually an additive one anyway, but one that lacks the kind of theoretical support that Martin's goal (e) provided for her vision for the reform of schooling.

This absence of a new and pressing sense of direction for reform of the kind one might expect to be derived from Martin's heightened awareness of the importance of gender and the place of women in educational theorizing is not the only weakness of Martin's view of a reformed academy. There is the even more surprising absence of reform proposals that draw upon the rich literature of feminist pedagogy and what it has to say regarding alternatives to the modus operandi of the academy upon which Martin tends to focus. Here there is a remarkable failure to envision reform that introduces, builds upon, or adds to what feminist pedagogy suggests. No attention is paid to the unique demands made by work, child rearing, and homemaking upon many women students and what feminist literature indicates may make the university responsive to their situation. Returning to the point made by Thayer-Bacon, the academy that Martin critiques seems to derive from a historical model of the university that excluded women; the one she envisions, moreover, shows no particular interest in women coming to school across a wide range of class, cultural, ethnic, and racial backgrounds. Thus, no special attention is paid to the unique requirements of older women attending university or other forms of adult education, such as those served by Mujeres Unidas en Accion,[63] and the responsiveness to student needs, participatory methods, and nonhierarchical forms of organization favored by such women. The same is true of women's liking for modes of teaching that emphasize storytelling or build upon what we have learned in recent decades of women's ways of knowing, such as small-group learning and teaching, intimacy in the learning setting, the importance of using autobiographical approaches to learning, and the importance of sharing, collaboration, and cooperative modes of learning. Neither is there anything on the implications of feminist pedagogy for such controversial areas as evaluation and assessment of learning. Likewise, little is said on such approaches to research or service to the community, and nothing on administrative procedures favored by women rather than men. In fact, it is difficult to understand why Martin's very different perspective does not result in a more innovative and substantial set of proposals. Even if located within existing structures, taken together they might constitute at least the beginnings of a genuine alternative to the academy and its modus operandi of which she is so critical.

While these are serious criticisms of Martin's prescription for the reforms of the academy, they are not serious criticisms of her general educational stance for the same reasons that Martin's proposals are weak: they do not go to the root of that stance or bring into question a crucial dimension of it. What does go to the root of Martin's general stance and is potentially a serious weakness is her reliance upon the distinction she draws between the productive and the reproductive processes in society. This distinction is at the heart of her epistemological critique, her gender critique, and her reasons for espousing the ideal of a gender-sensitive education as set forth in *Reclaiming a Conversation* and elsewhere. It is also central to *Coming of Age in Academe*. It is time, accordingly, to seek further clarification of what this distinction entails. Clarification is also needed in regard to the related question of Martin's view of what she terms "the educational realm" and the role of women in it, a view that also relies on this distinction.

Production and Reproduction

A number of commentators have drawn attention to Martin's distinction between the productive and the reproductive processes in society, though they have not always drawn out the implications for Martin's position.[64] Kallman-Roemer, for example, points out that Martin has stipulated the meaning of the reproductive and productive spheres in terms of private and public arenas. The term "reproduction," Kallman-Roemer grants, is ambiguous and includes childbirth, household and subsistence work, and all relations outside productive relations that are required to maintain the capitalistic system. While she accepts that Martin's choice of vocabulary may be problematic because of this ambiguity, she also maintains that what is important for Martin's argument is that we understand how she is stipulating the meaning of these terms. As far as Kallman-Roemer is concerned, it seems that Martin's position "is compatible with an analysis of household relations of production and consumption and an examination of the way in which seemingly private experiences of different families mask the shared experiences of households reproducing class relations." It may also be true, she continues, that understanding the relations between the ideal of an educated person and the various notions of reproduction already mentioned "is essential for formulating a gender-just ideal."[65]

More than Martin's choice of vocabulary is problematic in this area, as has been pointed out by McClellan. McClellan is of the opinion that if we were to view human beings as other animals, then production and reproduction are essentially complementary. But this is not so in a capitalist society, he contends. Here all of production is carried on exclusively to maximize the profits going to the capitalist class. While this may cause Martin no difficulty, its consequences could where reproduction becomes strictly ancillary to production and "nurturance is valued only as a necessary condition for the social reproduction of the existing class system."[66] If this were to lead to a perpetuation of the status quo in the social and economic spheres, there would be little hope for Martin to realize her goal of equal treatment for people of all sexes, races, and economic circumstances, a criticism Martin did not fully rebuff when she turned her attention to it a few years ago in "The Wealth of Cultures and the Problem of Generations."[67]

Problems with Martin's position arise for Hilary Davis due to what she refers to as Martin's conflation of the feminine with caring and emotions. Davis then considers its implications for Martin's position. "By linking it solely with reproductive processes and emotions," Davis writes, "Martin's understanding of the feminine is monolithic and universalist, even though she refers to reproduction in its broadest non-biological sense. Such a stance unintentionally omits other understandings of the feminine (for example, psychoanalytic definitions based on sexuality and desire, or Foucaultian analyses of power/knowledge relations)."[68] This appears to support the allegation that Martin conflates the feminine with caring and emotions but Davis is not quite correct in asserting that Martin links the feminine solely with reproductive processes and emotions. Martin clearly acknowledges that women can operate within the productive realm and men within the reproductive.

There are other aspects of the relationship between the productive and reproductive processes as described by Martin that also need attention. At the extremes it may be possible to distinguish between the productive and reproductive social processes. Childbearing is clearly reproductive; nursing and housekeeping are nearly as clear-cut. Identifying a clear-cut case of a productive process is more difficult. Take the economic concept of "the production of goods and services." Right away the notion of services is ambiguous as regards production and reproduction, including as it does health services, and local, state, and federal government services as they pertain to welfare and disaster-relief services, for example, all of which could be said to fall within the realm of the reproductive processes. Leaving education aside, there are other such services, too, including community services in which even business sometimes engages. Moving beyond service, which notion perhaps already includes an element of the reproductive, how does one categorize the production of goods such as agricultural goods, that is, the food needed to sustain life, not to mention biological reproduction? Does the farmer engage in the productive or the reproductive processes of society? And what about the world of communications, including radio, television, telephone, and the Internet? Does communication belong only to the public world of production and not at all to the world of conversation, counseling, and "reaching out," that is to say, the world of reproduction? What does one say of the construction industry that builds the houses we live in, the schools and hospitals in which we teach and provide health care, and the automobile industry that can do as much for family well-being as for corporate profit? What about the seemingly clear-cut case of the production of firearms, bombs, and missiles? Is defense of the nation—be it in times of peace, war, or terrorist attack—in no sense a reproductive or community-maintenance enterprise? In fact, it is not easy to come up with a clear-cut case of an industry engaged in a purely productive process. The tobacco industry comes to mind, but many of its workers depend on it to feed and raise their families, as its defenders often remind us, and recent scientific findings that it may contribute to certain health products does not ease the decision.

The alternative analysis that I introduced earlier, in terms of a public/private dichotomy in place of Martin's gender analysis, draws attention to some further ambiguities or apparent confusions in Martin's own analysis. In general, these arise in the context of Martin's identifying different "worlds," "spheres," and "domains," using them more or less interchangeably and speaking of them as being variously "public," "private," "women's," "men's," and "domestic."[69] In particular, confusion arises from Martin's attempt to clarify her position on the distinction she draws between the productive and the reproductive processes in society and how it bears on the distinctions made by others as between home and work and between private and public.

In a discussion of the productive/reproductive divide in her consideration of Peters's concept of the educated person, Martin accepts that theorists have put different labels on "the two parts into which the social order has traditionally been divided." Some refer to "the split between work and home, others to the public and private domains, and still others to productive and reproductive processes." She continues by defining her terms. The reproductive process she takes to include "not simply childcare and rearing, but the related activities of keeping house, running the household, and serving the needs and purposes of all the family members. Similarly, I interpret the term 'production' broadly to include political, social and cultural activities and processes as well as economic ones."[70] Although she appears ambivalent as to whether the distinction is one of substance or merely of terminology by saying that one can use the public/private or work/home distinctions if they are preferred over her productive/reproductive distinction, she is not ambivalent. It is the definitions that count for her and they must remain. Yet she does introduce some confusion by indicating that the terminology is a secondary matter while also maintaining that the other two forms of framing the issue are, for different reasons, unsuitable to the discussion on hand. If they are unsuitable, it is more than a matter of terminology.[71]

Education and Ambiguity

But the ambiguities do not end here. In the distinctions just drawn by Martin, she makes no mention of education, even though one gains the distinct impression throughout her work that education would be a fairly clear-cut case of a reproductive social process; one also gets the impression that for her, education pertains to the private rather than the public world. But are these impressions well founded or illusory, and of what consequence is it one way or the other? Whether she maintains it or merely gives the impression that education is considered the woman's domain, throughout her work Martin insists that women are excluded from the education domain. Among these exclusions are their exclusion from the philosophy of education at least in the analytic tradition, their exclusion from the subject matter of the history of educational thought, their exclusion from the subject matter of the academic disciplines and consequently from liberal education, and their exclusion in spirit and often in practice from the academy. If exclusion is so prevalent the obvious question arises, how can education be thought of as the woman's domain?

A number of examples of Martin's maintaining that education is considered the woman's domain are found in *Coming of Age in Academe*. According to Martin, one of the overall effects on feminist theory of the pro-male-gendered value system of the academy is to deny it sources of richness and creative imagination. For her part, she believes that feminism should feel free to pursue a broad agenda, including traditional women's issues such as family, mothering, and education, as long as it avoids the traps of sentimentalism and victimization.[72] Then when speaking of the academy's dismissive attitude toward the three subjects of nursing, education, and home economics, she has this to say: "View the academy's ratings of these three fields as independent, isolated events and one sees three separate areas of questionable academic repute. Look at the three together, and one perceives that old double standard at work." She continues a little later, "Considered women's domains, these areas are tainted in the academy's eyes by the second-class citizenship of the people who practice them. Even more telling, the historical association of these practices with the world of the private home sullies them."[73]

Elsewhere, however, Martin herself casts doubt on her account of education as being considered to belong to the domain of women and the home. This she does when she describes the productive processes as including "political, social and cultural activities and processes" as well as economic ones. Education is not only a cultural activity par excellence, and as normally understood, the sole deliberate means of perpetuating culture. As such, education is now listed by Martin among the productive not the reproductive processes, and if the terms are somewhat interchangeable, considered to belong to the public world of work and distinct from the private world of the home, the domain of women. Linking education and culture with the productive processes, as Martin has now done, raises the prospect of a range of unlikely interpretations of her position, such as putting her in the same position as Hirst and Peters, agreeing that child-rearing that goes on in the private world of the home is not education. It makes one wonder, too, why she rails against recent reports on education and educational institutions alike for emphasizing preparation for the public world of work rather than the private world of the home. If education is a cultural activity, and if cultural activities are deemed by Martin to belong to the world of production, is this not to be expected? Martin's association of women historically with the home rather than the public world could also explain, and perhaps lend some justification to, why women, traditionally associated with the private world of the home, have been excluded from education. Perhaps it would also throw light on some other ill-fitting parts of the picture of the interrelations between education and the private and public worlds that Martin draws for us, such as her refusal on occasions to see that the public world has always been involved in education. Most strikingly, there is the seeming contradiction of holding that education is the woman's domain and yet maintaining that it is dominated by men, as in the academy! Accordingly, one asks: is there a deeply rooted inconsistency in Martin on this issue of whether education belongs to the domain of women or to the public world and the productive processes of society?

Perhaps not. It is a pervasive theme in Martin that both the study and the conduct of education are located in the professional lowlands because they have been historically considered to be the sphere of women. As we know, for Martin the reproductive roles such as parenting are not intuitively known. When we refuse to allow for them in the curriculum through a subject such as family studies or home economics, we create a negative image of these roles, leading the educational establishment and theorists alike to dismiss them as not rising to the level of education.[74] This is why Peters could deny that rearing children qualified as education. It is also why, in part, politics is taken seriously as an academic discipline but education is not. But how can this be so, you may well ask, if, according to Martin, men control and dominate the academy, which is after all considered an educational institution? As Martin sees it, in our culture politics has the advantage that it is situated in the public world and placed in the care of men. Although school has succeeded in removing education from the private home into the public world, it is faced with the problem that "its 'natural' site is still considered to be the near side of Woolf's bridge and its 'natural' practitioners are still assumed to be women."[75] It is therefore because of its association with women, Martin is saying, that the subject matter of education is downgraded, notwithstanding the fact that through its removal from home to the school, the practice of education came to be located within the public world and placed under the control of men (or so she says in regard to the academy). Now at least we can see how Martin claims that on the one hand education is the woman's domain, they being its "natural practitioners," while on the other hand that it is located in the world of production, the public world, since its being moved out of the private home.

To say that women are the "assumed" natural practitioners of education would appear to contradict the new reality. Yet by invoking this very assumption, Martin veils what she is trying to tell us: is she saying that assuming women to be the natural practitioners is a false assumption or a correct one; and what of the implied distinction contained in the term "natural practitioners?" Is this intended to indicate that once upon a time education was a reproductive process located in the woman's domain but with social progress has since been moved to the productive and the realm of men and the public world? This would fit in with her theme of exclusion of women from the educational domain while also allowing her to maintain that education belongs in the woman's sphere.

In the final analysis, these questions may be unanswerable, yet it might have helped if Martin from the beginning had paid closer attention to a distinction between education and schooling that is clearly evident in Adler and others such as Giroux, who distinguish between these concepts in different ways. Martin does emphasize the distinction in her later work, especially when she speaks of "multiple educational agency." When in her cultural wealth thesis, for example, she argues that schools are but one agent of education, she draws attention to the range of agents that exist. But the emphasis is on the range of agents as distinct from the degree to which any one or all combined, including the school, can carry out all tasks of education.[76] Neither does she contemplate the possibility that education is not well-suited to being institutionalized, and clearly she does not agree if that is intended to convey that the condition is irremediable.

An example of how the failure to distinguish between education and schooling causes difficulties for Martin, and for the reader, can be drawn from *Coming of Age in Academe* where she writes that we in the West assume that "love, nurturance, and the 3Cs of care, concern, and connection—all qualities associated with the private home and with women—run counter to education's raison d'être. Indeed, we take these to be such obstacles to the achievement of the objective of preparing people for membership in the public world that we make one of school's main tasks that of casting off the attitudes and values, the patterns of thought and action associated with home, women, and domesticity."[77] Implicitly, she says, we divide social reality into two worlds and assume that the function of education is to transform children who live in the world of the private home into members of the world of work, politics, and the professions. "Perceiving the public world as a human creation, and membership in it as something at which one can succeed or fail and therefore as problematic, we make preparation for carrying out the tasks and activities associated with it the business of education." By contrast, "assuming that the private home is a natural institution and that, accordingly, membership in it is a given rather than something one must achieve, we see no reason to prepare people to carry out the tasks and activities associated with it."[78]

The point that Martin is making here is that we need to prepare children for family living and that even the school should be called upon to help in this work. But the language she employs fits the point I am addressing, namely, that she fails to distinguish adequately between "education" and "schooling." It may be true, as Martin contends, that we make one of the main tasks of schooling that of casting off the attitudes and values, the patterns of thought and action associated with home, women, and domesticity. To claim, as Martin does (as when she writes that we assume the 3Cs associated with the private home and with women run counter to education's raison d'être), that we also view this as one of the main tasks of education is quite a different matter, however. We may see it as a task of schooling but not of education. This may be especially true of education that occurs in the home or, for that matter, in the church or youth club. One may say the same of Martin's claim that we make preparation for carrying out the tasks and activities associated with the public world the business of education. We may see preparation for carrying out the tasks and activities associated with the public world as the business of the school without seeing it as the responsibility of education provided in the home or elsewhere.

Such a distinction between education and schooling is even implied when Martin talks of "assuming" women to be the natural practitioners of education, as is a distinction between schools and other educational agents in her cultural wealth thesis. But while distinctions between one educational agent and another are usually made because different agents may be considered suitable for carrying out different tasks of education, Martin often uses "schooling" and "education" interchangeably. This may not only be the root cause of her ambivalence in assigning education variously to the public and private spheres, to the productive and reproductive processes, and to men's and women's domains. It may also be a root cause of her unwillingness to accept certain incapacities in schools (having acknowledged their existence as a matter of historical record) to take on educational roles of the home, assigning them to schools without more fully acknowledging the limitations of schools in this regard or examining other possible alternative and potentially more suitable courses of action. This tendency is pronounced in *The Schoolhome*, although it is subsequently heavily modified in *Cultural Miseducation*.

The fact that education, understood at times to belong to women and the private world of the home, takes place also in the public world of the school (in somewhat the same way as nursing, for example, takes place in hospitals as well as homes) challenges Martin's strong distinction between the public world defined as the preserve of men and the productive processes, and the private world of the reproductive processes. Clearly, the distinction between reproductive and productive processes is not as tight as Martin would have us believe, even if she does suggest that it is only a convenient theoretical device.[79] Neither is Martin consistent in assigning education to one sphere or the other, the sphere of men or that of women. But if the sharp distinction that she wishes to draw between the productive and the reproductive processes in society does not hold up well to scrutiny, or if such scrutiny suggests that there are no more than degrees of difference between the two, Martin is fortunate as far as the consequences for her theorizing go. The upshot is more one of confusion than of a serious flaw in her general position, and the consequences for her critiques are not in all cases detrimental or even adverse. If the productive and reproductive processes are not so sharply cut off from one another as Martin seems to think, for example, this hardly lessens the need to remedy the narrow intellectualism contained in Peters's conception of the educated person, or the need to join reason, feeling, and emotion in a "broader intellectualism."[80] Neither does it lessen Martin's arguments for greater attention to the 3Cs, the importance of including women's experience in education, and the elimination of gender bias in all forms and levels of education.

NOTES

1. It is not out of place here to draw attention to the gradual introduction of material dealing with the contribution of women educators and educational theorists of the past into conventional textbooks and anthologies in the history of educational thought since Martin first began to draw attention to its exclusion. See, for example, Gerald L. Gutek, *Historical and Philosophical Foundations of Education: A Biographical Introduction* (Upper Saddle River, NJ: Prentice Hall, 2001); *Historical and Philosophical Foundations of Education: Selected Readings*, ed. Gerald L. Gutek (Upper Saddle River, NJ: Prentice-Hall, 2001); Ronald F. Reed and Tony W. Johnson, eds., *Philosophical Documents in Education* (New York: Longman, 2000); and Howard O. Ozmon and Samuel M. Craver, eds., *Philosophical Foundations of Education* (Upper Saddle River, NJ: Prentice-Hall, 1999).

2. Jane Roland Martin, *Reclaiming a Conversation: The Ideal of the Educated Woman* (New Haven, CT: Yale University Press, 1985), 195.

3. Martin, *Reclaiming a Conversation* 71.

4. Martin, *Reclaiming a Conversation* 70–75.

5. Martin, *Reclaiming a Conversation* 76. See also Mary Wollstonecraft, *A Vindication of the Rights of Woman* (New York: W.W. Norton, 1975).

6. Martin, *Reclaiming a Conversation* 76–78.

7. Martin, *Reclaiming a Conversation* 79.

8. Martin, *Reclaiming a Conversation* 78.

9. Martin, *Reclaiming a Conversation* 80–84.

10. Martin, *Reclaiming a Conversation* 87; see also 84–89, 100.

11. Martin, *Reclaiming a Conversation* 91–99.

12. Martin, *Reclaiming a Conversation* 99.

13. Martin, *Reclaiming a Conversation* 100–101.

14. Martin, *Reclaiming a Conversation* 101–102.

15. Martin, *Reclaiming a Conversation* 103–138.

16. Martin, *Reclaiming a Conversation* 104.

17. Martin, *Reclaiming a Conversation* 109.

18. Martin, *Reclaiming a Conversation* 111–116.

19. In this connection, see Catharine Beecher, *A Treatise on Domestic Economy*

(New York: Schocken Books, 1977) and *Miss Beecher's Housekeeper and Health-keeper* (New York: Harper and Brothers, Publishers, 1873). The extended title or subtitle of the latter indicate the strong "domestic economy" thrust of this work: "Containing five hundred recipes for economical and healthful cooking; also, many directions for securing health and happiness. Approved by physicians of all classes."

20. Martin, *Reclaiming a Conversation* 114–115; see also 109–116.

21. Martin, *Reclaiming a Conversation* 123.

22. Martin, *Reclaiming a Conversation* 125.

23. Martin, *Reclaiming a Conversation* 116–125.

24. Martin, *Reclaiming a Conversation* 127–128, 134–138.

25. Martin, *Reclaiming a Conversation* 128–132.

26. Martin, *Reclaiming a Conversation* 132.

27. Martin, *Reclaiming a Conversation* 140–141; see also 139–148.

28. Martin, *Reclaiming a Conversation* 149.

29. Martin, *Reclaiming a Conversation* 151.

30. Martin, *Reclaiming a Conversation* 141.

31. Martin, *Reclaiming a Conversation* 151. See also Charlotte Perkins Gilman, *Herland* (New York: Pantheon Books, 1979).

32. Martin, *Reclaiming a Conversation* 151–161.

33. Martin, *Reclaiming a Conversation* 170 and 166–171.

34. Jane Roland Martin, "Women, Schools, and Cultural Wealth," *Women's Philosophies of Education*, eds. Connie Titone and Karen E. Moloney (Upper Saddle River, N.J.: Merrill/Prentice-Hall, Inc., 1999), 155.

35. Jane Roland Martin, "Bringing Women into Educational Thought," *Educational Theory* 34 (Fall 1984): 345–349.

36. Martin is not alone in taking such a view but others have taken a more moderate stance. See, for example, the discussion of the impact of gender in higher education in regard to such matters as curricula, institutional culture, and the challenges and possibilities in the inherent contradictions they contain for women in Elisabeth Hayes and Daniele D. Flannery, with Ann K. Brooks, Elizabeth J. Tisdell, and Jane M. Hugo, *Women as Learners: The Significance of Gender in Adult Education* (San Francisco: Jossey-Bass, 2000), 23–52.

37. Jane Roland Martin, *Coming of Age in Academe: Rekindling Women's Hopes and Reforming the Academy* (New York: Routledge, 2000), 67–75.

38. Of particular interest here are those features of formal places of learning, such as modes of classroom discussion, that threaten to undermine self-esteem among women learners especially. See Hayes et al., *Women as Learners*, especially 73–74; and Mary Field Belenky, Blythe McVicker Clinchy, Nancy Rule Goldberger, and Jill Mattuck Tarule, *Women's Ways of Knowing* (New York: Basic Books, 1986).

39. Martin, *Coming of Age in Academe*, 25–43. In this connection, see also Jane Roland Martin, "Methodological Essentialism, False Difference, and Other Dangerous Traps," *Signs* 19 (1994): 630–657; and Jane Roland Martin, "Aerial Distance, Esotericism, and Other Closely Related Traps," *Signs* 21 (1996): 584–614.

40. Martin, *Coming of Age in Academe* 132–139, 179–182.

41. Martin, *Coming of Age in Academe* 62.

42. Martin, *Coming of Age in Academe* 55–56, 81–84. For an account suggesting that the actual roles played by women in the so-called traditional women's fields

Knowledge, Gender, and Schooling header

such as teaching may be less traditional than often assumed, see Linda Eisenmann, "Reconsidering a Classic: Assessing the History of Women's Higher Education a Dozen Years after Barbara Solomon," in *Minding Women: Reshaping the Educational Realm*, eds. Christine A. Woyshner and Holly S. Gelfond (Reprint Series No. 30, Harvard Educational Review, 1998), especially 277–279. The contributions of Black women educators such as Anna Julia Cooper and Nannie Helen Burroughs further bear this out. See, for example, Karen A. Johnson, *Uplifting the Women and the Race* (New York: Garland Publishing, Inc., 2000).

43. Martin, *Coming of Age in Academe* 47. See also Martin, *Changing the Educational Landscape* 28. While the setting may be different from that on which Martin is focused, a recent study in England raises some questions about the limiting effects of accepting existing educational structures and so-called refeminization. Attempting to account for the successes of girls in closing the gender gaps that traditionally shaped schooling in Britain, the authors of a recent study conclude, "successive generations of girls have been challenged by economic and social change and by feminism," and they attribute greater influence to the feminization of the teaching profession than to national equality strategies or formal educational measures in causing these changes. On a pessimistic note, the authors also detect a hostility to feminist efforts to improve conditions for females, with the effect of converting "girls' educational successes into a moral panic about boys' failure," thereby rendering these successes problematic. See Madeleine Arnot, Miriam David, and Gaby Weiner, *Closing the Gender Gap: Postwar Education and Social Change* (Cambridge: Polity Press, 1999), especially 150–151.

44. Martin, *Coming of Age in Academe* 47, 103–109.

45. Martin, *Coming of Age in Academe* 125–133. See also Martin, *Changing the Educational Landscape*, 120–129, 170–186.

46. Martin, *Coming of Age in Academe* 139. See also Martha C. Nussbaum, *Cultivating Humanity: A Classical Defense of Reform in Liberal Education* (Cambridge, MA: Harvard University Press, 1997).

47. Martin, *Coming of Age in Academe* 57, 141–150.

48. Martin, *Coming of Age in Academe* 101–109.

49. Martin, *Coming of Age in Academe* 159–177.

50. Martin, *Coming of Age in Academe* 179–182.

51. Martin, *Coming of Age in Academe* 180.

52. Martin, *Coming of Age in Academe* 62. See also 46–47, 55–63.

53. See, for example, Martin, *Coming of Age in Academe* 132–139 and 179–182.

54. This is a point that Martin possibly overlooks as, for example, in Jane Roland Martin, "Redefining the Educated Person: Rethinking the Significance of Gender," *Educational Researcher* 15 (June/July 1986): 6–10. That is to say that one may arrive at many conclusions similar to Martin's regarding the content of the school curriculum, such as the limitations of academic education and the importance of practical forms of education, including home economics, without depending upon an analysis of gender. See, for example, D. G. Mulcahy, *Curriculum and Policy in Irish Post-Primary Education* (Dublin: Institute of Public Administration, 1981).

55. See Martin, *Changing the Educational Landscape* 79, endnote 34.

56. Recent scholarship suggests that equating men with the public and women

with the private sphere has become an outdated view. See Maxine Baca Zinn, "Feminism and Family Studies for a New Century," in *Feminist Views of the Social Sciences* (*The Annals of the American Academy of Political and Social Science*, 571), eds. Alan W. Heston and Neil A. Weiner. Special Editor Christien L. Williams (Thousand Oaks, CA: Sage Publications, Inc., 2000): 43–44.

57. Martin, *Coming of Age in Academe* 115–121.

58. Barbara J. Thayer-Bacon, book review of *Coming of Age in Academe*, in *Educational Studies* 31 (Winter 2000): 463–469.

59. Martin, *Coming of Age in Academe* 159–177.

60. See, for example, Hayes and Flannery et al., *Women as Learners*, especially 155–183.

61. Martin, *Coming of Age in Academe* 175–176.

62. Kathleen Weiler, "Freire and a Feminist Pedagogy of Difference," *Harvard Educational Review* 61 (November 1998): 117–145.

63. See Eva Young and Mariwilda Padilla, "Mujeres Unidas en Accion: A Popular Education Process," *Harvard Educational Review* 60 (February 1990): 97–115.

64. In this connection, see Barbara J. Thayer-Bacon, *Transforming Critical Thinking* (New York: Teachers College Press, 2000), 86–91.

65. Eleanor Kallman-Roemer, "Harm and the Ideal of the Educated Person: Response to Jane Roland Martin," *Educational Theory* 31 (Spring 1981): 118, endnote 18.

66. James McClellan, "Response to Jane Martin," *Educational Theory* 31 (Spring 1981): 114.

67. Jane Roland Martin, "The Wealth of Cultures and the Problem of Generations," in *Philosophy of Education*, ed. Steve Tozer (Urbana, IL: Philosophy of Education Society, 1998), 33–34.

68. Hilary E. Davis, "Docile Bodies and Disembodied Minds," *Educational Theory* 46 (Fall 1996): 534.

69. See, for example, Martin, *Changing the Educational Landscape*, 79; see also the discussion, 13–14.

70. Martin, *Changing the Educational Landscape* 79; see also the discussion, 13–14.

71. See also the discussion of this very point in Martin, "Bringing Women into Educational Thought," 344–345 and Martin, *Changing the Educational Landscape*, 13–14.

72. Martin, *Coming of Age in Academe* 45–63.

73. Martin, *Coming of Age in Academe* 53.

74. Jane Roland Martin, *The Schoolhome: Rethinking Schools for Changing Families* (Cambridge, MA: Harvard University Press, 1992), 140.

75. Martin, *The Schoolhome* 139.

76. See, for example, Martin, "Women, Schools and Cultural Wealth," especially 172–174.

77. Martin, *Coming of Age in Academe* 49.

78. Martin, *Coming of Age in Academe* 48.

79. See Martin, *Changing the Educational Landscape* 79, endnote 34.

80. Martin, *Changing the Educational Landscape* 48.

CHAPTER 4

Gender-Sensitive Education and the New Problem of Curriculum

It was in the early 1980s that Martin first recognized the extraordinary transformative potential for educational thought and practice of including women in the discourse on education, the impact of which she writes about in a number of places.[1] It would take her some time to draw out the implications for the curriculum, culture, and schooling, and more specifically, for the education of both girls and boys. Central to the position she develops is the idea of a gender-sensitive education as a "governing educational ideal," a concept that is sensitive to the individual and collective educational needs of boys and girls as well as to those educational needs that derive from their interdependency.[2]

Although it has roots in her early work in the epistemology of the curriculum, Martin's cultural wealth thesis, especially that aspect of it that bears most heavily on the question of curriculum—what she has termed the "new problem of curriculum"—remains a work in progress. This notwithstanding, the cultural wealth thesis and the ideal of a gender-sensitive education constitute Martin's contributions of greatest substance to educational thought that are essentially positive and novel. As ideals they are mutually supportive but there are also serious tensions between them.

A GENDER-SENSITIVE IDEAL

The basis for setting forth Martin's gender-sensitive ideal of the educated person has now been laid, and its determining characteristics have already been adumbrated in the preceding chapters. Its roots are to be found especially in the epistemological critique. In fact, this extensive critique, and not just Martin's positive ideas regarding her gender-sensitive ideal, is itself grounded in her educational predilections, even though these were not fully verbalized as readily or as early as the critique. Take "The Disciplines and the Curriculum," first published in 1969.[3] It goes almost unnoticed within this sometimes technical discussion of the academic disciplines as curriculum content that Martin indicates her educational preferences, as when she invites the reader to consider "a curriculum conceived as embracing a wide and varied range of human activities and conduct—as encompassing forms of living or activity and not just forms of knowledge."[4] Academic education was clearly important to Martin, but even in this early piece education for human conduct was no less so; high culture was necessary but so also were other aspects of our cultural wealth.

These same leanings can be found at a more developed level in Martin's critique of Hirst's theory of a liberal education in "Needed: A New Paradigm for Liberal Education," and in a still more fully developed form in the final chapter of *Reclaiming a Conversation*. Most recently they appear in *Cultural Miseducation*.[5] In all cases the reader is led to conclude that valuable as traditional liberal learning is, it is inadequate as a complete educational ideal, and it may even be of secondary importance. This is well-captured by Martin when she speaks of liberal education as a starting point for developing a broader idea of education, one in which there is no wedge driven "between thought and action, between reason and emotion."[6] The central elements contained in the early and more sketchy treatments of these ideas are revisited by Martin in later works, notably *The School-home*.[7] Yet to fully grasp what they suggest, and to comprehend the scope and structure of her gender-sensitive ideal, it is helpful to return to the critique that derives from these early and understated beliefs.

Accentuate the Negative

In the epistemological critique, we are presented with Martin's rejection of the opposites of qualities found in the educated person that she will later come to idealize. To see these qualities in this light enables us to grasp more fully her positive idealization. The three main criticisms of Hirst's forms of knowledge theory of a liberal education are a good place to begin. The criticisms are as follows: (a) the forms of knowledge theory of a liberal education was guilty of the epistemological fallacy, that is, of putting curriculum content before educational goals; (b) it created ivory tower people, that is, people who knew but could not act, do, or make anything; and (c) it created an untenable dualism by separating mind from body and reason from feelings, leading to the creation of uncaring and apathetic human beings. In her critique of the disciplines, Martin also argued that discipline knowledge of the kind one associates with liberal education excluded many different kinds of knowledge that she considered essential to living well. These included commonsense knowledge, practical wisdom, and a range of knowledge relevant to the lives of young people, such as knowledge regarding family and relationships. And in the "Curriculum and the Mirror of Knowledge,"[8] Martin was critical of traditional learning because it excluded from the curriculum, and hence as shaping influences on the person to be educated, the experiences of women, minorities, and the underclasses.

If you ask what are the opposites of these failings or negative characteristics of traditional or liberal learning identified by Martin in (b) and (c) above, it is possible to construct the outlines of a more positive image. One may also fathom in her earlier writings Martin's own but as yet unarticulated ideal of the educated person. What do we learn of Martin's ideal of an educated person by looking at the opposite of the ivory tower person, a lopsided and incomplete human being? In the first place, such a person would not be the object of ridicule, the butt of jokes, the "bashful man" of Charles Lamb or the incompetent houseguest of Richard Pring.[9] This person would have a fund of common sense and a measure of practical wisdom. Such a person would be reasonably well educated in a formal sense but would also possess knowledge and skills not found in the disciplines yet considered essential by most people to meeting the demands of everyday living. Such knowledge and understanding would include attitudes, values, and skills indispensable in the conduct of interpersonal relations with a wide range of people of different economic, racial, social, religious, and ethnic backgrounds, for example. This person would possess "knowledge how," be willing and prepared to engage in action, and be sufficiently knowledgeable and grounded to eat and drink wisely. (In curriculum terms, such an ideal implies subjects such as physical education, vocational education, artistic performance, languages, and education for moral action rather than merely those with an exclusive focus upon propositional knowledge and the narrowness of mind to which it leads, in Martin's view.)

What do we learn of Martin's ideal of an educated person by looking at the opposite of the untenable dualism she sees manifest in Hirst's idea of a liberal education? Let us remind ourselves of the educational implications of the dualism. It separates reason from emotion, thought from action, and education from life by "banishing both knowledge-how and noncognitive states and processes from its conception of mind." It makes education of the body non-liberal, thereby, according to Martin, denying any value to such education and education for action. Lastly, it commits one to political models that require, or at least desire, people "to be passive rather than active participants in the political process."[10] This leaves us with people who are uncaring, inactive, and unwilling and incapable of taking action for any cause, even in the face of injustice and hardship for themselves and others. Turn this around and we see the makings of an ideal in which reason is combined with emotion, thought with action, and education with life, one that embraces education of the body and education for action. We see also a person who is caring, and both prepared and willing to be active in the political process and in the search for justice for all. In Plato's terms, we would see not merely philosophers but kings too, kings with feelings and emotions and the capacity to act.

In "The Disciplines and the Curriculum," Martin challenges the notion, held notably by Phenix and in lesser degrees by many others, that the curriculum should be confined to the academic disciplines or subject matter drawn from them.[11] One of her arguments is that the disciplines are not sufficient to meet the relevance needs of young people, firstly because the focus is on the inner structure of the disciplines rather than on their outward relevance. Such an inner focus may be acceptable from the point of view of educating specialists but not so when one is concerned with general or liberal education. The disciplines are not sufficient to meet the relevance needs of young people, secondly, because along with practical skills, feelings, and emotions, much of what the young need to know about falls outside the scope of the disciplines. In a manner that is unusual for writers on curriculum, and that is consistent with her later work on cultural wealth, in this early article Martin points to a wide range of learnings that fall outside the bounds of the disciplines but are considered by her to be indispensable in everyday life and consequently in education. They include learning about war and peace, marriage and divorce, violence and poverty, and love and friendship. They pertain to a wide and varied range of human activities and conduct, not just forms of knowledge. They include the arts and the professions, various kinds of work, and all sorts of other practical activities along with a variety of social activities and roles and matters pertaining to the personal realm, such as character development.[12]

Martin's ideas on cultural wealth are set out at greatest length and are best integrated with her general educational thought in *Cultural Miseducation* but they are also found in "Women, Schools, and Cultural Wealth" and elsewhere. These ideas are an area of development in Martin's theorizing about the nature of knowledge with implications for curriculum that extend beyond the boundary of critique and they are influenced by Adam Smith's concept of economic wealth. According to this concept, wealth includes more than the money, gold, and silver to which it was limited in the mercantile system of which Smith was so critical. Our stock of cultural wealth, Martin argues, can similarly be expanded; according to the cultural wealth thesis, our cultural stock comprises more than the high culture such as is found in the academic disciplines and higher learning. It is more in line with the anthropologist's understanding of culture. This additional stock of culture includes folk knowledge as well as cultural beliefs and practices, and includes cultural wealth often unrecognized because it emanates from minority populations and ordinary folk, and from the activities and pursuits of everyday living. It contains assets as well as liabilities. This cultural stock is possessed and normally transmitted by a wide range of cultural or educational agents other than the school, such as churches, the Internet, and the media. Because they are not seen as educational agents, some of these agents are not held accountable for the cultural liabilities they transmit, liabilities that take the form of violence and abuse of others, for example. In the recommendations for action that Martin derives from this analysis lie possibilities for assigning moral and cultural accountability to those agents that transmit cultural liabilities without flinching. This, Martin believes, can be achieved by heightening community awareness of the actual educational functions of these agents and by setting up a scheme of accounting for our cultural stock and for those agents that deal with its different component parts.[13]

Having characterized disciplines as confined to knowledge about things, Martin writes that education "is not and ought not to be limited to learning about: there are skills to be acquired, techniques to be mastered, activities to be learned, works of art to be appreciated; there are emotions to be fostered, attitudes to be developed, convictions to be encouraged, ways of acting to be promoted."[14] Although this quotation is taken from "The Disciplines and the Curriculum," it could as easily have come from *Cultural Miseducation*. In her cultural wealth thesis, Martin resurrects this theme, once prominent in her critique of Hirst's theory of a liberal education and other early writings, and also central to her gender-sensitive ideal. Accordingly, as we move forward with the portrayal of Martin's ideal of the educated person, it becomes evident that she increasingly characterizes this person in terms of behavioral, attitudinal, and practical knowledge and skill rather than conceptual knowledge. She seeks education for participation, not mere spectatorship, serving to underline further the distance that exists between her and mainstream philosophical thinking about curriculum in the second half of the twentieth century.

Accentuate the Positive

It is a persistent theme in Martin, as is evident in "Needed: A New Paradigm for Liberal Education" and "Two Dogmas of Curriculum," and one that is articulated more specifically in "The Radical Future of Gender Enrichment," that educational programs ought to be determined by educational goals, purposes, and educational considerations and not simply by the existence of knowledge. In order to decide what knowledge an educational program should contain—rather than beginning with assumptions regarding that knowledge—where does it lead us if we are to ask, as Martin would wish, what are the goals and purposes of education and what ideal of the educated person do they envisage? In this case it leads us straight to Martin's own discussion of the goals of education in "The Radical Future of Gender Enrichment," where she identifies what she considers to be the normally accepted goals of education in our society, adding to them, as we have seen, goal (e), that of developing each person as a member of a home and family. It is by these goals as amended that her ideal is framed, with particular reference to the goal of education for family living.

In delineating the central characteristics of Martin's idealization of the educated person up to this point I have written in general or categorical terms, indicating her desire for the development of attitudes and skills as well as theoretical knowledge. It is now necessary to be more specific about the kinds of learnings associated with Martin's ideal of the educated person, and to speak of particular attitudes, values, skills, knowledge, and understandings. As one attempts to be more specific, Martin's position regarding the traditional learnings associated with the academic disciplines and a liberal education begins to appear ambivalent. By contrast, she is committal and specific in treating of those learnings that fall outside of the subjects normally associated with liberal education. Accordingly, it is largely to these that I shall pay attention, especially those pertaining to family life and domesticity, because it is to these that she devotes greatest attention in positively delineating her ideal. In fact, the elements highlighted by proceeding in this way constitute both the distinctive and most challenging features of her position. When it comes to the specifics of her alternative ideal, it is not the nature of the academic studies, liberal education, or cognitive growth that receives attention. Instead the focus is largely on how the ideal is shaped by these factors: domesticity and its associated values of care, concern, and connection; inclusion, as it applies to gender, race, ethnicity, religion, sexual orientation, class, and socioeconomic status; the integration of the productive and reproductive processes in the formation of boys as well as girls; and cultural wealth and the role of various educational agents in transmitting its assets and its liabilities.

It is because she found Hirst's theory of a liberal education to be unduly narrow as an account of "that education deemed valuable" that Martin called on philosophers of curriculum to broaden their horizons and consider other forms of education besides liberal education that might be deemed valuable. Martin herself attempts to do this when she calls for a new paradigm of that education deemed valuable, presenting her conclusions in embryonic form in the article on Hirst and in a developed form in *The Schoolhome*.

Hirst, along with Peters, I have suggested, conveys the impression that liberal education is the most valuable and true form of education and, moreover, that there is little or no distinction between it and general education.[15] As was also argued already, much of the force of Martin's critique of Hirst's theory derives not from any shortcomings in his theory of a liberal education in itself but from the shortcomings of that theory judged as a more comprehensive or all-embracing theory of education. It is this that makes Martin's critique so telling and which invites the construction of an educational theory to challenge the dominance of Hirst's theory of a liberal education. If the force of Martin's critique of liberal education derives from the shortcomings of Hirst's theory judged on broader grounds, the question arises as to how one might construct a more broadly based theory or concept of education. In the article on Hirst, Martin makes a start on this. In summary, she says,[16]

> Begin with a conception of liberal education as the development of a person, add to it an analysis of the concept of a person in which mind and body are inseparable, mix in the value judgment that the purpose of a liberal education ought to be to develop us as persons and not simply as minds. Guidelines for a liberal education that drive no wedge between thought and action, between reason and emotion, begin to emerge.

If the concept of liberal education set forth by Hirst, a concept of education based fairly and squarely on the nature of knowledge itself, is not adequate for all possible forms of education, is there not some basis other than the nature of knowledge itself upon which an adequate concept might be developed? There is, but it does raise further questions. In particular it raises the question, "adequate for what purpose?" The purpose with which Hirst is concerned is the development of mind; for Martin, it is the development of a person, a particular kind of person.

In "The Radical Future of Gender Enrichment," Martin carries further the analysis of purpose. An omission from educational thinking and policymaking that by the 1990s she had come to argue was quite unacceptable is corrected by adding on and even incorporating the goal of preparing children for family, goal (e). It is a goal of education, in Martin's view, that like the others considered in "The Radical Future of Gender Enrichment" ought to be sought after by the school. Yet even by Martin's own account of domesticity repressed, schools are unlikely candidates to house such education, putting proficiency in the 3Rs before the 3Cs, ignoring home, and preparing students for the public world. It is not merely that home skills are not taught in school; if anything the school is expected to help out in casting off the attitudes of domesticity associated with the home. Schools are also sites of misogynist messages and violence.[17]

But the times, they are a-changing, changing radically. Dewey asked what educational response the changes in the household he witnessed necessitated. His answer, namely, placing the occupations of the once traditional home in the school, Martin believes, is no longer the right answer to the changes taking place about us. The issue today "is not the removal of work from the household into factories but the domestic vacuum that is created when mothers as well as fathers leave home each day to go to work."[18] Notwithstanding the school's hitherto pronounced disinclination to con-

cern itself with the affairs of the home, then, for Martin, the task of education for domesticity, for preparing children not so prepared to live in the
home, is one which must now be taken over by the school.

Martin's concerns that Hirst's theory ignores "the development of such
central aspects of human existence as action, feeling, and emotion"[19] is
echoed in "The Radical Future of Gender Enrichment," although she is less
than committal when it comes to identifying specific values. Even though
she demurs when it comes to identifying a range of particular values to be
taught pertaining to home there, in *The Schoolhome*, written a year or two
earlier and in "Women, Schools, and Cultural Wealth" written several
years later, she has no doubt that to attain the goal of developing each
person as a member of a home and family, some values ought to be chosen
over others. In *The Schoolhome* she recognizes that Montessori had already
indicated her choice, as Martin herself had in the article on Hirst.[20] Referring to the kind of home she has in mind, she writes in "Women, Schools,
and Cultural Wealth" along the lines she had earlier done in *The Schoolhome*: "when I propose that our schools be home-like, I have in mind ideal,
not dysfunctional, homes." She continues by spelling out what she means
by ideal or best. In doing so, she conveys the broader sense of domesticity:
in recommending that school be a moral equivalent of home, she writes,
"I assume a home that is warm and loving, and neither physically nor
psychologically abusive; and a family that believes in and strives for the
equality of the sexes."[21]

In the article on Hirst, Martin tells us a little more about her ideal when
she elaborates on the kind of person and the kind of society she wishes to
create. Whether her alternative theory may be considered a paradigm of
liberal education or not, it will be "one that does not ignore the forms of
knowledge, but reveals their proper place in the general scheme of things
as but one part of a person's education; one that integrates thought and
action, reason and emotion, education and life; one that does not divorce
persons from their social and natural contexts; one that embraces individual autonomy as but one of many values."[22] Her words resonating with
sentiments she expressed a quarter of a century earlier, in *The Schoolhome*
she writes once more, accordingly: children must be educated in ways of
living in the world as well as knowing about it,[23] in action as well as
thought.[24] Citing a range of sometimes conflicting voices, such as George
Eliot, Rodriguez, James, and Dewey, Martin sounds once more the refrain
that to base education on academic studies exclusively is to teach our young
merely about life: it is to fall into the trap of turning out observers *of* it
not participants *in* it. If we do not teach the young to apply intelligence to
living, they will fall victim to its challenges.[25] The point is reasserted in
"Women, Schools, and Cultural Wealth" and again in *Cultural Miseducation*. No further elaboration of Martin's idea of home is provided beyond
what we have been told before, however: that it is an ideal, not dysfunc-

tional home, warm and loving, non-abusive, and striving for equality of the sexes.[26] What is needed, unfortunately, is not a reiteration of this aspiration but a very considerable elaboration upon it: what is it to be "ideal," "warm," and "loving," and how do we recognize and promote these in varying kinds of home and family? Are those parents and homes that scold teachers who discipline their children for "defending themselves physically in the school playground," for example, to be considered warm and loving or abusive? And what of the government or the nation as family when it calls for a war on terrorists? Is it to be considered violent or a loving protector of its citizens?

Reinventing Domestic Tranquillity

It is made abundantly clear by Martin that the Schoolhome is committed to education for living and living together. The Schoolhome also recognizes the need to work through with the young the cultural resistances to domesticity, and it wishes to make all children feel at home in it.[27] But how can we foster the care for every human being of the kind one seeks in the private world of the home if it is out of step with the values, priorities, and modus operandi of the public world? How can the school become, as one representative of this public world, President George H.W. Bush, put it in his Presidential Address to the Governors at the Education Summit in 1989, "a beacon of excellence, a sanctuary from violence, a model of good character, sound values, exemplary ethics"?[28] In a crucial and imaginative move in *The Schoolhome*, Martin invokes the nation's past and turns to the U.S. Constitution to find the answer: acknowledging that the notion of the school as a moral equivalent of the home necessitates "a remapping of the logical geography of education as well as a revisioning of the public world," she believes the Schoolhome can play its part in bringing the values of the home, the school, and the world into alignment "by deriving its overarching aim from a rewritten domestic tranquillity clause."[29]

In Martin's search for a gender-sensitive ideal of education, the concept of domesticity and the 3Cs of care, concern, and connection are central. She makes it clear that while a domestication of education is her goal, achieving it will necessitate a re-domestication of the nation, a return to the ideals of the founding fathers. Ask not, she demands, if the role of the school is to prepare children for the "real" world, no matter how ruthless and heartless the "real" world may be. Ask instead how we may set about a "remapping of home, school, and world" in which we may make the school a moral equivalent of the home and the values and behaviors of the public world conform to those of the Schoolhome.[30] Martin knows that for Plato and Rousseau, each man's theory of education was part of a broader political philosophy in which education played an indispensable role in attaining his idealization of the just state. Martin devotes less attention to setting forth a broad political philosophy, yet she does indicate that the just state or desirable society would be characterized by care, concern, and connection. She does, moreover, make it clear—even if she appears less than emphatic—that for her educational ideal to be attained, the wider society has a crucial role to play: it must embrace a revitalized interpretation of the constitutional ideal of domestic tranquillity and become a caring society.[31]

What have the 3Cs or caring got to do with domestic tranquillity, and why should Martin's aspirations stand a greater chance of being realized than those of former President Bush? While, for Martin, what she terms "the *civic* form of domestic intranquillity" about which the founding fathers were concerned is not extinct, "domestic intranquillity" of another kind poses the greater threat today. This is an antisocial form that seemed of little concern to the founding fathers, and it tears the social fabric just as rebellion unties civic bonds. Domestic violence of all kinds, Martin maintains, "violates the very rights of life, liberty, and the pursuit of happiness" that the Constitution sought to protect.[32] For many today—the homeless, the poor, the abused—there is no domestic tranquillity, in Martin's opinion. For the framers of the Constitution, however, the public or civic realm was the domestic realm. "Domesticate" the concept of "domestic tranquillity" and you have a society—a citizenry—in which social and personal values of caring replace those of cold politics and economics. To teach such domesticity in schools will require teachers to go beyond their subject, to be concerned for the welfare of all life in the school—manners and morality as well as subjects.[33] This is the morality of domestic tranquillity, one of caring and feeling for others. It does not idealize independence and separation from others, but neither does it call for forfeiting individuality any more than intimate relationships with others. In fact, domestic tranquillity might better promote individuality; keeping love at arm's length, conversely, might do more to breed conformity.[34]

Many may doubt the wisdom of such political philosophizing, but domesticating the nation at large can also draw support from the principles of democracy, not just from caring. It is true, Martin agrees, that a political theory derived from families, such as Filmer's, could lead to autocracy rather than democracy, but not necessarily. Besides, today the remembrance and the affirmation of our nation as a home is not what poses a danger to democracy. Rather, "our peril lies in the repression of domesticity."[35] The ideal of domesticating the nation at large also draws support from the notion of independence itself, Martin believes. Democracy requires a degree of self-governance of its people; but this is not self-sufficiency, a theme taken up again and elaborated further in *Cultural Miseducation*. We still depend on others—even Thoreau, the great advocate of self-reliance, did, as Martin points out. Lastly, there is a free speech argument to support a revitalized ideal of domestic tranquillity. The strongest point in favor of showing that free speech is not in conflict with the 3Cs is that in homes where spouses view each other as equals there is less violence.[36] So the question arises: how do we get there from here? Enter the Schoolhome.

At the point where Martin introduces the idea of a reinterpretation of domestic tranquillity, she makes it clear that the role of the school should not be to prepare students for the "real" public world as it now stands. But neither does she plan to leave this world untouched. The whole point of advocating a reinterpretation of the domestic tranquillity clause is to indicate that such a reinterpretation allows for a social and political ideal supportive of the Schoolhome through education grounded in the 3Cs of care, concern, and connection. So the work of social reform must also be undertaken. Martin puts it very explicitly when she writes, "we can remap the public world." Rather than rejecting the Schoolhome because there is a conflict between the values, attitudes, and patterns of behavior it seeks to promote and those of the public world, she suggests, let us attempt to reshape the values, attitudes, and behaviors of to the public world in accordance with those of the Schoolhome.[37] This is also why she says that no progress will be made toward making the school a moral equivalent of the home without a remapping of the home, the school, and the world, suggesting the need to develop new relationships among them.

Martin makes clear that she realizes the Schoolhome on its own cannot transform a culture adhering to a philosophy of radical disconnection, in which domesticity is repressed, into one that views the nation as a home and thinks of its citizens as family. The Schoolhome cannot work alone through the resistances; yet she maintains that it can work in concert with our other institutions "to prime the process of collective remembering."[38] In this way, for Martin, a reformed society may be seen as a mutually dependent ally to the school as both school and society seek together to enact the new social and educational ideals, a thought that is expanded upon by the recognition in Martin's later writings of other educational agents for which she begins to see a crucial educational and cultural role. It is a thought that in *Cultural Miseducation* and elsewhere gains further strength from the view that when the school is seen as but "one among many educational agents, it will no longer be in a position to treat the aims and procedures of other institutions as automatically subordinate to its own."[39] If this is so, to dismiss Martin's Schoolhome on the grounds that it would be out of harmony with the society in which it exists carries little weight. Indeed Martin's vision of society ultimately ranges beyond the nation to embrace the whole world. The Schoolhome wants to share with its inhabitants a vision not just of the nation but of the whole world as home. Thus its students and teachers can be found picturing their Schoolhome as the "innermost point in a set of concentric circles, each one of which is a moral equivalent of the home."[40]

It would be a mistake to underestimate the interconnection Martin envisages between the school, society, and the all-embracing extent of her educational ideal, even though she does not set forth a political philosophy at length. One thing is for sure: the notion of domesticity is fundamental to both her gender-sensitive educational ideal and her view of how we ought to set about the remapping as well as the regenerating of home, school, and society. In this the influence of Montessori on her thinking is profound. Kilpatrick and educational theorists in general may have been blinded to the insights of Montessori by the misleading cultural definition of school as a place that prepares students for the public world. Perhaps Martin herself was blinded for a while, but no more.[41] Now she follows Montessori, who wished to bring the atmosphere and affection of home into school, even though doing so conflicts with what society expects from education.[42] In doing so, Martin fills out a little further the particular values to which her ideal is committed.

According to Martin, "when it is understood that Montessori thought of school on the model of home, the elements of her system take on a different configuration."[43] Of course, Montessori did not model her school on just any home. She modeled it on a version that many of its inhabitants would not have known, that is, a caring, nurturing, warm, welcoming, joyful place, thereby, unlike Dewey, imparting values to students drawn not from their own homes. For Montessori the children belonged to the school; the school belonged to them; and they were all part of the one school family. She also thought of the home as a "second womb," where children were transformed into "peaceful" persons, not the vandals they were likely to become if left to the streets. In Martin's account of Montessori, insofar as the home stopped teaching its "domestic" lessons, the school should step into the breach. Montessori being a domesticated romantic in Martin's characterization, the lessons taught in Montessori's school would emphasize protection from harm, social connectedness, and harmony with nature. They would be much the opposite from the martial virtues admired by James, such as obedience to command and contempt of softness.[44]

According to Martin, Montessori was anticipating a time in the United States when many mothers would also have to leave home and children to go to work; she was also anticipating the curse of family homelessness described by Kozol. This is not to say that Montessori's Casa dei Bambini can be simply transplanted into the United States today, for while many of its curricular elements, such as the 3Cs, can be, many cannot. Martin now intends to do with Montessori's philosophy and practice what Montessori did with the findings of Itard and Séguin—modify and build upon them for our day.

The Ethos of the Schoolhome

Martin sets the tone for dealing in a practical manner with these matters when, in the Prologue to *The Schoolhome*, she asks, what do we do to provide for the children who are left behind and neglected as women join men in leaving the home? Her answer: we need a new educational ideal, not just a traditional one gendered in favor of males extended to women; we need a gender-sensitive educational ideal. Degenderizing the qualities built into our cultural concept of the educated person has never been an educational aim, she maintains. If we need a gender-sensitive idea of education, we also need gender-sensitive schooling, and our policymakers must address the gender issue if we are to succeed. Not that doing so is a cause for alarm. On the contrary, "we should not underestimate the changes to be wrought by redefining the function of education and restructuring the ideal of an educated man or woman."[45] Who knows what we might come up with?[46]

Yet gender sensitivity is not sufficient for domesticity; there must also be sensitivity to race, ethnicity, religion, class, physical abilities, sexual orientation, and other salient dimensions of young people's lives.[47] Because of neglect in this area even now, for many, the school curriculum is unrelated to their lives. They feel excluded and underperform, though some such as Rodriguez master its content. Criticizing the excluding and self-focused character of Hirsch's plan for "cultural literacy," Martin wishes to include the voices and stories of all, not just those of the dominant, cultural elite.[48]

Martin elaborates on this idea in "Curriculum and the Mirror of Knowledge" as she stresses putting goals before content. She is particularly concerned about the White man's excluding perspective that pays little or no attention to the experience of more than half of the population, namely, women and people of color. For this reason, she would likely disagree with Scheffler, who appreciates the ideal of gender-sensitive education—a "new unitary conception of the educated person," as he terms it—but denies that Peters's ideal of "the educated man" rejected it. The concept of the educated man, Scheffler suggests,[49]

is no less opposed to popular stereotypes than the feminist critique. As we have seen, this concept is no narrow defense of popular notions of science or theory. It incorporates the ideas of passion, care, activity and engagement, the idea of self-respect and respect for others, the life of art and intellect, as well as the notion of community within which intellectual and moral agency is given birth. In abstracting from sex difference, the defense of this concept of education as normative projects its ideal both for men and for women, challenging all to expand and enrich human culture in its many dimensions.

Martin's contention would surely be that the ideal that "the educated man" projects is one that has been shaped on the basis of men's experience and the exclusion of women's, and that Scheffler, like Siegel and McClellan, fails to grasp that the traditional concept of the educated man excludes women's experience.

Once again, the reasons for her concern are derived from—and hence permit us to perceive more fully—her idealization of the educated person. Such an exclusive curriculum as the elders have in store for us is objectionable because it excludes subject matter that enables us to be more accepting of one another in all aspects of life.[50] A mirrorless concept of curriculum, one guided by educational purpose rather than prejudicial content loaded in favor of the elders and their exclusionary values—and justified by their hollow and illusory claims of internal curriculum coherence— is important, then, because at least "it allows us to ask those questions about external meaning, disconnection, incompleteness that our elders have been avoiding. In particular it lets us ask if a nation worried about falling apart does not require a *unifying* curriculum—one that develops kinship bonds among girls and boys of different races, social classes, ethnicities— far more than a *unified* one."[51] By so allowing, it may enable one to attain to Martin's ideal of an educated person in which connection, care, and concern are central values, certainly as important as academic achievement.

As we have seen already, Martin believes that many educators, notably Kilpatrick, did not see the deeper message in Montessori's philosophy, because they saw school as a place that prepares students for the public world of work. For Montessori, by contrast, school (her Casa dei Bambini) was to be a home, with all of the affective, moral, nurturing, educative and positive connotations; hence her wish to bring the atmosphere and affection of home into school. It was not merely a house or building, and this is the meaning of home that Martin now wants captured in her idealized Schoolhome. In any culture, that which is labeled education is valued, and since our schools have focused on preparation for the public world, it is this "public knowledge," unlike domesticity, that is valued and is put into the curriculum. How silly that we are willing to dispense with half of our cultural capital! The Schoolhome, by contrast, has designed a curriculum that will prepare boys and girls for life in both the public and private worlds.[52] It considers that to deny boys domesticity education is positively immoral, though that is what the preservers of the traditional curriculum wish to do.[53]

Money may be needed to establish schools in the mold of the Schoolhome, but so is a refocusing of attention, and more besides. The Schoolhome is not seen as a marketplace assembly line making products such as workers and consumers. Rather, emphasizing domesticity and the 3Cs, there is a focus on matters such as classroom climate and a reorienting of practice. Martin accepts that recreating the school as a moral equivalent of the home means having to address the issues of whether this can be done in a place of such diversity and violence. It means having to recognize that postindustrial homes often lost the ethic of caring. Indeed it means having to recognize that the school may have to replace the lost "ethic of caring" and the respite and recreation from the cruel world once found in the home, at least the idealized, model home.[54] At the same time, it is possible, with hard work by faculty, to develop a suitable curriculum. This would be a curriculum that (a) speaks to all students, (b) addresses common themes and the great questions, and (c) unifies all. It is also possible to "treasure the uniqueness of a whole range of perspectives without losing sight of commonalities."[55] This will require a teaching faculty that exemplifies an inclusive stance. It will mean a school that is experimental to a degree, since the issue of what differences make a difference to education cannot be settled in advance.[56] It will also entail demands from society at large for a much greater degree of accountability from the media—educational agents in disguise, as Martin has come to view them. These now bombard the young with unwholesome, antisocial models of living, making these appear fatally attractive. Greater success must be achieved in holding the media accountable for the damage they do in preserving and transmitting cultural liabilities rather than cultural wealth.[57]

The Curriculum of the Schoolhome

It is ironic that for Martin, as for Montessori, it is the school and not the home that is seen as leading the charge in the domestication of the nation, hence the very idea of the Schoolhome. Thus to her own question, what must be done to fill the "domestic vacuum" caused by the removal of work from the home that requires both parents to leave the home for work, Martin responds that changing homes are not up to teaching children about family. It must be done in the schools where boys and girls alike must learn the values of the home. The curriculum will be enriched in the process.[58] There is room for optimism that the transformation from schoolhouse to Schoolhome can take place. It will take time but the reform of American education can begin right way. It does not have to be nationwide or even district-wide to begin. One school, even one classroom at a time, will be a beginning.[59] If we are to judge from *Cultural Miseducation*, there is also the newly found hope that some of the added burdens may be shared by hitherto unrecognized educational agents such as the media.

How, then, might an ideal education be translated into practice and be reflected in the school curriculum? Will domesticity be a school subject, and be derided as domestic science once was and home economics often is today, even by girls? Finding what to incorporate in the Schoolhome will be difficult but there are many sources to which we can look. Since Martin has long argued that we should not base school programs on the basis of what knowledge exists but on the basis of what our goals or purposes are, curriculum content is to be chosen on the basis of our educational purposes.[60] Knowledge can be viewed as a human or social construction, and all knowledge or any particular subject does not have an a priori claim on the curriculum. Accordingly, Martin will seek a curriculum that emphasizes a commonality of attitudes, skills, and values rather than bodies of knowledge,[61] that blends science with humanity and affection, that recognizes individuality and tolerance, and that has a respect for nature and joy.[62] But what specifically are the subjects of the Schoolhome or of a good education? While the subjects she recommends certainly are not set out in tabular form, and one may have to rake through several years of her writings to grasp them all, an attempt can be made at representing them.

Unexpected as it may be, for all its failings, it appears that liberal education and the disciplines of which it is composed in one form or another is a sine qua non of the educated person and therefore of the curriculum. Whether this component is to be organized in the form of "the discipline" that Martin spoke of in "The Disciplines and the Curriculum," it will need to be supplemented with education for domesticity and the 3Cs. What education for domesticity consists of is mentioned at various points and, along with the attitudes, values, and practical skills she wishes it to incorporate, it includes home economics or family studies, journalism, and drama. We are also told that, in general, the Schoolhome will feature reading, writing, friendship, conversation, music and singing, camaraderie, and spontaneity. It will also include gym. The Schoolhome will be a happy place where all can achieve and form positive memories of the experience. All will belong.[63]

Turning to the question of domesticity and whatever one might call a subject in domesticity, if there is to be one, Martin argues for the inclusion of the study of a subject entity embracing gender, women, domesticity, and the 3Cs. It is difficult, she admits, to find a suitable name for such a subject entity—perhaps home economics or family studies.[64] Care is needed, moreover, that such a study would not fall prey, as other practical subjects do, to being just a study of theory—with students becoming mere observers. It is important, therefore, that "boys and girls alike learn to exercise the virtues which our culture thinks of as housed in our private homes."[65]

What would be the content of such a study? Once again, Martin is not expansive, though she offers examples of how such material might be incorporated in the curriculum. It would appear to have three main elements. Given the abusive attitudes toward girls and women that boys are universally exposed to from their earliest years in school, firstly there would be a focus on gender intended to promote respect for others of both sexes. Secondly, there would be a study of domesticity: child-care, housework, and the reproductive processes of society in general. Thirdly, there would be attention to the 3Cs.[66] Aside from this, no extensive analysis is provided regarding the epistemological and moral character of these areas and the pedagogical characteristics and methodological aspects of them receives only slight attention. Having indicated that we need to teach children human activities, since they are not born with them, Martin mentions theater and journalism as suitable for this purpose. She also sees these, in turn, as leading into language, literature, social studies, and even science, math, building, designing, and every human emotion, joining head and hand to heart. They have the potential to lead to political science and civics too. In another example, a class in literature is considered suitable for teaching boys to be caring and nonviolent and girls to speak up for themselves and to look out for themselves as well as others.[67]

Martin realizes that the Schoolhome cannot do all the work of the home or fully replace the home: it cannot buy the groceries or do the housework; and it cannot tend to the young during their waking and sleeping hours in the home.[68] The Schoolhome, it seems, is to focus on roles that are largely educational ones. One of these will be to teach boys to take on domestic roles or activities that culture—not nature—has assigned to women. All will learn domesticity, and not just in theory but by doing and doing joyfully. This is not to be training for a professional career, but for living in the home. The manual side will be balanced by attending to the intellectual side, often in the library. Domestic and related intellectual activity will focus upon and develop around food, shelter, and nutrition.[69] While Martin may still be short on elaboration when it comes to the content of family studies or home economics, she does add another important point having to do with the hidden curriculum. Just to neglect or exclude family studies from the curriculum is not merely to leave students ignorant of its content. Whether we include it in the curriculum or not, we are teaching home economics, for to omit it is to teach that it has no value. The very fact that we are unsure of what to name this subject area is itself evidence of its already marginal status.[70]

The inclusion of home economics in the school curriculum, or at least some of the elements of it such as cooking, might not rise to the order of a challenge to all schools today; for theorists such as Hirst, Phenix, and Adler, it does. Their theories marginalize if not entirely debar it. Yet Martin clearly wants to go much further than conventional home economics or even conceptions of the subject as held by recognized scholars in the field today.[71] In a word, she wants to bring the culture of the home—the right or ideal home—into the school curriculum, along with its associated values of the 3Cs and respect for gender differences, as well as cooking; and through the school she wants to bring it into the world. She expands the concept further when she adds that "when the civic 'sphere' is seen as a domestic domain, as I am recommending it should be, domestic education in the limited sense of home economics becomes one among many elements of domestic education writ large."[72] Seeing matters in this way is not merely a challenge to the theorists; it may be even a greater challenge to the schools themselves, to those who make school policy, and to the politicians.

THE IDEAL CONSIDERED

Speaking to the depth and breadth of Martin's educational ideal, Kallman-Roemer had this to say:[73]

> Following her pragmatic argument which appeals to the harmful consequences for women and men of a contemporary and dominant educational prescription, Martin challenges us to take up the task of developing a "gender-just" ideal of the educated person. She also provides a model for proceeding with her careful and provocative analysis. Developing a gender-just ideal involves uncovering the depths and pervasiveness of our sexual ideology, its relationship to our social structure, and its influence on our lives, particularly the development of personal and group identity. It involves examining our ideals of truth, our standards of evidence, and our foundations of knowledge in terms of our social-political context, as well as considering anew our ideas of the good person, a good society, and what it means to live a life of scope, both productively and reproductively.

These are high expectations that captured well many facets of Martin's educational ideal when they were written in 1981. Today, however, they provide but a partial measure of the challenge that Martin has taken upon herself as her ideas evolve. She is not satisfied merely to explore or develop the ideal; now, however wisely, she wishes to provide a model for its implementation as well.

Domestic Tranquillity

In the course of her gender critique of mainstream educational thought, Martin concluded that, as a society, we use schools to prepare children for the transition from the private to the public world. We assume, moreover, that preparation for home and family life is unnecessary, that we are by nature fit for it. The evidence of abuse of children in their own homes is sufficient to convince Martin that this is not true. There is an urgent need to prepare the young for family living, for life in the private world of the home, just as there may be a need to prepare them for the public world. If, as Martin maintains, homes are no longer capable of providing such education and the job must be given over to the schools, the question arises as to what authority the schools have to undertake it, and what are the prospects for success if homes are not up to preparing those who dwell in them for life in those very homes. For Martin, the authority derives from

the Constitution, from a revitalized interpretation of the domestic tranquillity clause; the prospects for success are rooted in a nation domesticated. With the nation viewed as home, and possessing the values and
characteristics of home, the school may absorb, reflect, and therefore dispense such values and qualities as are embodied in domestic tranquillity.
Presumably we may expect no less from all other educational agents.

While this may be a noble aspiration it is at best an ideal as we speak.
If all the conditions required for it to be realized were met in the first place,
moreover, there may be no need for the schools to do anything. Besides,
for such a happy state of affairs to exist, homes themselves would possess
the very values, aspirations, and characteristics of domesticity that Martin
now finds lacking in them. Yet even ideals can be realized, through force
of circumstance or exceptional leadership and sacrifice. Revolutions bear
testimony to this, and on several occasions Martin is calling for nothing
less than revolution. Viewed in this light, her appeal to a revitalized interpretation of the domestic tranquillity clause is a startling breakthrough,
perhaps more powerful than she herself realizes. She shows concern over
the possibility that a society governed by tranquillity may be prone to an
autocratic form of government, and seeks support for her novel idea in
appeals to the principles of independence, freedom of speech, and even
democracy itself. Yet she is reluctant to rejoice in the realization that one
of the goals of democracy, as of any just society, is the attainment of that
very peace and tranquillity. While she explores the implications of peace
and tranquillity for school and society, ironically, her vision and the likelihood of its attainment are impeded by nothing less than her focus on
domesticity itself, urging her to put the private world before the public.

Impeded or not, it is a powerful vision from the point of view of the
educational goals it defines and the educational measures it envisions. First
as to goals: Martin perceives educational goals very much in terms of their
social significance. Her all-embracing aspiration is a just and caring society,
characterized by respect for all and violence and abuse toward none. Hence
the call to domesticity, to peace and tranquillity: so that we all may come
to possess the 3Cs, showing care, concern, and connection in our daily
activities in both the public and private worlds, nurturing the young, tending to the elderly and the infirm, and connecting with all of whatever race,
gender, or economic circumstance.

These goals are admirable and almost entirely unobjectionable. They may
be as relevant and pressing in any age as in our own but when there is a
growing concern regarding the breakdown of family life, of violence and
incivility, and of social stratification and discord, they are surely no less
pertinent today than ever. Yet traditionally they have not been so highlighted among the goals of education as those more readily associated with
the public world, where considerations of economic competitiveness, technological superiority, and individual achievement and personal fulfillment

take precedence. Unlike others, such as Adler, who have assented to the goals she highlights, moreover, Martin recognizes that they have implications for education that have not always been recognized, leading her to call for education to balance the theoretical and the practical, the rational and the emotional, the public and the private. In many respects the broad measures she calls for in regard to the implementation of her ideal are both innovative and encouraging. These include the addition to the commonly accepted goals of public schooling of goal (e), preparation for home and family living, for which she has made a strong case. They include a broadly based concept of culture that is consistent with her advocacy of a curriculum deriving from goals rather than preconceived conclusions about its knowledge content. It is a view of culture that fits well with broadly conceived goals that address the emotional and practical as well as the academic formation of the young. Martin's concept of multiple educational agency gives recognition to the role of sources of education other than the school, a view that also blends well with her concept of culture.

Yet to pick out those features of Martin's alternative view of education that are both compelling and innovative must not blind us to its weaknesses, even if these pertain to the details and to the implementation rather than the scope of her ideal. Such are the implications of peace and tranquillity and such are the hopes and wishes held out for it by society and individuals alike that its attainment has been an aspiration for the ages, sought after by philosophers, statesmen, and social and religious leaders alike. It has meant different things at different times and for different people, including its negative construction as the absence of war and poverty and other forms of suffering. Construed more positively, it has variously meant the attainment of personal joy and fulfillment through prayer and meditation, artistic achievement, the liberal pursuit of knowledge, and familial and social harmony. The implications of these and other possibilities for education are considerable both in terms of idealization and practicability, and they merit far greater consideration than can be given here. But more demanding still, and a prize that has escaped mankind itself, is that of divining the path to peace and tranquillity from where we find ourselves in the present; to snatch even a glimpse of an educational program designed to set us on our way has proven equally elusive. Yet the search goes on. For Martin it takes the form of a search for a gender-sensitive ideal of education defined in terms of the standards that apply within the private world, the world of family and of women.

There is the hope that peace and tranquillity will at once sustain it and emanate from this kind of education; but how the public world outside of education will impinge upon the realization of this ideal is often overlooked by Martin, as are its ramifications for promoting peace and tranquillity. Aside from her call to recognize a multiplicity of educational agents along with schools, she gives little attention to considering the obstacles that exist and the measures that may need to be taken within key areas of the public world if a revitalized interpretation of domestic tranquillity is to prevail. These include measures such as gaining political support, the willing co-operation of economic interests and the subjugation of self-interest, and the education of governmental, business, professional, military, and other leaders of the public world who will promote or at least accept peace and tranquillity.

One notable exception to this general oversight is found in the attention that Martin has begun to give to the role of various educational agents. In *Cultural Miseducation* and "Women, Schools, and Cultural Wealth," for example, Martin details the enormous impact of the range of educational or cultural agents that exist and which lie beyond the normal control of the school. One listing that Martin provides includes the following: "Church, neighborhood, museums, libraries, zoos, symphony orchestras, banks, businesses, the stock market, newspapers, magazines, book clubs, record companies, publishing houses, sports organizations, billboards, government agencies, TV, the Internet, and the media in all its multitudinous forms."[74] Martin goes further to suggest ways of generating some form of educational and cultural accountability among these various bodies, including some means of keeping track of those aspects of cultural stock for which the various agents may be considered responsible. In this way one may be able to keep track of those elements of cultural stock that become neglected or forgotten. In what would undoubtedly be an ambitious undertaking, Martin believes that one may also make visible to all that these various agents have a moral responsibility to the community to ensure that the cultural stock they transmit is an asset and not a liability.

Admirable and ambitious as this proposal of Martin's may be, it still seems inadequate in the face of the kind of countercultural forces that concern Martin. Some general sense of the power of the public world in determining the success of the private world in promoting peace and tranquillity, the 3Cs that are expected to go along with it, and even Martin's aspirations for the Schoolhome, can be gleaned from a glance at the exercise of power in conducting the affairs of the nation and the world of nations. Political, military, and economic goals and strategies dominate the interests of states and governments. Benevolent political leadership as measured, if it can be, by the standards of Western democracies, for example, wages constant battle with the forces of crime, greed, and control. It does this in its efforts to balance international diplomacy, a global competitive edge for the business community, tax relief for the wealthy, and a powerful military presence with the interests of health care for the sick, economic support and assistance for the elderly and the needy, adequate educational resources for the young, social welfare, and civil rights for all. Initiatives to promote neglected and needy endeavors vie with established policies and procedures. Ideally, they are handled in such a way as not to create imbalances that jeopardize them. It is for this reason that such initiatives need to be considered and treated in the context of the public world settings in which they must make their way, and the ideals of peace, tranquillity and gender-sensitive education spearheaded by the Schoolhome are clearly such initiatives. It may be true that in an altered world, one in which Martin's reinterpretation of the domestic tranquillity clause holds sway, promoting her educational ideals would be more readily realized. We are still at the point where such a reinterpretation needs to be put in place, however. Given the competing interests that have so far existed, how the primacy of domestic tranquillity as a political and social ideal is to be advanced in a way that it has not to this point in history is therefore unclear.

In one instance where Martin attempts to draw out some practical implications of a revitalized interpretation of the domestic tranquillity clause by drawing on the friendship shown by the people of Le Chambon, France, toward the Jews in World War II, difficulties lurk on the horizon right away. There may never have been a golden age of domestic tranquillity in America, she tells us, but the ideal can be realized, and it does not have to consign women to be second-class citizens to come about. It can be embraced by men, who also can be trained to care, and many of whom are already so disposed. One may question if the kind of community or group care she has in mind is possible, yet the case of Le Chambon is one instance of where it seems to have occurred. While Martin is quick to add that we must be careful not to produce care that leads to colonization, the interplay of the notions of individuality and community needs far closer scrutiny by her. Take the poor, for example. Proclaiming the necessity for love of one another as part of any reclamation of the domestic tranquillity clause, Martin inquires if such love for one another means that we should take the poor into our private homes. She immediately replies that it does not. It is enough, according to Martin, to make them part of the larger family, "and provisions would therefore have to be made for them."[75] Not only does this smack of "love by edict" but it raises the question about who is going to make "provisions"—people who love or agencies that may not? Even if we are to put the problem "at the top of our public agenda" one must still ask if this is sufficient. Or are we to take comfort from the fact that, after all, domestic tranquillity on a national scale is but an ideal?[76]

Because Martin's appeal to domestic tranquillity—and its implications for home, school, and society—is framed within concerns for domesticity, she fails to explore fully the public context in which, perhaps, from today's starting point, it can only be attained. She could have framed her concerns for domesticity and a revitalized interpretation of the domestic tranquillity clause within a social, political, and economic philosophy rooted in the public world in the manner that both Plato and Rousseau located their educational theories. If she had done so, it may have enticed her to consider at greater length those dimensions of the broader society—of the public world—necessary to explore adequately the ramifications of peace and tranquillity for home, school, society, and gender relations, and the measures needed to be taken in the public world to conduct the kind of education that Martin herself seeks to promote by locating it within the public world of schools. This is not to dismiss the revolutionary potential of Martin's appeal to a revitalized reinterpretation of the domestic tranquillity clause. This much her appeal has for sure. Neither is it to overlook Martin's more recent focus on the need for accountability by educational agents beyond the school, and her recognition of the broad social context in which education and schooling take place. But the social, political, and educational possibilities which her reinterpretation of domestic tranquillity contains may not be realized unless even greater emphasis is given to the broad public contexts in which these possibilities come to life and, like schooling itself, must themselves continuously be refashioned.

Implementation

It may be objected that the means of implementing Martin's educational ideal are set forth by her in the educational proposals she advocates in her gender-sensitive ideal of education, notably in *The Schoolhome*. Not so. Through both her epistemological and gender critiques, Martin tellingly portrays the critical weaknesses of conventional thinking and makes a powerful case for a new idealization of education. She elaborates on the idealization in *The Schoolhome*, colors it by sketching in a teaching scenario here and there, and bolsters it with a powerful appeal to a reinterpretation of the domestic tranquillity clause. In *Cultural Miseducation* she imaginatively and cogently articulates the richness and range of curriculum content that may be called upon to further the new idealization. But that's as far as she goes. Concrete proposals for actual implementation as distinct from theorizing about or imagining alternatives are few and weak. The one contained in "The Disciplines and the Curriculum," namely the adoption of a subject called "the discipline" to deal with academic studies in which the focus would be upon the nature of disciplinary study remains one of the more tangible. A great deal of what Martin has presented by way of proposals for curriculum reform in the intervening years still fits within the framework presented in that article. She adds to it in matters of detail while at the same time calling for an experimental stance in regard to organization, curriculum, and instruction. But much greater elaboration is needed, notwithstanding Martin's recommendations in regard to assigning different educational and moral responsibilities to the various educational agents she more recently recognizes to have a role in education. Bewildered at the prospect of teaching affection, friendship, camaraderie, conversation, and spontaneity rather than bits and bodies of knowledge, for example, one is left with more questions than answers on issues of justification, methodology, organization, assessment, and overall practicability. Even in the specific proposal for liberal education based on a study of "the discipline," one has to ask can one ever provide the liberal education dimension of the broader education that Martin now seeks through such a vehicle? If so, she has not told us how,[77] nor added much in her later writings to the stance she adopted in regard to "the discipline."[78]

While any such treatment needs to address the liberal education dimension of Martin's curriculum thinking, it also needs to attend to the many considerable omissions in her account of the components of her favored curriculum learnings. Once Martin leaves her role as philosopher and assumes that of reform guide, as she does in *The Schoolhome*, for example, it's no longer quite sufficient to send the reader off to change the world with the "reminder" to adopt an experimental stance in regard to matters of organization, curriculum, and instruction. What is needed are guidelines at least on how to combine science, humanity, and affection, how to ensure that students go beyond mere observation and delve into the exercise of the virtues of the good home, and how you not only employ the study of theater and journalism to lead to a wide range of human activities but also to language, literature, social studies, science, and mathematics, not to mention building, designing, and every human emotion. Guidelines, or some indication that what she proposes can be realized, are also needed, since past practice seems to have been unsuccessful in how literature can be taught in such a way that it will at once enable girls to speak up for themselves and boys to become more caring and nonviolent, and how the study of home economics, the bane of many students' lives, can be engaged in joyfully.

While Martin's treatment of these matters is deficient from a pedagogical standpoint, not to mention the many issues crucial to transforming her ideal into reality not raised at all, in *The Schoolhome* she does attempt to give a sense of the ethos of Schoolhome. She is also somewhat more explicit on the subject of home economics or family studies, a core dimension of her reform curriculum. Here the goal is for all to learn practical and joyful domesticity for living, not just the theory, through a balanced program of hands-on experience and academic study centered on food, shelter, and nutrition. Elsewhere the range is extended specifically to include gender, women, and the 3Cs. Hence the three core constituent parts of a home economics or family studies curriculum that have already been identified: gender; domesticity, meaning child care, housework, and the reproductive processes of society in general; and the 3Cs of care, concern and connection.[79]

In a nutshell, this is the essence of Martin's gender-sensitive education and of a significant aspect of her entire reform vision. Reduced to its most central element, it represents a rich concept of domesticity combined with a gender-sensitive school ethos; it also suggests a more comprehensible overall project. Yet it remains deceptively difficult to manage and is in need of considerable elaboration as to its implementation. This is especially so when the "civic 'sphere' is seen as a domestic domain," as Martin recommends, and when citizenship education in the limited sense of education about government is combined with domestic education in the limited sense of home economics, in a broadened and revitalized conception of domestic education.[80] Such elaboration must address the kind of experimental and creative stance Martin envisages in regard to organization, curriculum, and instruction. It may need to pay particular attention to her view that while we may wish to teach subject matter derived from both the productive and reproductive processes in school, the split between the two ought not to be replicated in the school curriculum.[81] Accordingly, it must surely address issues of evaluation and assessment, not least the role of testing in perpetuating gender bias. It may also be advisable to take cognizance of the legacy of rejection associated with home economics specifically and practical subjects as distinct from theoretical in general. Once family studies have been fully admitted to the school curriculum, the complexities of teaching the practical must also be addressed. Yet before any of this, Martin must show that education in domesticity, in the 3Cs, and in gender relations is a job for the school rather than the home.

Alternatives

Not only are the tangible proposals for implementation that Martin makes few and weak, there is a wide range of possibilities that she never considers. These are, at the least, readily conceivable if not revolutionary. One has to wonder, therefore, why she rushes to the conclusion in *The Schoolhome* that the main alternative to the existing state of affairs is to turn to the school to do the job of preparing the young as members of homes and families. One has to wonder, too, why the very first question that comes to her mind in seeking to remedy the neglect of family life education is "where does the responsibility lie?" Why should one assume it lies anywhere but primarily with the family? When hospitals do a bad job of healing patients or financial institutions produce a poor return on investments, we don't ask right away where the responsibility for these activities lie and then seek new institutions to attend to them.

When, in *Cultural Miseducation*, Martin recognizes the existence of a wide range of agents beyond the school that may share in the work of education, remarkably the family and its educational role still gets short shrift. Yet when it comes to education for family living, there is no escaping the central role of parents and family. No consideration of how deficiencies can be remedied by schools or other educational agents that does not take a closer look at their roles can be considered realistic. In so doing, not surprisingly, it readily emerges that the situation is rather complex. In her writings on the subject, Martin frequently refers to the connection between education for family life and the fact of women as well as men working outside the home; she adverts also to the additional demands this outside work makes on mothers in particular, and to what it all means for the children who are left behind. Above all, she is convinced that for many households it leads to an inevitable neglect in child rearing, a central theme in *The Schoolhome*. Yet even if one accepts that both parents working outside the home is a relevant factor, we still need to account for those homes where preparation for family living is alive and well, even with both parents out to work, and for those where nothing of the sort exists even though neither parent goes out to work. This clearly raises questions about the impact of different kinds of parenting, and it raises questions concerning Martin's assumptions regarding the effects on children of both parents working outside the home and about her assumptions about child rearing neglect being caused by absentee or working parents. It also raises the question of the role of the school—and with the appearance of *Cultural Miseducation* that of other educational agents too—as envisioned by Martin as a counterbalance to both parents working outside the home. Most importantly, perhaps, it raises the question as to whether it is to the reform of parenting and the social provisions we make for it, as well as the educational agents in society that Martin more recently wishes to bring into the picture, rather than the reform of schools to which we should look in search of the primary mode of addressing the neglect of education for home and family. Other sorts of questions also arise. What might be done to assist homes experiencing parenting difficulties in doing a better job? What educational role might the school have as an ancillary and partner with the home rather than as the lead agency in preparing for family living? Or, as one promising recent study framed the question, what might it do to improve "home involvement"?[82]

Before turning to examine possible answers to some of these questions, it may be helpful to look at what Martin has to say herself about the conditions of women working outside the home. It is true that women, including mothers, the traditional educators in the home, are now sometimes required to work outside of the home as men first were. Yet, not all women are so required. For many it is a matter of choice, sometimes even a choice between material prosperity and other priorities but a choice nonetheless. If the situation they encounter is so dismal as that described by Martin, and the problems created in the home so catastrophic, one has to wonder why we as a society should exacerbate the problem by encouraging their expulsion from the home?[83] Why not seek to save the home and the job of homemaking—which is often the alternative goal that is sacrificed to material prosperity or other goals besides child rearing—and elevate both the home and the roles associated with it? Does equality among men and women require women to follow men into the conventional workplace instead of carving out, somewhat along the lines attempted by Beecher, for example, a new if not uniquely woman's domain in which to be leaders in new forms of family-related work? Or is Martin actually falling into the trap of defining success for women in terms of what counts as success for men? Is "setting women free" to work outside the home just like men at once part of the problem? Of course, to argue that one parent should stay home to rear the children does not mean that this should be the mother, in which case some of these questions may not arise at all.

There are many alternatives to be explored before one has to acquiesce in the dismissal of women—or either parent in a two-parent home if one does not wish to confine full-time child rearing to women—from the home. Such alternatives may necessitate a less ready willingness to accept as economic truths or "demands of economic necessity" beliefs so accepted by Martin, such as her belief that both parents are required to work outside the home.[84] Possible answers exist along with questions. One such possibility would be a greater sharing of the work of the home between men and women, and Martin has made clear that she believes this ought to be done anyway. Another would be to have one parent give up working outside the home and stay at home attending to both the domestic work of the home and to domestic education, as is still done in some homes today, sometimes by men. This would certainly conform to the expectation that the home is where the responsibility lies for child rearing and family life education, not the school to which this work is often left when parents devote less time rearing their children than may be necessary. It then becomes a matter of deciding which parent stays at home, a matter that may be more contentious for participants in the academic debate surrounding this question than for the actual parents involved.[85]

A more difficult case, of course, is that of single parents or those two-parent homes for which one income is actually inadequate. Here again alternatives to the school as the major source of providing family education are imaginable. These include forms of sharing as between school and home, home and church, home and youth organizations of a kind that may also be compatible with Martin's new emphasis on a multiplicity of educational agents, and of course parent education. There is, too, the possibility of financial support in the form of providing a parent a stipend to stay home. There are also those cases where parents are abusive or incompetent and where such a solution may not apply. This may call for parent education or, in cases of abuse or serious incompetence, intervention by social work agencies. In some cases, adoption or foster care might need to be considered. Any such solution would have to allow for variations to meet different cases. A variation that merits particular mention for better-off families is that of allowing tax relief for a parent as an inducement to stay at home, accompanied by efforts aimed at combating glorified if unrealistic media images, typically of mothers who can "do it all."

Lastly, there is the complex issue of women's need as much as men's to feel genuine accomplishment in whatever field of endeavor attracts them. Of those—men or women—who find that looking after family fulfills this need, little more needs to be said here. Where this is not, more needs to be said and done. In an age of extraordinary communications such as ours is, and the possibilities for social interaction between a caregiver in the home and others outside that accompany it, there are grounds for optimism that promising new alternatives may exist on this front, however.

An obvious avenue of exploration regarding the central question of education for domesticity and the 3Cs related to some of the measures just identified is to ask what can be done to improve parenting. If we are willing to add a whole new burden and expense to schooling, as might be necessitated by adopting the Schoolhome for all, surely it would merit first inquiring if time and effort would not be better invested in parenting education for existing parents and parents-to-be. Today, in-service education is found in all spheres of the workplace, yet we ignore anything resembling it in regard to parenting. Even when Martin herself calls for "the education of a whole range of cultural custodians themselves in accepting their educational responsibilities,"[86] parents are not included. Do we have to give up so readily without trying out such a possibility? Besides, if children suffer educationally without parental involvement, how can the school ever hope to give home education or education of any kind by taking it away from the home? There is also the crucial issue of it not simply being a matter of how much time parents spend with their children but what is done by both parents and children in that time, and the quality of the relationships and mutual respect that exists. If this confirms for us that parent education may be as important as time, it also raises once again the issue of it taking a village to raise a child,[87] for where a vibrant community exists, parents can serve other parents' children as well as their own. This may be every bit as important as providing home education in the school. If the task of education for family life and the 3Cs is to be passed on to schools, they may be no more successful than many existing homes without the aid and support of local and more broadly based communities as well as parents that can successfully contribute.[88]

Martin's recognition of agents of education other than the school, such as the media, come to mind here as an area where they may have much to contribute to community well-being. It could alter the situation created for parents from the unrelenting competition presented by the media. For all the so-called control measures such as the V chip that can be put in place to give parents a greater say in the education of their children, for example, there is in fact very little control exerted over what children are exposed to in the way of television and Internet viewing. Both are largely driven by advertising: what is made available for public viewing is what business is willing to support in the way of advertising revenue; and much of the time, appeal to base instincts seems to be what creates revenue. In other words, what is made available for public viewing is dictated by economic considerations rather than those of peace and tranquillity or concerns for the welfare of the community. The control of weapons of destruction—firearms to be more specific—is also a matter of economics. Business interests make guns because guns make money. If these two economic forces alone actually could be controlled, whether by measures such as those that Martin presents when calling for greater accountability among the various educational agents, or any others, the issue of the exposure of children to the glamour, allure, and ultimately the degradation of violence and personal indulgence could be seriously addressed. This is but another way of saying that civic-minded business and community values shaped by an aspiration to domestic tranquillity rather than narrow economic interests also present alternatives to the school as a mode of teaching civility.

There may be objections to alternatives of the kind mentioned here, some even on the grounds of government invading our lives. Of course the government has been invading our lives in this area ever since compulsory schooling entered the scene, and one could argue that the alternatives mentioned are less rather than more invasive than those offered by Martin. Yet there are practical difficulties of another kind also facing Martin's ideal of gender-sensitive education to which she makes reference but for which any remedy is hard to envisage. One is the kind of problem Martin encountered in Plato, namely, requiring men to acquire traits now genderized in favor of women. Perhaps Martin's ideal of a gender-sensitive education will tackle this problem successfully, but up to this point nothing has been said that makes one hopeful. There is also the related matter of rejecting and putting in place an alternative to what Martin describes as the narrow intellectualism contained in the Hirst and Peters concept of the educated person. Any such alternative is unavailable, she maintains, as long as the criteria for what falls within the educational realm mirrors the distinction between the productive and reproductive processes in society. Already I have pointed to difficulties with Martin's distinction between production and reproduction. I have also considered one of the specific guidelines that Martin presents as a way of broadening education beyond the narrow intellectualism of which she complains, namely, her suggestion that goal (e), the development of each person as a member of a home and family, be added to the goals of schooling. Such an addition may broaden Peters's concept of education but might still do little to address Martin's wish that such education be taken over by schools, at least until it can be demonstrated that schools are likely to be successful in this area. To add on (e) as an additional goal to education, in other words, does not equate with attaining it in practice.

The issue is not merely one of arguing for a broader concept of education or schooling but of showing that the broader dimension can be taken care of in school or even in the Schoolhome. Neither does it solve many problems to say, as Martin does, that it is a matter of uniting thought and action, reason and emotion, self and other, or of making women visible in the educational realm. To do all of this may be helpful but ultimately the question is can these elements of education be handled successfully in school or any agency besides the home. It is true that in *The Schoolhome* Martin addresses this practical issue in relation to schools, and in *Coming of Age in Academe* does likewise in regard to the university. Yet it remains to be seen if she can convince the reader—more importantly, demonstrate—that this goal can be handled successfully in both of those institutions, notwithstanding the miserable record that Martin claims both have demonstrated in this regard up to this point in history.

Before leaving the consideration of alternatives, one other aspect of gender-sensitive education raised by Martin merits attention. One of the complexities to which Martin makes frequent reference is coeducation, the question of equality among the sexes that accompanies it, and the different educational needs of boys and girls.[89] For Martin, the assumptions upon which coeducation exists today need to be questioned: that is, "same role, same education," since the "same" education may validate one sex and not the other, and the same methods may work well for the one and not the other. Additionally, according to Martin, females live in a different and more vulnerable world, and this also affects their learning. Thus to offer the same education to women as to men, such as Adler advocates, solves nothing since the same education for all will not yield identical results in all instances.[90] If we want sex equality, "we must start to worry less about the sameness of the education of girls and boys, women and men, and more about its equivalency."[91] Besides, there are circumstances where boys and girls need to be taught separately, such as when the treatment of certain masculinity-femininity issues dictate.

One may agree with Martin on these matters. Yet as is true of her unfinished philosophizing regarding the idea of a common curriculum, as we shall see presently, here, too, one is left with the clear impression that the issues these matters raise are not clearly resolved by Martin, at least in programmatic terms.[92]

Feasibility and Desirability

While Martin acknowledges her critics, she does not dwell upon potential criticisms or set forth an elaborate defense of the bold stand she adopts in regard to her view of an expanded educational role for the school.[93] Given the limitations of schools, especially in regard to providing practical forms of education,[94] and Martin's own recognition of their failings, the question nonetheless arises if schools can be realistically expected to mend their ways, change tack, and, even in the case of the Schoolhome, become more homelike than homes themselves? Even in *The Schoolhome*, Martin recognizes that the Schoolhome cannot do it all by itself. This said, the fact that she now draws attention to the roles of other educational agents and admonishes educators not to equate schooling with education does not change the fact that she had already laid out an agenda almost without limits for the Schoolhome, one in which little, if any, distinction between education and schooling is drawn by herself.[95] Such is her continuing pessimistic portrayal of the home, moreover, that by now we are led to ask if it is capable of carrying out even its non-education jobs, such as health care, nutrition, clothing, and shelter? Are otherwise incompetent homes quite competent in these areas? If not, what are the effects on the Schoolhome and education in general? What are the implications for homes and society itself, and what do we do about it?

When all is said and done, the evidence favoring schools substituting for homes or, as Martin puts it in "Women, Schools, and Cultural Wealth," becoming surrogates for them as places of family affection and domesticity,[96] is bleak. Anecdote alone portrays even well-intentioned boarding schools, where children are more continuously under the supervision of the school, as nothing like home. Often they are cold and lonely places. Sometimes, as with other custodial institutions, they are even cruel in a manner reminiscent of *One Flew over the Cuckoo's Nest*.[97] Added to these are additional constraints on the kind of individualized care and attention that schools can give to individuals. One, to which Martin adverts, is school size; another and more serious is the legal prohibitions on teachers interacting with students in schools in ways normally associated with expressing the kind of intimacy and affection that Martin believes children need to experience and that good homes presumably engage in. This being the case, one has to ask how schools can educate for family living and affection if teachers cannot demonstrate or express it or extend comfort to those in distress. Of course it is to be presumed that unlike the schools we now have, the Schoolhome can overcome such difficulties and strike out in a bold new direction. Yet one must ask what progress any school can make if homes are so inadequate that the school is to "take over" a large share of their responsibilities. How can any school or Schoolhome prosper if home and parental neglect or deficiency continues? Can calling the media to task, as Martin now proposes, and looking to other educational agents realistically be expected to make up for such deficiencies? Even if peace and tranquillity exist in the greater society, and provide the broader context and support structures for civility in society at large, there will still be a need for good and competent parents in order to fulfill their end of meeting the educational needs of the young. After all, it is to actual homes that children return every day from the Schoolhome. If these remain unreformed, what hope is there for the Schoolhome to succeed?

Even if one grants that in basic schooling there should be a place for

144

Knowledge, Gender, and Schooling

education in the 3Cs, for family, and for domesticity as broadly portrayed by Martin, questions still arise. For beyond the narrow question of feasibility, there is also the question of desirability of handing the task to schools. When Martin writes in critical terms that the thought never struck the authors of national reports on education that the school should "take over" the responsibility for preparing young students for life in their homes,[98] she seems remarkably unaware of the desirability aspect of the issue. If the matter had not been raised by Martin in this way, this same thought would not have occurred to many outside or inside of government, not least parents and educators, for the very reason that it seems a highly questionable practice in a free society or one that aspires to be free. Taking over the responsibility of parents for the education of their children in domesticity and the 3Cs raises very many questions as to the values to be promoted under the auspices of the school or governing authority, as was seen already. Even if one accepts that there is a role for the school in teaching home values, or values of any kind, and that it can fulfill this role, there are still questions as to which values and how we get agreement by the parties involved. Martin does say she wishes the values of an ideal, not dysfunctional, home, one characterized by love and respect and sustained and justified by the appeal to peace and tranquillity. She even gives the clear impression that we all know what we mean by the ideal home when she writes that it is important for boys and girls alike to learn "to exercise the virtues which our culture thinks of as housed in our private homes."[99] But which version of love and respect does she have in mind, and which version of peace and tranquillity? Martin's own versions? And which version of caring does one seek if, as Noddings puts it, there are no recipes for caring?[100]

This is the crux of the value question, and it brings us right back to the issue of how committal Martin is when it comes to identifying the values of the "ideal, not dysfunctional home," as she puts it. To say that the ideal home is characterized by love and warmth and by the absence of abuse is to give the appearance of being committed to certain specific values. In actuality, it is only identifying very broad value categories. To say you want to teach love or the 3Cs in school or in the home is akin to saying you want to teach knowledge. As Martin acknowledges, however, there is an abundance of knowledge in our culture and even schools have a tendency to focus only on the theoretical aspects of it. This is not to say that this makes education in knowledge a hopeless enterprise, just that it calls for much greater specificity if the directive to teach it is to have any meaning. That is why schools and school districts, and even state departments of education, have "a curriculum" that names subjects and why there are syllabuses for different subjects. Difficult as teaching is in regard to the academic subjects, it is daunting when it comes to the realm of domesticity and the 3Cs, the domain of action and of the affective from which schools, as Martin has often told us, tend to shy away. There is need, accordingly, for a clearer idea of the values to which the Schoolhome is committed, and a far greater specificity regarding the associated behaviors and attitudes that we are making judgments about, if there is to be any prospect of success in promoting them. There is, furthermore, the need for corresponding sets of justifications.

If there is need for an advance on Martin's ambivalence and lack of specificity as to the type of home she sometimes wants to advocate, there is reason to believe that such an advance will not be forthcoming. Despite her concerns regarding the role of various educational agencies in perpetuating cultural liabilities a similar ambivalence on Martin's part can be detected in regard to the transmission of knowledge or cultural wealth in general. In a consideration of whether trivial knowledge is to be included in the curriculum or not, in "Women, Schools, and Cultural Wealth," Martin writes that a democratic definition leaves open the question of what is the relative value of various items of wealth, and is neutral on the question of which parts of the cultural wealth should be passed on.[101] This is a passage that brings to mind her willingness many years earlier to suggest that there was a place for chance in education.[102] It is difficult to see, however, how one can be neutral or welcome chance in curriculum matters and yet be committed to particular values at one and the same time. To be neutral on the question of which parts of the cultural wealth are to be handed down is not going so far as to accept handing down cultural liabilities. Yet it does fail to pick out which particular values or parts of the cultural wealth define one's concept of curriculum or ideal home.

Martin has made it clear that in her view for schools to overlook the goal (e) of preparing children for living in families and homes is a serious mistake. Notwithstanding the force of her critique or the fact that she grants "the inability of home and family to be effective transmitters of the 3Cs and the ethics of care," leading her to the conclusion that "new guardians may have to be appointed,"[103] in the final analysis, Martin fails to demonstrate that whatever the failings of the home, schools can actually do the job of family-life education by taking children out of the home so as to prepare them for living in the home. In *The Paideia Proposal*, Adler recognized that the objectives of schooling are distinct from the objectives of education. In dealing with education for domesticity in *The Schoolhome* and elsewhere, Martin talks about the goals of education and of schooling without making any such distinction, however. Neither does she distinguish between the overarching aim of education and of the Schoolhome. As I have discussed elsewhere, an education that claims to be a general education, at least in the sense of a broad education for living, necessitates the inclusion of preparation for family living or domesticity.[104] To this I would add that a demarcation of the role of the school—and a recognition of its limitations—vis-à-vis the home and other agencies in providing such education may be crucial. Even though Martin has since modified her stance, it is still not clear if, and to what extent, she would agree.

Clearly, one can educate outside of school, as in homes and churches and youth organizations and the wide range of other such educational agents that Martin herself recognizes.[105] Even if the failure to distinguish between education and schooling may lead one to think otherwise, it does not follow, however, that one can educate for family living outside the home or that schools will ever be able to take over the job of doing so. This is especially true in the face of opposition or even mere lack of co-operation or support from neglectful or incompetent parents and from the community. To expect that in such circumstances schools should take over the job, in fact, may be to raise unrealistic and damaging hopes. Yet this is precisely the kind of scenario for which Martin's remedies are in good part scripted. Having called home and school partners in education in *The Schoolhome*, Martin later writes that what she did not say enough about there is that, "for all their importance, these are but two of society's edu-cational agents,"[106] and she does attempt to correct this in her multiple-educational-agency thesis. At the same time, she talks of the school as a surrogate home[107] and she has not accommodated her original ideas re-garding the almost monopolistic view of the Schoolhome as *the* agent of education to her new way of thinking.

There is no denying that in the economic and social culture of our day, attitudes toward women and gender issues, domesticity, and the 3Cs are often a cause for great concern. Martin has made a case that there are grounds for such concerns, and that gender biases in society and schools contribute to the problems that exist. In drawing attention to the possibil-ities contained in a reinterpretation of the domestic tranquillity clause of the Constitution, Martin provides a philosophical, moral, and legal basis for seeking and supporting political and educational action favoring the values of peace and tranquillity, although the exact form in which these are to be advocated is not spelled out. From our discussion of Martin's philosophy, the question that arises is how we should deal with the prob-lems with which we are faced. Should we do so by reforming the school, the family, or the social contexts that undermine family and the 3Cs, or a combination of all? Recognizing the limits faced by schools in the absence of peace and tranquillity, the general counter-stance to Martin that seems to have greatest promise is one in which greater attention would first be given to exploring ways of assisting parents and homes in their task of education for home and family living, one of which would be encouraging a more positive attitude toward schools as sources of support rather than as the lead agent in promoting the 3Cs. Gender-sensitive education, after all, is an ideal that may be promoted in homes as well as in schools and other agents of education, and perhaps more successfully so.

Broadening the Discourse

As I have just said, whether schools can or should provide education for family living or domesticity is open to question; it is a separate matter whether the broad general education of the young should include such a goal. Martin has made a powerful case that it should. She has also made the point that this view is not reflected in the goals commonly adopted for schooling in our society today. This is not to say that other educational theorists do not accept it, for some do. The line between those who do and do not usually has two prominent characteristics: the inclusion or exclusion of practical education, and the inclusion or exclusion of what Martin has labeled the concerns, interests, and ethos of the private world of the home. Mainstream curriculum thinking, with its emphasis on academic knowledge and preparation for the public world has insisted, by and large, on the exclusion of practical and family life education; Martin and the minorstream, that small group of educational theorists of broadly similar persuasion, tend to include it in varying degrees.

As I have pointed out already, Martin does not sing the praises of a liberal education or dwell upon its desirable qualities. She does, however, draw attention to the emotional, behavioral, and attitudinal rather than cognitive nature of the more practical forms of education that she argues ought to be added to liberal education if we are to provide a good general education. She singles out for special attention the benefits of such education for both the public and the private worlds. In doing so she also broadens out very considerably the range of legitimate discourse on general education as we enter the twenty-first century, adding serious weight to the minorstream tradition in educational theory whose voice has been muted over the years.

Martin broadens out the range of legitimate discourse in a second and related area as well. Whether one agrees or not with the particular values and the strong commitment to education for domesticity and the 3Cs that she wishes to advance in the Schoolhome, her stance raises serious questions for her to deal with. Yet she can take some solace. If schools are to be schools, that is, places of education, they have to stand for something. As Purpel and Ryan put it some years ago in speaking of moral education, "it comes with the territory."[108] This being the case, the question is not whether schools should embrace or reject any particular values, be they values of domesticity or any other values; rather, the question is what values and how. Thus the kinds of questions of practice and principle posed here for Martin will still need to be faced up to whatever the stand of the school. It is to Martin's credit that she has vigorously challenged those who theorize about these matters to consider an extended range of these values. The challenge could not be more timely.

Of the concepts introduced by Martin, none is more original or far-reaching in its suggestive potential than the ideal of a gender-sensitive education. The outgrowth of her insight that once women are brought into the debate on what constitutes an educated person—gender-sensitive education, in its strictest construction—means simply taking gender differences into account in the design of educational programs. These differences will sometimes necessitate differences of approach to ensure equality for all. One thing is for sure: "so long as women and men live in the world together, their education must be designed, and continually redesigned, together."[109] Thus, while in some respects the ideal of how to educate women will differ from the ideal of how to educate men, in Martin's view such differences exist to ensure equality, for to be treated equally sometimes means being treated differently. In Martin's hands, the ideal of the educated woman—and one might add, the ideal of the educated man, too—merges rather than conflicts with her ideal of a gender-sensitive education.

Ironically, gender-sensitive education may have greater implications for the education of boys and men than it does for girls and women. It may also encounter even greater opposition than the ideal of a woman's education, for it requires that the education of the softer side of human nature that society has often intended for girls and women be extended to boys and men. This ideal has never enjoyed the kind of crusade that women such as Mary Wollstonecraft led on behalf of the academic education of women, for few have argued as Martin has to extend to boys and men an education in the 3Cs. Indeed, one of the challenges of the quest for gender-sensitive education is fighting off the cultural resistance to such a "feminine sounding" education for young men.[110]

CULTURAL WEALTH AND THE NEW PROBLEM OF CURRICULUM

Since elaborating the notion of a gender-sensitive education in *The Schoolhome*, Martin has added substantially to the fundamentals of her educational thought by developing her cultural wealth thesis. This being so, the thesis and the related notions of multiple educational agency, the educational problem of generations, and what she terms "the new problem of curriculum,"[111] all of which are set forth at greatest length in *Cultural Miseducation*, have important implications for her gender-sensitive ideal. Although several aspects of the thesis are open to question, as I shall argue, the cultural wealth thesis nonetheless adds considerably to the constructive dimension of Martin's educational thought. This is especially true of what she has to say of the new problem of curriculum, namely, "transmitting to our young a more democratic, in the sense of more inclusive, vision of our cultural heritage without sacrificing the ideals of political democracy and social equality."[112]

The critique of mainstream curriculum thinking implicit in the cultural wealth thesis—namely that it conceives of culture largely in terms of high culture such as that found in the academic disciplines—is muted. It gives way, more readily than in works of Martin focused on critique, to a consideration of alternatives and solutions. The broader concept of curriculum to which Martin is led by her cultural wealth thesis, and the sharper distinction between education and schooling to which it also leads, is presented as a basis from which to set about a redefinition of education in society at large. This view of education is intended, in part, to heighten awareness of the manner in which society unwittingly accepts transmitting to the young cultural liabilities rather than cultural wealth. According to this view, the transmission of cultural liabilities is accomplished most conspicuously through various media agencies and technologies that are not held to the same standards of accountability or responsibility as educational agents such as schools and universities that are expected to transmit cultural assets, not liabilities.

Martin's concept of cultural wealth as incorporating aspects of culture other than merely high culture or the higher learning—parallel to Adam Smith's concept of economic wealth—is perfectly consistent with the position she adopted in her earliest work on curriculum, "The Disciplines and the Curriculum." With cultural wealth as distinct from cultural liabilities seen as the positive part of our overall cultural stock, Martin now compares her sense of culture to that of the anthropologist. She writes, "an old farmer's know-how, an artisan's craft, a mother's daily lessons to her offspring in the 3Cs of care, concern, and connection are all, therefore, grist for an anthropologist's mill. As cultural assets, these also fall squarely in the category of cultural wealth."[113]

Because educators have erroneously tended to equate schooling with education, Martin now writes, the existence and even the proliferation of educational agents outside the school has gone unnoticed. Yet these too are powerful teachers of the young and sometimes, as in the case of the television and the Internet, they pass on cultural liabilities as well as cultural wealth. This being so, what is needed now is some way of ascertaining how we can at once minimize the transmission of cultural liabilities and maximize the passing-on of cultural wealth. This leads Martin to conclude that we need a system of "cultural bookkeeping," analogous in her view to the human genome project, to track the culture's wealth and liabilities and record which educational agents are responsible for the preservation and transmission of various aspects of the cultural stock.[114] One consequence of this is that schools may have a less dominant and supervisory role in the educational affairs of the community than it now has or than was attributed to it in *The Schoolhome*. Such an accounting would also aid in minimizing the transmission of liabilities and maximizing the transmission of cultural wealth, Martin believes.

Perhaps the crucial measure to be taken to reduce the cultural liabilities currently passed on in our society, in Martin's view, is ensuring that television and other forms of communications technology are recognized as de facto educational agents. Even though they may not meet the conventional requirement of education as a purposeful undertaking rather than a casual or even accidental occurrence, they ought to be viewed as agents of education, Martin argues. Once accorded such status, society may be more willing to hold them accountable for the cultural stock they transmit, she suggests.

In the course of determining how we can most effectively maximize the transmission of cultural wealth, Martin embarks on one of the more creative and imaginative explorations in all of her educational theorizing, matching her quest for gender-sensitive education in its potential for fresh avenues of educational inquiry and controversy. Central to the ideas that emerge is the proposal that, contrary to the widely accepted view, the one curriculum for all is not the best path to follow in seeking new and improved directions for general education. She favors, it appears, an entirely elective or differentiated curriculum free of compulsion.[115] If such a differentiated curriculum brings charges of elitism, they would be misguided she believes. Whether there is to be a similar absence of compulsion as regards attending school or being educated at all is less clear, although the logic of the argument employed by Martin suggests there should be no compulsion in these regards either.

The idea of a differentiated or elective curriculum finds some support in the theory of multiple of intelligences propounded by Howard Gardner,[116] according to which students may differ from one another in their talents or ways of knowing and understanding the world. It also departs from a notion of democracy in which each individual is seen as supremely self-reliant. According to Martin, such a view of individual self-reliance flies in the face of both community experience and the advancement of science where the community or team draws upon the varying kinds of expertise of its participants, which expertise in turn reflects the interests and talents of community and team members. Given the cultural superabundance we possess, the existence of multiple intelligences, the precedent of teamwork and its dependency upon varying areas of expertise among the participants, and rejecting the notion of supreme self-sufficiency, Martin argues as follows against the idea of a compulsory curriculum for all: rather than attempting to transmit the same selected fraction of cultural wealth to every individual, leaving to chance that which is not passed on to all, seek instead to transmit all or a much greater proportion of the cultural wealth to the community as whole. This may be done and justified in the knowledge that not all will possess the same cultural stock or knowledge but all do have a contribution to make to the goals and purposes of the community as a whole. Martin acknowledges that this does bring with it the serious challenge adverted to already, that of transmitting different portions to each rather than the one identical portion of our cultural wealth to all "without sacrificing the ideals of political democracy and social equality." That is to say, those who possess the most valuable cultural stock may be at an advantage over others, and there is the risk that they will not share its benefits freely with all others, thereby threatening political democracy and social equality.

Having spent most of the final part of *Cultural Miseducation* arguing the case for a differentiated curriculum, and having earlier indicated the same general stance in "The New Problem of Curriculum," toward the very end of the book, Martin turns the table on the reader. She asks, to the reader's surprise, if there are any core elements of curriculum or culture that should be required learning for all. She surprises further by not answering the question right away, opting instead for a future opportunity to examine it more closely. For the reader following her argument, this very question is foremost in one's mind throughout her discussion of a differentiated curriculum. Not only has the idea of a common curriculum become the norm in curriculum theorizing, it has led to a sea change in governmental policy in education on both sides of the Atlantic. England has abandoned its long-standing approach of local control of curriculum in favor of a national curriculum and national examinations, and similar tendencies are detectable in the United States arising from the emphasis on national goals for education and national standards for curriculum content and student performance. Now Martin wishes to challenge the thought.

Although Martin is fully aware of the risks in allowing different people to pursue different curricula,[117] the arguments that she brings forward against a common curriculum for all are themselves telling. They include the theory of multiple intelligences, the manner in which teams made up of individuals possessing different specialisms can work effectively—perhaps most effectively—in solving complex social and scientific problems. To this may be added the important consideration she brings forward of preserving the full scope of the cultural stock which might not be so easily achieved if the same selected portion of it is to be presented to all in the form of a compulsory curriculum. But the greatest weight in coming down against a common curriculum for all seems to be given by Martin to a claim she makes on the basis of her personal experience. In her experience, she relates, students taught the same subject matter in school do not always remember it in the same ways, if at all, several years later. From this and other such observations, she concludes that to depend on a common curriculum to generate a common body of learning is to be misled.[118]

Even if she wishes to postpone final judgment, Martin's argument in *Cultural Miseducation* clearly leans toward a differentiated or wholly elective curriculum, not a common core curriculum with electives. Despite the considerations just outlined to the contrary, there are good reasons why Martin should not reject the idea of a core of common learning for all. In the first place, an entirely elective curriculum is not the only alternative to a common curriculum of the kind suggested by Adler or that proposed by Hirst and Peters, which requires all students to be exposed to all of the same forms of knowledge. There is plenty of room for a moderate stance between the extremes. In the second place, while Martin did consider and reject arguments that are sometimes presented to bolster the idea of a common curriculum in *Cultural Miseducation*, she did not consider some of the more telling arguments set forth to support and justify it. In the third place, while Martin did express reservations in the past regarding the idea of a common curriculum, even in *The Schoolhome* she held that, as distinct from an entirely elective curriculum for all, there ought to be merely a modicum of curriculum differentiation as between boys and girls.[119] This she held in order to treat both equally and to be sensitive to the difficulties experienced by members of one sex (usually boys) being exposed to curriculum content traditionally considered proper to the other, and its possible detrimental effects on the learning intended. Most importantly, when distancing herself from the idea of a common curriculum in *The Schoolhome*, it was from a commonality of bits or bodies of knowledge, as she put it, that she did so, not a common curriculum alternatively conceived. She actually rejoiced in a curriculum comprising commonality of attitudes, skills, and values. Even commonality of this kind in the curriculum, however, is now brought into question as she considers the new problem of curriculum.

A standard argument supporting the idea of a common curriculum for all, with or without electives, is that no man (or woman) is an island. It seeks to justify both common learnings and, if necessary, compulsion, to implement them. As with Martin's argument to the contrary, it, too, is an argument from community, not from individuality. That is to say, being a member of a community requires having at least some common grounds among the members. These common grounds entail common beliefs, common values, common attitudes of the kind that Martin considered necessary in *The Schoolhome*, and the common knowledge and skills upon which they are founded. Such common grounds do not justify the same curriculum for all but they do justify a common core for all. They justify it on the grounds that such learnings are necessary not merely to attain one's full potential, but because such common beliefs and values are necessary to sustain communication and understanding between and among individuals and consequently to the existence of any community or society. The price of admission to, and the process of attaining full membership in, the community is the acquisition of these common learnings; the aspiration to such membership is the justification for compulsion in their acquisition if necessary.[120]

These are not the only considerations that could lead Martin to answer affirmatively whether there needs to be a common core in the curriculum she supports or advocates, although she rejects them in "The New Problem of Curriculum" because "they constitute dangers only when rejection of the postulate of curricular sameness is conjoined with an ideal of absolute self-reliance and a possessive individualistic conception of learning."[121] Other considerations include the following. Consistently throughout her writings, Martin has not sought preparation for mere community membership, personal development, or advancement as the goal of her educational enterprise. As she insists in her criticisms of those who fall foul of the epistemological fallacy, there ought to be purposes beyond the acquisition of knowledge that justify content selection in the curriculum. Such purposes are shaped, in turn, by the kind of community one seeks and by the kinds of individuals one wishes to people it. Yet the kind of unified community that Martin seeks, and the kinds of individuals she wishes to inhabit and shape it, is gravely jeopardized by the arguments against a common curriculum presented in "The New Problem of Curriculum" and *Cultural Miseducation*.

What kind of society, and what kinds of individuals to enliven it, does Martin envision? The answers to these questions are readily found in the central themes that recur throughout her writings. They revolve around what is needed to prepare the young to participate in the public and private worlds, to engage in the productive and reproductive processes of society. Concerned that undue attention has been paid to the preparation of the young to engage in the productive processes—those associated with the public world of work—she has emphasized those aspects of preparation that focus on those processes associated with the world of the private home. The society that Martin envisions appears to have much in common with the ideal home to which she alludes. It therefore emphasizes the 3Cs of care, concern, and connection; it is characterized by the absence of violence; it is respectful of gender, racial, religious, and ethnic differences; and it is respectful toward nature and the natural environment. The attainment of an ideal state conforming to these ideals, in turn, calls for a gender-sensitive education to bring it about and a public life characterized by civility and domestic tranquillity to sustain it.

In setting forth as she has the values and ideals by which her ideal society is to be characterized, Martin has made choices that determine both the purposes and the content of education. In arguing as she has for a gender-sensitive educational ideal of the kind portrayed above, she remains by and large consistent with the social and educational ideals of respect for others and the 3Cs that she has long espoused. This cannot be said of her cultural wealth thesis, however, specifically the aspect of it that raises the prospect of an entirely elective curriculum. Put differently, to the extent that Martin's cultural wealth theory of education necessitates a curriculum free of core requirements, it is intrinsically incompatible with her broader social and educational ideals, not least her ideal of a gender-sensitive education, for these ideals, and the values they contain, imply particular learnings. Martin herself recognizes this even in "The New Problem of Curriculum" when she argues on the one hand for an elective curriculum and, without seeing the contradiction, argues on the other hand for requiring that all learn the 3Cs. She writes, "In my view, the best way that a curriculum can contribute to the manufacturing of unity is by . . . providing everyone with a solid foundation in the 3Cs of care, concern, and connection."[122] Since the 3Cs imply particular learnings if they are to mean anything, it is non-sensical to talk of students being free to choose otherwise in what Martin describes as a democratic view of knowledge and the curriculum. Under such a democratic view, students of course may choose to be guided by Martin's gender-sensitive ideal, but they would also be free to become ivory tower people and quite lacking in the 3Cs, outcomes entirely at odds with the ideal of a gender-sensitive education.

The crux of the problem is Martin's dual but seemingly incompatible aspirations: democracy on the one hand, her tranquil, gender-sensitive ver-sion of loving community on the other. The gender-sensitive society to which Martin aspires must be freely chosen. If it is to be freely chosen, there is no guarantee that it is Martin's version that will be chosen in the end. But even if one sets this difficulty aside, the cultural wealth philosophy that she espouses in relation to the curriculum still encounters serious dif-ficulties arising from the elective nature of the curriculum that she believes it necessitates. In what is an attractive dimension of the cultural wealth philosophy of curriculum, one rarely if ever highlighted by curriculum the-orists in the mainstream, Martin goes beyond the position just referenced that she adopted in *The Schoolhome*, where the commonality in the cur-riculum she espoused is found not in bits and bodies of knowledge but in attitudes, skills and values. The goals of the preservation and transmission of a wide range of cultural wealth, the satisfying of students' interests and talents, and meeting the many needs of the community that depend on a variety of specialist inputs may be accomplished, she now argues, without insisting on the same curriculum for all. Each student, she maintains, does not need to possess the same knowledge as every other, just as all members of a scientific research team do not need to possess the same specialist knowledge.

Not requiring the individual to be supremely self-reliant as envisaged in Martin's cultural wealth thesis, the educational needs of the individual are viewed differently from how they are typically seen in the mainstream. There may be advantage in this while viewing the role of education as promoting the full growth and development of the community rather than, as is normally envisaged, the full development of the individual. It may, as Martin herself suggests, contribute to less social atomism, a greater social bonding, and a greater integration of individuals into their local commu-nities and local communities into larger communities. In such a scenario, what one individual lacks either by educational achievement or personality may be compensated for through the achievements and personalities of other members of the community. This, after all, is how teams of scientists and practitioners in a range of fields proceed, as Martin points out. While waxing eloquent on the crucial contribution that varying specialisms may make to the advancement of science, in *Cultural Miseducation*, however, she downplays a crucial facet of communities and team members, one to which she gave careful recognition in *The Schoolhome*: the commonalities of values, skills, and attitudes shared by the members of teams and communities. As she herself points out in *The Schoolhome*, and as she demonstrated so acutely in her negative portrayal of the academy, these commonalities comprise aspirations, values, assumptions, and modus operandi, among others, as well as commonalities of knowledge and understanding. To hold to the example she herself employs, moreover, there are few research teams or academic institutions—or corporations, political parties, or religious organizations—willing to invite new members aboard because of the specialties they possess, if they do not also share these additional commonalities.

It is the same in the broader community, as the important decisions revolve around choices regarding those values to be sought and taught. Yet here again Martin demurs. Having sought to make clear the kind of society she seeks and the kind of educational ideal by which it is to be guided, when it comes to decisions regarding the content of the curriculum, she once again backs off. She is reluctant not merely to be specific on certain values, but even to acknowledge openly and consistently that certain values need to be chosen over others. If they are not, not only does gender-sensitive education become a mirage, community-focused educational ideals such as those considered in relation to her cultural wealth philosophy of curriculum become a hollow aspiration. Unless content choices are made in accordance with specific values that reflect such idealizations, they may never be attained, and a philosophy of curriculum that attempts to justify it is a deception.

Lack of attention to the commonality of shared values and aspirations is not the only problem attaching to the idea of an all-elective curriculum. Commonality of knowledge, understandings, and skills also comes into play, although this may be concealed in the examples of cooperation among community and research team members offered by Martin. No community or community project group will get very far if the members do not, by and large, speak the same language and share the key concepts it houses. Teams of translators could be employed, of course, but reliance upon them will take from the flexibility and spontaneity that many such community or team projects require in order to prosper, or in times of crisis where immediate action and directness of communication may make the difference between life and death. And as Martin herself points out in regard to the deaf community in Martha's Vineyard, such commonality is necessary to insure that all members of the community are included and treated equally.

It was to ensure that all students were provided the opportunity to develop such varied knowledge, skills, and understandings that curriculum theorists in the mainstream such as Adler, Hirst and Peters, Phenix, and Broudy, Smith, and Burnett argued for a curriculum of general education that mandates a wholly or partially common curriculum for all students, as was essentially true over the ages with the tradition of a liberal education. Despite its rejection by Martin and more recently even by Hirst himself, the principle that Hirst's theory of the forms of knowledge asserted, namely, that all students ought to have a common understanding of the forms of knowledge, has the merit of addressing the common knowledge and understandings required by all for the purpose of communication. Similarly, the distinction between the interpretive and applicative uses of knowledge made by Broudy, Smith, and Burnett not only recognized the importance of the application of specialist knowledge, but each individual's need for a fund of broadly common interpretive knowledge to understand the contexts and justifications in which specialist knowledge is and may be employed. The knowledge favored by those such as Broudy and Phenix and others may be open to the criticisms of exclusiveness leveled by Martin against the elders. As with Hirst's forms of knowledge, however—and quite independently of whether it falls foul of the epistemological fallacy or not— it presents a more compelling argument for a common core of knowledge for all than Martin's argument to the contrary. The case for such commonality of knowledge and understanding, moreover, does not rely for its justification on the notion brought into question by Martin, namely belief in a supreme self-reliance concept of democracy. On the contrary, the greater the interdependency among citizens, the more crucial it is that there be an adequate basis for communication and a sharing of common knowledge and understandings along with values and aspirations.

Curriculum theories of the mainstream such as those of Hirst and Peters and Broudy, Smith, and Burnett may be guilty of the same errors as those of the elders singled out for attention as such by Martin, such as Bloom and Hirsch, when they call for a common curriculum for all that is insensitive to or exclusive of the experiences of those other than the "White, European, male." Martin herself has drawn attention to the fact that some have failed to draw a distinction between the idea of a hidden curriculum and a particular form of the hidden curriculum.[123] She now needs to be careful herself not to fall into a similar trap here. That is to say, if Broudy, Smith, and Burnett and Hirst and Peters, along with Bloom and Hirsch, are guilty of perpetuating a culturally exclusive curriculum, it is necessary to distinguish between their positions and that of a common core curriculum that aims to incorporate the broader experiences of all. As with the hidden curriculum, all common core curricula are not, or need not be, the same nor are they guilty of the same errors.

Reference was made earlier to the notion presented by Martin in laying out her cultural wealth concept of education that even though the cultural stock passed on by the media may not meet the conventional idea of education as a purposeful undertaking rather than a casual or even accidental occurrence, the media nonetheless ought to be considered an educational agent. She elaborated by adding that definitions or conceptions of education that ruled out such instances of education were effectively flying in the face of the fact that these agents generate a great deal of learning amongst the young, a point that brings us back to the disagreement between Martin and Siegel regarding the rationality theory of teaching and the connection with education. It also brings Martin into conflict not only with the strict requirement presented by Hirst and Peters—that education consists in knowledge and understanding in depth and breadth—but with the very definition of education as an undertaking that is essentially purposeful or intentional in character.[124] Martin's chief purpose in widening out the notion of education to include unintended learnings was to bring about a situation where the media, if seen as educational agents, could be viewed by society in general as having to become more accountable for the learnings they do promote.

There can be no denying that the media generate a huge amount of learning on the part of the young and that they could be held more accountable for any liabilities that they transmit. Whether viewing media agencies as educational agents leads to a greater likelihood of this happening is hard to say, and it raises questions as to the benefits to be gained from a departure from viewing education as a purposeful undertaking. What is not changed by any of this, however, are the tensions evident in Martin's own thought. They lie in the relentless striving for a society characterized by brotherly/sisterly love and tranquillity, and her view of education as not only committed to, but guided by, purposes and values upon which such a society is predicated. Competing with these is her reluctance to be specific when it comes to the identification of values and educational content for fear of conceding the principles of freedom of thought and action associated with her persistent commitment to a democratic form— as distinct from a "supremely self-reliant" form—of self-rule and a sense of individual self-determination.

Martin, as we saw, argued that Hirst is guilty of the epistemological fallacy when he dispenses with the primacy of purposes in curriculum-making and assumes that knowledge must necessarily comprise the school curriculum. Yet in her democratic approach to knowledge as set forth in the context of her cultural wealth thesis, Martin argues against the inclusion of any particular knowledge or required content, while justifying the inclusion of trivial content as a candidate for curriculum space on the grounds that it may have unforeseen benefits. To argue against the inclusion of particular knowledge or content in the curriculum, however—to accept the principle of an entirely elective curriculum—renders the adoption and justification of educational goals or purposes redundant. The very point of having goals, after all, is to guide such decision-making. As for the inclusion of trivial content, not only may the unforeseen turn out to be liabilities as likely as benefits, but if the benefits are unseen, by what values (other than a love of chance or the unknown, perhaps) is such content to be admitted to the curriculum? Matthew Arnold may have sounded elitist when advocating that we pass on the best of what has been thought and said, yet the principle on which he relied is crucial: education, and curriculum-making specifically, entails selection. That can only be done—and as Martin herself has advocated strenuously, should only be done—on the basis of educational purposes and the values that sustain them. In an age of cultural superabundance, to make way for the trivial in the process of curriculum selection is not only farcical; it encourages educators to be less than exhaustive in the selection of curriculum content to achieve their purposes.

There are tensions evident in the contradictory requirements of a society characterized by domestic tranquillity, the 3Cs, and a gender-sensitive education, on the one hand, and the persistent appeal to individual freedom represented by the ideals of the democratic pursuit of knowledge, the absence of compulsion, and freedom of choice on the other hand. These tensions are reminiscent of Martin's failure to be explicit about the values to which she was committed in portraying the ideal home. Such tensions may be viewed in different ways, some positive, some negative. Depending on how they are viewed, Martin is faced with a great contradiction or a grand ideal. Viewed negatively, they may be seen as manifestation of an underlying indecisiveness in choosing between two powerful but ultimately inconsistent or contradictory themes running throughout Martin's social, political, and educational philosophies. The one theme is a quest for a society governed in the manner of a political democracy, guided by a democratic education where, free of compulsion, one may pursue one's interests freely. The other is a society characterized by love and tranquillity, respect for differences, and equality for all in harmony with nature. Viewed more positively, Martin envisions a society that is free as in a democracy, and being free chooses—as she wishes it to choose—a democratic society epitomized by care, concern, and connection: a victory of hope over contradiction.

NOTES

1. See, for example, Jane Roland Martin, "Women, Schools, and Cultural Wealth," *Women's Philosophies of Education*, eds. Connie Titone and Karen E. Moloney (Upper Saddle River, NJ: Merrill/Prentice-Hall, 1999) 151–159; Jane Ro-

land Martin, *Reclaiming a Conversation: The Ideal of the Educated Woman* (New Haven, CT: Yale University Press, 1985); Jane Roland Martin, "Bringing Women into Educational Thought," *Educational Theory* 34 (Fall 1984): 345–349; and Jane Roland Martin, "Redefining the Educated Person: Rethinking the Significance of Gender," *Educational Researcher* 15 (June/July 1986): 6–10.

2. This latter point is especially well brought out in Martin, "Women, Schools, and Cultural Wealth," 150–155.

3. Jane Roland Martin, *Changing the Educational Landscape: Philosophy, Women, and Curriculum* (New York: Routledge, 1994) 133–153.

4. Martin, *Changing the Educational Landscape* 148.

5. Martin, *Changing the Educational Landscape* 170–186; Martin, *Reclaiming a Conversation* 171–199; and Jane Roland Martin, *Cultural Miseducation: In Search of a Democratic Solution* (Forthcoming from Teachers College Press). An important formulation that gives particular attention to the importance of developing appropriate models of moral reasoning is presented in Jane Roland Martin, "Transforming Moral Education," *Journal of Moral Education* 16 (October 1987): 204–213.

6. Martin, *Changing the Educational Landscape* 180–181.

7. Jane Roland Martin, *The Schoolhome: Rethinking Schools for Changing Families* (Cambridge, MA: Harvard University Press, 1992). The connections alluded to here between the earlier and later work are also accepted by Martin herself: see Martin, *Changing the Educational Landscape* 23–24.

8. Martin, *Changing the Educational Landscape* 212–227.

9. Richard Pring, *Knowledge and Schooling* (London: Open Books, 1976) 92–93. For a further discussion of these issues, see Pring, *Knowledge and Schooling*; and L.R. Perry, "Commonsense Thought, Knowledge, and Judgment and Their Importance for Education," *Readings in the Philosophy of Education: A Study of Curriculum*, ed. Jane R. Martin (Boston: Allyn and Bacon, 1970) 187–200.

10. Martin, *Changing the Educational Landscape* 179–180.

11. Philip H. Phenix, *Realms of Meaning* (New York: McGraw-Hill, 1964) especially 311–321.

12. Martin, *Changing the Educational Landscape* 139, 148, 218; Martin, "Women, Schools, and Cultural Wealth," especially 169–171.

13. Martin, *Cultural Miseducation*; Martin "Women, Schools, and Cultural Wealth;" Jane Roland Martin, "The Wealth of Cultures and the Problem of Generations," *Philosophy of Education*, ed. Steve Tozer (Urbana, IL: Philosophy of Education Society, 1998) 23–38.

14. Martin, *Changing the Educational Landscape* 143.

15. P.H. Hirst and R.S. Peters, *The Logic of Education* (London: Routledge and Kegan Paul, 1970) 19, 25, 66–67.

16. Martin, *Changing the Educational Landscape* 180–181.

17. For important new scholarship on violence in schools, see Ronnie Casella, *"Being Down": Challenging Violence in Urban Schools* (New York: Teachers College Press, 2001); Ronnie Casella, *At Zero Tolerance: Punishment, Prevention, and School Violence* (New York: Peter Lang, 2001).

18. Martin, *Changing the Educational Landscape* 233, 235–240.

19. Martin, *Changing the Educational Landscape* 176.

20. Martin, *The Schoolhome* 12; Martin, *Changing the Educational Landscape* 180–182.

21. Martin, "Women, Schools, and Cultural Wealth" 159–164. Martin, *The Schoolhome* 46; Martin, "Women, Schools, and Cultural Wealth" 159–164.

22. Martin, *Changing the Educational Landscape* 183; Martin, "Women, Schools, and Cultural Wealth" 163.

23. Martin, *The Schoolhome* 86.

24. Martin, *The Schoolhome* 85–87.

25. Martin, *The Schoolhome* 87–91.

26. Martin, "Women, Schools, and Cultural Wealth" 162; Martin, *Cultural Miseducation*.

27. Martin, *The Schoolhome* 203.

28. George H.W. Bush, "Remarks at the University of Virginia Convocation in Charlottesville," Charlottesville, 28 Sept. 1989.

29. Martin, *The Schoolhome* 203.

30. Martin, *The Schoolhome* 161–162; Martin, "Women, Schools, and Cultural Wealth" 165–167.

31. Martin, *The Schoolhome* 161–204.

32. Martin, *The Schoolhome* 165–166.

33. Martin, *The Schoolhome* 167–174. See also Jane Roland Martin, "Reforming Teacher Education, Rethinking Liberal Education," *Teachers College Record* 88 (Spring 1987): 406–410.

34. Martin, *The Schoolhome* 180.

35. Martin, *The Schoolhome* 186.

36. Martin, *The Schoolhome* 184–192. Other thoughts of Martin on the issue here fall into the category of wishes rather than arguments.

37. Martin, *The Schoolhome* 162.

38. Martin, *The Schoolhome* 204.

39. Martin, "Women, Schools, and Cultural Wealth" 174.

40. Martin, *The Schoolhome* 204; Martin, "Women, Schools, and Cultural Wealth" 167.

41. Martin, *The Schoolhome* 9–18.

42. Martin, *Changing the Educational Landscape* 94.

43. Martin, *Changing the Educational Landscape* 89.

44. Martin, *Changing the Educational Landscape* 88–99; Martin, *The Schoolhome* 5–24.

45. Martin, *Reclaiming a Conversation* 198.

46. Martin, *Reclaiming a Conversation* 193–199; Martin, *Changing the Educational Landscape* 104–106.

47. Martin, *The Schoolhome* 118.

48. Martin, *The Schoolhome* 65–70; Martin, "Women, Schools, and Cultural Wealth" 149–177.

49. V.A. Howard and Israel Scheffler, *Work, Education and Leadership: Essays in the Philospophy of Education* (New York: Peter Lang, 1995) 95–96.

50. Martin, *Changing the Educational Landscape* 225.

51. Martin, *Changing the Educational Landscape* 226.

52. Martin, *The Schoolhome* 76.

53. Martin, *The Schoolhome* 5–17, 70–77; Martin, *Changing the Educational Landscape* 92–94.

54. Martin, *The Schoolhome* 40–49.

55. Martin, *The Schoolhome* 56.

56. Martin, *The Schoolhome* 49–57, 118–119.

57. Martin, "Women, Schools, and Cultural Wealth" 174.

58. Martin, *Changing the Educational Landscape* 231–233.

59. Martin, *The Schoolhome* 205–211.

60. For example, see Martin, *Changing the Educational Landscape* 133–153, 170–199, 212–227.

61. Martin, *The Schoolhome* 84.

62. Martin, *The Schoolhome* 18–19, 31–40.

63. Martin, *The Schoolhome* 91–98, 150–160, 205–211; Martin, *Changing the Educational Landscape* 228–241.

64. Martin, *The Schoolhome* 91–98, 150–160; Martin, *Changing the Educational Landscape* 228–241.

65. Martin, *Changing the Educational Landscape* 233.

66. Martin, *The Schoolhome* 91–98, 150–160; Martin, *Changing the Educational Landscape* 228–241.

67. Martin, *The Schoolhome* 91–98, 111–119; Martin, "Women, Schools, and Cultural Wealth" 164–165.

68. Martin, *The Schoolhome* 154.

69. Martin, *The Schoolhome* 153–159, 204.

70. Martin, *Changing the Educational Landscape* 230, 239. A similar point regarding the name of the subject "home economics" is made in Linda Peterat, "Family Studies: Transforming Curriculum, Transforming Families," *Gender In/forms Curriculum*, eds. Jane Gaskell and John Willinsky (New York: Teachers College Press, 1995) 175.

71. Peterat, "Family Studies: Transforming Curriculum, Transforming Families" 174–190.

72. Martin, "Women, Schools, and Cultural Wealth" 166.

73. Eleanor Kallman-Roemer, "Harm and the Ideal of the Educated Person: Response to Jane Roland Martin," *Educational Theory* 31 (Spring 1981): 124.

74. Martin, "The Wealth of Cultures and the Problem of Generations" 28.

75. Martin, *The Schoolhome* 178.

76. Martin, *The Schoolhome* 178–184.

77. One memorable proposal for a liberal education based upon the study of one subject, English literature, is that suggested in F.R. Leavis, *Education and the University* (London: Chatto and Windus, 1948).

78. Jane Roland Martin, "The New Problem of Curriculum," *Synthese* 94 (1993): 85–104.

79. Martin, *The Schoolhome* 153–159; Martin, *Changing the Educational Landscape* 228–241.

80. For example, see Martin, "Women, Schools, and Cultural Wealth," 166.

81. Martin, *Changing the Educational Landscape* 209–210.

82. Common themes in the literature on parenting education are the complexities and the difficulties faced by those wishing to promote such education and the lack of public responsiveness on the issue. See, for example, Gill Jagger and Caroline

Wright, eds., *Changing Family Values* (London: Routledge, 1999); Sylvia Ann Hewlett and Cornel West, *The War against Parents* (Boston: Houghton Mifflin, 1998); Kedar Nath Dwivedi, ed., *Enhancing Parenting Skills* (Chichester: John Wiley, 1997). See also Gerardo R. Lopez, Jay D. Scribner, and Kanya Mahitivanichcha, "Redefining Parental Involvement: Lessons from High-Performing Migrant-Impacted Schools," *American Educational Research Journal* 38 (Summer 2001): 253–288.

83. The European Union, for example, has been considering taxation policy measures that could have the effect of further enticing both parents to work outside the home.

84. Martin, "Women, Schools, and Cultural Wealth" 159–160.

85. On this point see Mary Roth Walsh, ed., *Women, Men, and Gender* (New Haven, CT: Yale University Press, 1997) 383–385; Penelope Leach, "Nurseries and Daycare Centers Do Not Meet Infant Needs," *Women, Men, and Gender*, ed. Walsh 386–390; and Diane E. Eyer, "There Is No Evidence That Mothers Harm Their Infants and Toddlers by Working Outside the Home," *Women, Men, and Gender* 391–397.

86. Martin, "Women, Schools, and Cultural Wealth" 175.

87. Hillary Rodham Clinton, *It Takes a Village* (New York: Simon and Schuster, 1996).

88. In this connection, see M. Elizabeth Grue, Janice Kroeger, and Dana Prager, "A Bakhtinian Analysis of Particular Home-School Relations," *American Educational Research Journal* 38 (Fall 2001): 467–498.

89. Martin, *The Schoolhome* 104–119.

90. Martin, *Reclaiming a Conversation* 34–37; Martin, *Changing the Educational Landscape* 105. For a controversial British and rather contrary view to Martin's in that it appears to favor essentialism and accept that the same education for men and women may not lead to the same results, see Anne Moir and David Jessel, *Brain Sex: The Real Difference between Men and Women* (New York: Dell Publishing, 1991).

91. Martin, *Reclaiming a Conversation* 36. For another statement that takes a broadly similar stand to Martin on this and related issues, see Ann Diller et al., *The Gender Question in Education: Theory, Pedagogy, and Politics* (Boulder, CO: Westview Press, 1996) 105–122.

92. For the student viewpoint, see Carole B. Shmurak, *Voices of Hope: Adolescent Girls at Single Sex and Coeducational Schools* (New York: Peter Lang, 1998).

93. For Martin's response to a number of critics and especially to the decidedly erratic remarks of Walker and O'Loughlin, see Martin, "Bringing Women into Educational Thought" especially 349–353. A somewhat similar set of responses and occasional dismissals is found in Martin, *Changing the Educational Landscape* 1–32. See also J.C. Walker and M.A. O'Loughlin, "The Ideal of the Educated Woman: Jane Roland Martin on Education and Gender," *Educational Theory* 34 (Fall 1984): 327–340.

94. Some of the methodological issues that arise in such practical forms of education are dealt with in several places in *The Schoolhome*. See, for example, Martin, *The Schoolhome* 91–98.

95. Martin, "Women, Schools, and Cultural Wealth" 159–165.

96. Martin, "Women, Schools, and Cultural Wealth" 164.

97. On this point see Penelope Leach, "Nurseries and Daycare Centers Do Not Meet Infant Needs," *Women, Men, and Gender* 386–390.

98. Martin, *The Schoolhome* 137. See also Jane Roland Martin, "Transforming Moral Education," *Journal of Moral Education* 18 (October 1987): 204–213 where she identifies these national reports by name. They include Mortimer J. Adler, *The Paideia Proposal: An Educational Manifesto* (New York: Macmillan, 1982); Ernest L. Boyer, *High School* (New York: Harper and Row, 1983); John I. Goodlad, *A Place Called School* (New York: McGraw-Hill, 1984); and Theodore Sizer, *Horace's Compromise* (Boston: Houghton Mifflin, 1984). Although not mentioned by Martin here, undoubtedly the most highly publicized report of this time period was the report of the National Commission on Excellence in Education, *A Nation at Risk* (Washington, DC: U.S. Department of Education, 1983).

99. Martin, *Changing the Educational Landscape* 233.

100. For a brief discussion of difficulties that arise here from the standpoint of an ethic of care, see Noddings, *Philosophy of Education* 188.

101. Martin, "Women, Schools, and Cultural Wealth" 171.

102. Jane R. Martin, *Choice, Chance, and Curriculum* (Columbus, OH: Ohio State University Press, 1975) 22.

103. Martin, "Women, Schools, and Cultural Wealth" 172.

104. D.G. Mulcahy, *Curriculum and Policy in Irish Post-Primary Education* (Dublin: Institute of Public Administration, 1981).

105. For example, see Martin, "The Wealth of Cultures and the Problem of Generations" 28; Martin, "Women, Schools, and Cultural Wealth" 172–175.

106. Martin, "The Wealth of Cultures and the Problem of Generations" 28.

107. Martin, "Women, Schools, and Cultural Wealth" 164.

108. David Purpel and Kevin Ryan, eds., "It Comes with the Territory: The Inevitability of Moral Education in the Schools," *Moral Education . . . It Comes with the Territory* (Berkeley, CA: McCutchan Publishing, 1976) 44–54.

109. Martin, *Changing the Educational Landscape* 8.

110. This is a point of which Martin remains well aware. Martin, "Women, Schools, and Cultural Wealth" 155.

111. For example, see Martin, "The New Problem of Curriculum," 85–104.

112. Martin, "The New Problem of Curriculum" 102; Martin, *Cultural Miseducation*, Part V.

113. Martin, "Women, Schools, and Cultural Wealth" 169–170; Martin, "There's Too Much to Teach: Cultural Wealth in an Age of Scarcity" *Educational Researcher* 25. 2 (1996): 4–10, 16; Martin, "The Wealth of Cultures and the Problem of Generations"; Martin, *Cultural Miseducation*.

114. Martin, "The Wealth of Cultures and the Problem of Generations" 34–36.

115. Martin, "The New Problem of Curriculum"; Martin, *Cultural Miseducation*, especially Part V.

116. Howard Gardner, *Multiple Intelligences* (New York: Basic Books, 1993).

117. Martin, "The New Problem of Curriculum" 100–102.

118. Martin, "The New Problem of Curriculum" 100–102; Martin, *Cultural Miseducation*, Part V.

119. Martin, *The Schoolhome* 77–84, 104–119.

120. See Martin, "The New Problem of Curriculum" 100–102. Although Martin recognizes these arguments, she is not persuaded by them. For yet a different view

of a common curriculum and the unacceptable uses to which it may be put, see Michael W. Apple, *Cultural Politics and Education* (New York: Teachers College Press, 1996) 22–41.

121. Martin, "The New Problem of Curriculum" 101.

122. Martin, "The New Problem of Curriculum" 102.

123. Martin, *Changing the Educational Landscape* 154–169.

124. For a cultural studies perspective on this question, see Ronnie Casella, "The Theoretical Foundations of Cultural Studies in Education," *Philosophy of Education*, ed. Steve Tozer (Urbana, IL: Philosophy of Education Society, 1998) 531–532.

CHAPTER 5

Beyond Implicit Vision

THE SIGNIFICANCE OF THE VISION

Giroux has said of postmodern feminism in general that in "its critique of patriarchy and its search to construct new forms of identity and social relations," it exemplifies the need for critical pedagogy to regain a sense of alternatives by "combining a language of critique and possibility."[1] He could have been speaking of Martin's work specifically and of its contribution to the creation of alternative cultural as well as educational ideals. Culminating in a vision for the reform of educational thought and practice, this work is firmly rooted in a critique of the epistemology and the gendered character of conventional thinking in education in general and curriculum in particular.

The strength and the weakness of Martin's work lies in the significance of the implicit vision she has created. It is a vision shaped by a philosophical respect for first principles and clarity of thought and motivated by a feminist inspiration. It is suggestive of a grand ideal yet remains more of a sketch than a detailed portrait.

Originality

One of the hallmarks of outstanding scholarship in any field is its degree of originality or innovation. It is a requirement that Martin's thinking meets handily as she pushes out the boundaries and opens up new issues for exploration within curriculum theory and the philosophy of education.

Hirst had fashioned an original and modernized idea of a liberal education based on a well-developed theory of the forms of knowledge. His critics were so mesmerized by the forms that they failed to advert to the educational dimensions of the theory they were employed to sustain. Whereas the critics failed to advert to the educational dimensions of the theory, Martin fixed her critical gaze on them so tellingly as to challenge the Hirst paradigm itself and suggest an alternative in its place. The most fundamental grounds on which Martin's critique of Hirst is based and the alternative proposal she presents are themselves rock solid, namely, the principle that goals precede the selection of content or, as Martin puts it, recognition of the epistemological fallacy. The other major elements of the critique, namely, exposing the narrow concept of knowledge itself, the narrow concept of mind, and the separation of reason and emotion, of knowledge and action that the theory entailed, are also compelling. The manner in which Martin took heed of the errors of Hirst's theory in developing her alternative concept of education, and the broadly based character of this new concept as developed in her gender-sensitive ideal, is also original.

Elsewhere I have argued that the theory of a liberal education elaborated by Cardinal Newman can be distinguished from his broader concept of a university education of which it forms the more celebrated component.[2] There is no need for such distinctions in Martin's work: for Martin, liberal education is so conceived as to embrace all the components necessary for a complete or broad general education. Gender-sensitive education blends elements of liberal education, education of the emotions, and education for action. It is because all of these components are not normally found in theories of liberal education that such theories are suspect as theories of a general education: they omit too much. Much the same is true of mainstream theory supporting the conventional academic school curriculum. Labeling her own stance "liberal education," as Martin once did in the article on Hirst, may pose problems of terminology and show disregard for historical precedent. Yet it also signals a break from traditional conceptions within the field that may outweigh such considerations. That is to say, whatever the terminology or the history, Martin has shown that traditional models of curriculum are too narrowly conceived to provide a complete or broad general education. These are dominated by rationalist conceptions of mind and are limited by correspondingly narrow conceptions of what counts as knowledge, legitimate curriculum content, and individual development. It is possible to overcome these limitations but it calls for a break from the mainstream.

The approach suggested by Martin makes such a break conceivable. The conceptions of mind, knowledge, and individual and social growth upon which it draws may not be original but they are such and are employed by her in such a way as to hold out the prospect of a curriculum model designed to respond to the changed educational requirements of a changing society. Such a model calls for establishing one's educational stance on an explicit commitment to goals, dictated by a broad concept of personal development and an inclusive social and economic philosophy. Following such an approach could lead to a concept of curriculum that embraces all facets of human development, and join feelings and reason, self and other, thought and action. To achieve this may be no small order, but to conceive and articulate it in the first place, as Martin does, is to beckon mainstream philosophical thinking in curriculum in a new direction from where Martin found it.

While conceptions of mind and of personal development play into their thinking, curriculum theorists allow other constraints to be placed on what counts as legitimate knowledge and legitimate curriculum content, constraints from which Martin wishes to break free. Thus she looks to students' needs and interests to find guidance in ascertaining what ought to be included in the curriculum. Mainstream philosophical thinking in curriculum, she argues, attempts to fine tune details of a curriculum that ignores the lives of students and what they need to know about war and peace, poverty and violence, love and relationships.[3] These are topics on which the discipline-based curriculum of which so many of the theorists are enamored remain mute. For her part, Martin is prepared to search farther afield than the academic disciplines, even if it is a failing of hers not to give an adequate account of such material or subject-matter as she is willing to include in the curriculum. Yet she does make the case for broadening out the curriculum beyond its conventional boundaries based on broader definitions of mind, knowledge, cultural wealth, and individual and social need. Holding that important skills, knowledge, and understandings inhere in many facets of our cultural experience besides the academic disciplines, she clearly wishes to provide access for students to these also. It is such knowledge and experience that enables people to develop in ways other than becoming mere ivory tower people, knowledge and experience that a strict interpretation of an academic curriculum would let to chance. It is to such a broadened range of cultural experience that Martin will also look to include material relating to the 3Cs, hence the importance that attaches to her justifying such content by appeal to the domestic tranquillity clause of the U.S. Constitution and its innovative potential.

Martin's willingness to go beyond conventional curriculum thinking in these ways is influenced by her capacity to accept that the kind of symmetry between the world we live in and the account of knowledge that one expects from a unified theory of knowledge is unlikely to reconcile. It is longings for some such unity, aided and abetted by a mixture of cultural and territorial imperatives that impels them to put a unified curriculum before a unifying one, that hinders the elders from embracing a broader curriculum, according to Martin. For Martin, it also reveals how epistemological considerations can merge with those of gender, ethnicity, race, and economic status in shaping curriculum and its social impact. The case of Rodriguez to which Martin makes reference reveals, in turn, the force of individual student response and its unpredictable emotional determinants. Just as important, if not more so, in enabling Martin to envision new curriculum possibilities in a space overwhelmed by powerful crosscurrents is the tenacity with which she holds on to the principle that goals must precede content. While this may seem the most basic of curriculum principles, Martin is exceptional in the manner in which she relies upon it to impart coherence to the variety of innovative curriculum possibilities she envisages.

These curriculum possibilities are shaped by yet another of Martin's creations, her ideal of a gender-sensitive education,[4] more than by any other influence. Inspired perhaps by the trait genderization she associates with such educational idealizations as Plato's guardians and Peters's educated man, for example, the gender-sensitive ideal attempts to come to grips with age-old and competing cultural aspirations and tendencies. These include the tendency to hold different and competing cultural expectations and roles for men and for women, the democratic aspiration to seek equality and justice for all, the favoring of male roles and experience over female both in society and in the curriculum, and the consequent imbalances, exclusions, and injustices it generates. Martin recognizes the enormous challenge faced in implementing her gender-sensitive ideal, not least the assumption by men of roles and educational experiences associated with women. Such are the stakes for the welfare of men as well as women, and even for the environment and the human race itself, that she is not prepared to broach any compromise. Even before its implementation can be contemplated, however, a number of misguided assumptions regarding equality of educational opportunity and provision need to be set right, she believes. Chief among these is the notion that while sex is a difference that often should make no difference at all, there are occasions when it does and where we need to act accordingly.

Martin's response to the challenge posed by the implementation of her gender-sensitive ideal and its innovative character is well-captured in *The Schoolhome*. There may be a novelty in the clever juxtaposition of familiar terms in the title but there is nothing trivial about Martin's overall vision. Many of the elements of the Schoolhome are not new. The idea of a school as a home away from home for youngsters Martin attributes to Montessori. The notion of domestic tranquillity as providing a political and moral ethos necessary to support the kind of value system essential to justifying her compassionate educational goals is derived from the Constitution. The distinction drawn between the productive and reproductive processes in society, the claims she makes for the centrality of education in the emotions and feelings alongside intellectual education in a complete education, and her objections to the exclusion of women and women's experience from the school curriculum, are all familiar themes in Martin and are often shared by others before her. It is the manner in which she brings these various elements together in propounding a curriculum vision, the very different circumstances in which she wants to adapt them, and the courage to wage battle with powerful traditions in the field in order to give her divergent views an airing that, taken together, contribute to the innovative thrust of the gender-sensitive ideal.

While I have drawn attention to limitations of the distinction Martin draws between the productive and reproductive processes in society, no one denies that there is a marked underlying tendency in our culture to treat men and women differently and to evaluate their achievements and spheres of influence differently. Insofar as it is this uneven treatment, and the serious threat that its continuing neglect poses for all as it affects our society's capacity to survive and prosper, that Martin's appeal to a gender-sensitive education is aimed at setting straight, the limitations of her distinction may be of little or no consequence. Neither does this distinction do anything to diminish the case for nurturing those qualities of the private sphere of home and family, the associated values of care, concern, and connection, and the particular knowledge and skills associated with domesticity. These are the core values that a gender-sensitive education aims to transmit to all students and in which it breaks most profoundly with the inherited traditions of academic education. They are the values of attention to and the care of the individual that impressed Montessori in the work of Itard and Séguin, and that are captured and highlighted by her in her own practical contributions in the education of the young. They are values that make Martin's embrace of the domestic tranquillity clause compelling.

Once again, there is nothing new in Martin seeking to locate her educational theory within a sustaining political philosophy, as Plato and Rousseau had done. If she had not settled on the notion of domestic tranquillity to ensure that her reform proposals have the kind of political and moral support that such a broader context supplies for Plato and Rousseau, and the kind of legal support her Schoolhome thesis may require, she would have needed to seek a source of justification elsewhere. While Martin finds it necessary to seek the support of the public world for her educational plan in this manner, it does imply, contrary to her argument and wishes, a relegation of the influence of the private sphere to one of secondary importance. Invoking the domestic tranquillity clause in order to provide a broader support for the values of domesticity that she wishes to advance requires Martin to seek support from the political and economic context— the public world—in which her educational ideas are to be played out. In doing so, she grounds her educational ideal in a uniquely supportive dimension of that self-contradictory conjunction of a democratic form of government and a capitalist economic system which undoubtedly contributes in no small way to why her gender-sensitive ideal is needed in the first place.

Siegel has challenged Martin's interpretation of the relationship between reason and emotion in Peters's educational thought, asserting that she over-looks the importance he attaches to the emotions. Right or wrong, Siegel's charge does little to alter Martin's own position in regard to the relation between the two and their place in the curriculum. Whether it can be said of Peters or not, Martin unambiguously claims education in the emotions and feelings, and education for action, to be as essential as intellectual education. It is as integral to her overall position as any other aspect of it. It is prominent, too, in the case she makes for education in domesticity being as necessary for boys as for girls. Education in the 3Cs, after all, is as vital and necessary for progress in the public sphere, the domain of men, as it is in the private, the domain of women.

Martin's stance on the place of education in the emotions, and the place of the 3Cs in the education of boys and girls, makes the kind of analysis needed to decipher Peters's stand on the place of the emotions in education unnecessary. Her unambiguous inclusion of it is one of the distinguishing marks of her educational stance, and it definitively sets her apart from the mainstream. This is not to say that educational practice always conforms to mainstream curriculum thinking either at the level of the school or the university. The fact that it often goes beyond it in the direction Martin urges only serves to underline how much more in tune with some aspects of actual educational practice Martin's position is, relative to mainstream theory.

Nowhere, however, does Martin do more to bring together reason and emotion, and thought and action, than in regard to education for mem-bership of a home and family and in making the case for its inclusion at the center of everyone's education. Nowhere is her stand more distinctive, for this is a unique vision for education that singles out Martin from all others. As Catharine Beecher was to the nineteenth century, so Martin is to the late twentieth and early twenty-first centuries: advocating a marriage of sorts between liberal education and education for domesticity. But Mar-tin wants to extend this to all, boys as well as girls. Martin's advantage over Beecher in having studied the great idealizations of women's education in the past leads her to seek a more comprehensive ideal not only of women's education but the education of all. In her study of earlier ideali-zations of women's education, Martin failed to uncover the perfect idea in any of them. Beecher seems to best approximate the ideal in Martin's eyes, combining Wollstonecraft's call for a liberal education for women with knowledge and skills in domestic affairs. Yet, even aside from not claiming such an education for men as well as women, Beecher, as Martin puts it, "having designed an education for Sarah to ensure the health of her 'cas-ket,' the powers of her intellect, and her self-control, gives short shrift to the very feelings and emotions she believes Sarah needs to have and to pass on to her own young."[5] It is education for these same feelings and emotions, along with everything else, that Martin now wishes to claim for all and which makes her position genuinely original. She also articulates well the major elements in education for membership of a home and family, showing the central place of education for the feelings and emotions through an ethic of caring: gender; domesticity, including child care, house-work, and the reproductive processes of society; and the 3Cs.

Another aspect of Martin's originality is her reinterpretation of the con-tributions of such figures as Plato, Rousseau, Hirst, and Peters and her critique of the academy itself. The critiques she develops are not set forth for the sake of novelty, having a much more serious point to them, namely, illustrating that women and women's experience have been treated preju-dicially to the disadvantage of all by educational theorists, historians of educational thought, and even educational institutions of great renown. Much of Martin's work has been directed at dealing with the undesirable consequences of such a mindset. The reinterpretation of Plato and Rous-seau has a distinctive flavor, one in which the interpretation is not merely of these figures themselves, but of the historiography. It is not Plato and Rousseau, Martin maintains, who overlooked the education of women, but the scholarship that chose to ignore what they had to say on the subject; as for Plato and Rousseau, the positions they took were in some respects simply mistaken. The upshot in each case was an underestimation of the potential and experience of women and their roles in education and society. This in turn involved not merely a devaluation of women and their expe-rience but a consequent denial of their value as persons and members of society in the eyes of future generations of both girls and boys. It is a denial that is perpetuated, wittingly or unwittingly, by educational theorists of Martin's own day. Alongside these, in Martin's view, go advocates of an unregenerated liberal education and the academic disciplines that sustain it. New scholarship revealing the biases of academic disciplines toward females has begun to rectify some of the problems inherent in earlier con-ceptions of the disciplines. Yet the denial persists and is further maintained through the power and mystique of the academy, the ethos that pervades it, and the modus operandi through which it asserts itself. For Martin, it is a denial with consequences of untold proportions with which we grapple today in its ongoing implications for the mistreatment of girls and women and our collective debasement as a society.

One may readily say of Martin's work that historical and philosophical analysis has been harnessed to the cause of an educational vision. Martin's is specifically an educational and cultural vision, for it is aimed at supplying through teaching what nature itself does not provide. Just as it holds out hope for improvement in the lives of women, so it also speaks to a better future for all peoples, young and old, rich and poor, Black and White, victorious and conquered, men and women. The ideal of a gender-sensitive education transcends division and injustice and aims to unify all as it elevates each. It may fairly be said to seek a new way forward.

Scope

How comprehensive is this implicit vision? One way of addressing this question is to consider the goals Martin's proposal is intended to attain. Is the proposal up to what is required to meet them, and how important are these goals in the first place? The problem that Martin has attempted to solve has often been referred to as the problem of a "general education," that is to say, determining what ought to be the goals and content of a broadly based education considered suitable for children and young adults. Because this term has been widely and variously used, sometimes for different purposes, I shall for present purposes label this concept of general education "complete education"; the term "total education" could have been chosen if it had not been employed by Hirst.[6] With this in mind, one may say that any such concept of education implies a wide-ranging set of goals. In Martin's own view, for example, it extends beyond the goals of a liberal education as Hirst understood it. Hirst's position, she has made clear, marked only a beginning point.[7]

So what are the goals that Martin seeks to attain, and are they sufficiently comprehensive to provide for a complete education? The goals highlighted by Martin are primarily of a personal and social kind and they grow out of her preoccupation with the 3Cs. The educated person of Martin, be it man or woman, will be a person of action as well as thought, will join emotion and feelings with reason, will be committed to the ideals of social justice, and be both able and willing to take action to attain them. This person will be educated to live well in the private sphere of home and family as well as the public sphere of government, business, and the professions. He or she will have an awareness of gender and its significance in our lives, possess the knowledge and skills of domesticity, and be caring, concerned, and connected. Beyond such personal formation, this person will also be attentive to social and environmental issues. He or she will strike an appropriate balance between the values of social unity and the satisfaction of personal or partisan desires, will be respectful to all persons and the racial, cultural, and economic sensitivities it calls for, and be considerate toward the world of nature.

It is by these goals that the ideal of a gender-sensitive education is directed and, as has been stressed already, the point of a gender-sensitive ideal is the fair and equal treatment of all. These goals necessitate a much greater awareness in education of values historically associated with women and the private world of the home and family rather than the public world. Martin's firm grasp of the wide sweep of the history of educational thought makes such a realization possible, and it transmits a corresponding breadth of scope to her thinking. The scope of Martin's conceptualization of the issues she addresses is further aided by the breadth of her critique of existing theories from which it grows, informed as it is by the range of historical, philosophical, and feminist perspectives she employs. The use she makes of literary sources adds further enrichment and clarification and, most importantly, the broadening of her justifying arguments by recourse to the domestic tranquillity clause lends an important and necessary theoretical dimension. It does not give her the support of so wide-ranging a social and political philosophy as those that Plato and Rousseau provide for their educational stances, but it does supply a dimension lacking before its presentation in *The Schoolhome*. Such scope notwithstanding, it is nonetheless true that while Martin has an innovative stance on the goals of a complete education, their domination by personal and social goals raises the question of whether the goals do justice to the requirements of a complete education. Do they pay sufficient attention to academic goals, such as knowledge and understanding in the sciences, mathematics, literature and the humanities, and other goals such as critical thinking traditionally associated with liberal education? To the extent that Martin's position on the place of liberal education in a complete education needs much further explanation for reasons already given, it is difficult to answer this question. What can be said is that just as Martin devotes inadequate attention to the elaboration and justification of the non-discipline knowledge and other experiences she wishes to include in a complete education, the same is true of her stance vis-à-vis the content and gendered nature of a liberal education. Even when some elaboration is provided by Martin, as in the proposal to roll all academic studies into one subject called "the discipline," as many questions arise as are answered.

One may conclude from this that while the goals of education to which Martin is committed embrace academic as well as practical and emotional goals, the ones upon which she elaborates are those personal and social goals distinctive of the gender-sensitive ideal that remains her priority. Since we know that Martin devises a plan to implement her goals for education, and addresses the curriculum aspects of it, are other aspects of it, such as teaching, evaluation, school organization and administration, and policy, all of which form a necessary part of any comprehensive educational plan, satisfactorily addressed? To answer this we need to turn to *The Schoolhome*.

The Schoolhome attempts to set forth both an outline plan and a supporting philosophy, the plan being the part to which Martin's previous work paid less attention. While greater attention is paid to the plan here than before, it remains inadequate in several respects. Teaching,[8] which Martin deals with at length in an earlier book, and school organization are touched upon at different points in presenting her plan, but little or no attention is given to evaluation and policy. These two being major categories under which any plan of execution for the attainment of educational goals is normally conceived and implemented, the failure to attend to them at greater length is an important omission. This omission is compounded by a failure to respond to secondary aspects of a plan of execution needed to ensure that the primary aspects can be properly attended to. A case in point is provision for the education of teachers. While it may be assumed that teachers would be exposed to the kind of gender-sensitive education intended for students themselves, it is unclear what else would be involved. In his proposal for educational reform, Mortimer Adler required of all teachers that before engaging in supervised teaching practice they pursue a liberal education. While Martin is critical of traditional liberal education in the preparation of teachers in "Reforming Teacher Education, Rethinking Liberal Education," she is nonetheless reluctant to dispense with it entirely.[9] Does she foresee special emphasis on the 3Cs and specialist studies in an academic or practical area of study during the collegiate years? How does she envisage the professional, and for that matter the continuing, education of teachers taking shape? If, as I argued earlier, there ought to be a greater emphasis on parent education to address the issue of family life education, what the proper education of parents consists of also needs to be addressed. The same holds true for those programs offered by supportive agencies such as youth programs, churches, and the like—not to mention the media—who may lend a hand in the formation of the young. Going beyond these matters, the broader aspects of any plan of change would need to attend to the particular economic demands of the plan and gaining the support of parents, teachers, and members of the general public for its adoption. Given the challenging, if not radical, nature of her ideas, strategies for dealing with dissidents who are likely to be many and vociferous would also be essential. Not men only but women of even mildly conservative persuasions are likely to have grave difficulty accepting the departures from conventional practice that Martin's stand entails, and their attitude to the many sensitive cultural and value issues that Martin deals with so readily are likely to be negative. Yet none of these matters, which need to be addressed if Martin's ideas are to have a wide appeal, and which themselves ironically smack of an ivory tower mentality, is given adequate attention. Still less attention is given to how such a plan might be envisaged for the nation at large. Martin is critical of national reports on education for not addressing the educational goals to which she is committed. For her own part, she is content to skip over any consideration of the particular requirements of a plan designed for the implementation of her ideas on a national scale, let alone on the international scale, to which she envisions her ideal somehow being expanded in the course of time.

I have suggested that in *Coming of Age in Academe*, Martin's proposals for reform do not match in scope the critique of the academy she presents, the proposals being insignificant by comparison. The fact that Martin extends both the critique and the reform proposals to include the levels of the public schools and the university certainly broadens the range of students to which her theorizing applies. So also does the willingness she demonstrates to have these proposals reflect the needs and interests of students, including those historically at a disadvantage. In *The Schoolhome*, as in *Coming of Age in Academe*, however, Martin talks of small and incremental change for the most part. In *The Schoolhome*, moreover, Martin's approach lacks the sense of urgency and the compulsion for revolution found in *Coming of Age in Academe*. It belies the urgency she attaches to the problem she sets out to address, and does so at the risk of allowing any momentum her plan achieves to run out of steam before it ever amounts to a widely accepted response.

Practicability

In one anonymous and skimpy review of *The Schoolhome*, Martin is dismissed without remorse for "an infuriating philosophical remoteness." With little else to add to the verdict, and having alluded to the repeated references in the text to viewing the other side of Woolf's bridge from some distance, the reviewer sarcastically cites Martin herself for a parting shot. "To borrow one of Martin's lines," the review concludes, "take out your binoculars and look for another book to read."[10] The frustration spouting from these few words underlines boldly the weakest aspect of Martin's ideal: a lack of elaboration on how to implement her ideas. Even those who are sympathetic to Martin's work advert to this weakness, as I have myself on a number of occasions. Levin, an important reviewer, says of *Changing the Educational Landscape* that it may help teachers, administrators, and policymakers to understand education, but gives little assistance in improving it. He reasons as follows:[11]

> Martin has not yet carried her critique to the next phase, which is formulating a program for schooling that would unite "thought and action, self and other, reason and emotion [*sic*]." (211). How is this to be done? How is the concept of "Schoolhome," developed in her 1992 book, to be realized? Martin's discussion remains abstract. Although the later essays do include some real examples and stories, they remain largely abstract discussion of concepts.

Not that she does, but it would not aid Martin to respond to such criticism by hiding behind the claim that she is not a school superintendent or principal, but a philosopher: what is needed is further elaboration of a vision, not its actual implementation by a gifted administrator.[12] Yet Levin suggests that the overall task undertaken by Martin "is too much to expect of one person" and that "others will have to take up the challenge of creating, in schools, the kind of education Martin so eloquently espouses."[13] While this may be true, one part of the challenge of turning Martin's sketchy vision into a more detailed portrait is to indicate where Martin needs to give greater attention to weaknesses in her position.

The most serious aspect of practicability may reside in a deep-seated conceptual, yet ultimately practical, difficulty that needs to be addressed even if it may never be fully resolved: determining with some greater specificity the values that represent Martin's ideal. Given its centrality to her educational vision, how is one to decide, for example, what kind of home constitutes the ideal, what are its values, and how does one achieve the necessary level of agreement upon these matters, whatever level that may be? In addition, one needs to deal with how the ideals and values adopted can be taught. While these may appear to be hopeless tasks, some way of dealing with them has to be reached as long as we live in a community. Deciding common values and how to attain them are among the most basic tasks faced by any society, and it is in how they are resolved that a community defines its own core values and character. This being so, the task that Martin sets us is not a merely educational one but a broad social and political one. It is because of this that recourse to the domestic tranquillity clause to support her educational ideal is both ultimately necessary and well-suited to the particular requirements of this broader task.

The appeal to the domestic tranquillity clause may provide the theoretical and moral basis for justifying Martin's ideal of domesticity and education in the 3Cs. The political support that it justifies may require a plan of political intervention, however. From time to time Martin points to the need for political action, even revolution in *Coming of Age in Academe*, but she never sets forth a matching plan in any detail. This is especially evident in her failure to devote attention to the organizational, administrative, economic, policy-making, and public relations dimensions of implementing her ideal at both the levels of the schools and the academy. If friendly critics have difficulties with her ideas on this score, one can only imagine the response of the unfriendly.

Beyond the questions of moral justification, constitutional support, and a plan of political engagement, the matter of practicability also brings us back to the curricular and pedagogical dimensions of Martin's ideal. Martin does address aspects of these in varying degrees and in different places, yet much that is necessary is left unsaid. One of the most glaring unanswered questions revolves around her intentions for the liberal education dimension of a complete education. One may ask, for example, how she can justify liberal education for boys or girls given the resounding critique of it that she consistently upholds throughout her writings. Uncertainty centers especially on the discipline-based content of a liberal education, given the equally resounding grilling that the disciplines have been accorded for the gender biases they continue to perpetuate in her opinion, and their exclusively theoretical orientation. These are less questions of implementation than they are having to do with the clarification of concepts, though they inevitably bear on practicability too. Also bearing on conceptual clarity as well as justification and practicability is the question of the content of those aspects of nondisciplinary subject matter to which I have drawn attention already, and about which considerable ambiguity exists in Martin's writings, in regard to both content and teachability. It is all well and good to talk of the need of students to know about relationships, violence, and war and peace, but what is it about these matters that needs to be taught and how? It is one thing for Martin to be unclear about some aspects of the academic disciplines that are to be taught. It is quite another to be mute on nondisciplinary knowledge and experiences that are likely to involve active participation, improvement through practice, and experiential learning when it comes to such matters as violence, relationships, and warfare.

Making the case for the inclusion of curriculum content drawn from a wide variety of sources other than the academic disciplines is important to Martin's position; it also marks a substantial departure from the mainstream. Such content may include material embedded in aspects of culture as diverse as folklore, time-proven customs and practices, language, music and other artistic pursuits, physical, vocational, and domestic skills, moral training, and emotional experiences honored in the community. Yet considerable elaboration on what may and may not, ought and ought not to be included is necessary, as are the accompanying justifications. This is where Martin falls down, and where earlier attempts at including such nontraditional content—such as the life-adjustment movement—ran into difficulties on the grounds that the material included was either trivial, objectionable, or unsuitable on other grounds. In the final analysis, not only is it necessary to elucidate the new content to be included, it is necessary that it be readily available for educational use by teachers and others. Only then, too, may one pass final judgment as to its desirability and suitability.

In addition to the identification, selection, and justification of such subject matter, the pedagogical aspects of this material have to be considered and provided for also. It is necessary to identify potential learnings and practical experiences, but no less necessary to arrange for the teaching and evaluation of such learnings. The efficacy of such curriculum content in meeting the needs and interests of students also has to be borne in mind, and the likelihood of this being the case in some instances given by Martin for use in the Schoolhome is questionable for many students in need. Students in greatest jeopardy are likely to be those coming from disadvantaged home backgrounds where the values and the experiences of the ideal home of which Martin speaks may not be found. They are highly unlikely to be able to participate in or even benefit from summer camps in the arts located in the Berkshires or the Hamptons. Content and experiences in journalism and drama may be highly desirable but are they suitable? How are children unable to read going to be attracted to editorial-room discussions and the like? How are students raised in the streets, sleeping rough, fending for themselves and accustomed from an early age to the cultures and effects of poverty, drugs, violence, neglect, and abuse ever going to comprehend the values and ethos of Martin's ideal home, not to mention assimilate them? The question is not whether these are desirable goals; it is how can they be attained. In a word, the examples of alternative activities for the School-home given by Martin are often suspect—being of the kind suitable for students coming from ideal rather than troubled homes—when it comes to addressing the very students who would appear to be in greatest need of the Schoolhome itself. The idea is admirable; ensuring its practicability needs further attention in order to find the right match between need and provision.

In addition to its teachability, one also needs to know if and how the kinds of nonacademic learning Martin has in mind can be assessed or eval-uated. Evaluation is a necessary element of any educational program. It need not be of a highly formal or technical nature and should not be con-fused with elaborate testing schemes that threaten teaching and learning themselves. But evaluation is necessary to ascertain if learning is taking place and what adjustments in teaching may be necessary.[14] The relative ease with which assessment takes place in the academic subjects, and the acceptance hitherto by the public of such standard reference points as SAT scores, contrasts with the difficulties of evaluating in practical areas which, in turn, probably serve as a further deterrent to practical education. Perhaps there is room for optimism in the greater use of portfolio assessment and other new forms of assessment in this area. Yet this is a challenge that Martin's proposals for the Schoolhome share with other forms of practical education.

Attention to these matters is lacking also in Martin's designs for the reform or reconstitution of the academy. Such is the gender bias of the academy that Martin talks of dismantling the academy in its entirety. Yet little or no guidance is provided for the improvement she has in mind; where it is given, for the most part, it tends to be concerned with rather minor modifications that apply within the existing structures and not the revolutionary new institutions she appeared to promise at times. Even less is said about the practicability of Martin's reform ideas for higher educa-tion than for schools.

Consistency

The coherence in Martin's educational thought is rooted in the firmness with which she stays true to her goals, ensuring a remarkable consistency among the various elements of her position. It is evident in the striking manner in which thoughts, reasoning, and examples appearing in writings of recent years, while very greatly expanded, are entirely consistent with those from the late 1960s through the early 1980s. Conversely, arguments made and positions taken in earlier work have a continuing applicability and provide helpful contextual support for more recent expressions of Martin's thinking.

This consistency of position and continuing relevance across contributions now spanning four decades represents one view of consistency. A second and perhaps more important consistency is the internal consistency among the various elements of Martin's thought. This is evident when, for example, she points to the epistemological fallacy in aspects of her epistemological and gender critiques and in her detailing of the ills of feminist theory and the academy. In the article on Hirst's theory of a liberal education, she does so to demonstrate his dismissal, and by implication that of his ineffectual critics, of the place of educational goals in curriculum theorizing. She does so again in critiquing the claims of the elders that there can be no curriculum unity without an underlying unified theory of knowledge. The common factor in these two different but related cases, for Martin, is that both the justification and the unity of curriculum emanate from goals of education, not from a theory of the nature and structure of knowledge.

This same consistency pervades the gender critique as well as those elements of critique that span epistemology and gender. Even as early as "The Disciplines and the Curriculum," Martin exhibits an awareness of the importance of what she would later refer to as the reproductive processes. In this early work, she sought to respond to the needs and interests of students by arguing for the inclusion of such topics as love and relationships, peace and war in the curriculum. A similar tendency is detectable in the critique of Hirst's theory of a liberal education. Here the product of such an education is considered limited for not being educated in emotions as well as reason, and for being inept when it comes to carrying out practical tasks or taking action on behalf of any cause. As the focus turns more directly to the gender critique itself in works such as the critique of Peters's concept of the educated man, "Excluding Women from the Educational Domain," *Reclaiming a Conversation*, *The Schoolhome*, and *Coming of Age in Academe*, the variety of themes developed and arguments advanced are both consistent and formidable. Take the notions of the exclusion of women's experience from education and the idea of a gender-sensitive ideal. Not only is Martin's thesis regarding the exclusion of women's experience employed in the critique of Peters's concept of the educated man to bolster the critique of a liberal education, but it is employed primarily to underline the gender-biased character of the academic disciplines upon which a liberal education is founded. The theme of exclusion is clearly maintained in "Excluding Women from the Educational Domain," and continues to be em-

ployed forcefully as recently as *Coming of Age in Academe*. The theme of
the exclusion of women's experience becomes a major influence in creating
the ideal of a gender-sensitive education, which in turn evolves through
Martin's study of the ideal of the educated woman in *Reclaiming a Conversation*. A further central element in the idea of a gender-sensitive education is that it ought to be for both boys and girls. The crucial element
of adequate attention to the 3Cs was missing from the great historical
idealizations of the educated woman, Martin argued, but this dimension of
Montessori's thought becomes pivotal in Martin's own thinking. Having
become convinced by the time her critique of Peters's ideal of the educated
man appeared in 1981 that a gender-sensitive education was the avenue to
pursue in order to promote equality of education for women as well as
men, from Montessori she drew much of the inspiration for the 3Cs, the
implications of which are spelled out at greatest length in *The Schoolhome*.
The 3Cs not only bring women's experience and the caring tendencies associated with them into the curriculum, but they become the key element
in the ideal of a gender-sensitive education.

The consistency found in the epistemological and gender critiques is carried forward into Martin's alternative conceptualizations of education and
her proposals for reform. This is hardly surprising given that they rely
heavily upon the critiques. The consistency is maintained in Martin's recourse to the domestic tranquillity clause to support her call for education
in the 3Cs and family life education. It is especially noteworthy that in the
course of Martin's study of the ideal of the educated woman, she does not
respond by advocating the logical counterpart of Peters's "educated man"
in the form of an idealization of the "educated woman." To do so would
have been to break with a higher logic, namely, that the ideal of a gender-
sensitive education sought equality for men and women in education by
advocating essentially the same education for males and females.

There is one area where there is an apparent breach in Martin's otherwise
impeccable consistency of position. It lies in the notion of the elective curriculum brought forward in *Cultural Miseducation*, which would be at
odds with her gender-sensitive ideal, as I have argued.

NEW QUESTIONS AND NEW DIRECTIONS

This inconsistency aside, the question arises as to what needs to be done
to make the implicit vision that Martin puts before us more explicit? One
way would be to extend the sketch of an alternative future for education
and society that Martin has presented by exploring alternatives or possibilities for additional forms of education not contained in Martin's perspective, for example. One could refine it by attending to its practicability.
One might even attempt both. Having already addressed the question of

refining the sketch by considering aspects of its practicability, I shall attempt here to identify aspects of where it might be extended.

If the focus here is not upon questions of the practicability of Martin's proposals but how her thinking might be extended in other ways, what does this entail? In this case, it involves elaborating on the emphasis in, as opposed to the general scope of, her thinking. The general scope of Martin's ideal is that of a complete education; the emphasis is upon promoting practical education, with special reference to the 3Cs, or education for family life, and the values associated with the world of women and the private home. Martin's distinctive contribution to educational thought is found in part in the attention she gives to the practical as opposed to the academic contents of curriculum. In the article on Hirst's theory, Martin spoke of a search for "a more general curriculum paradigm, whether that be a paradigm of liberal education or not" and she even adverts to some of the "new questions"[15] that such a search raises. When I speak of extending Martin's thinking on curriculum, new questions, ones that expand the discussion and elucidation of practical forms of education in particular, immediately come to mind. Martin clearly considers additional forms of practical education, such as vocational education, to be important, but has not devoted as much attention to them as to education for family living.

While we ridicule the ivory tower person and book learning, we show disdain for the practical. Because it is the proponents of academic and liberal education that have held sway for so long in the institutions of formal education, practical education has been the more publicly scorned, though this appears to be changing, and Martin is a crucial voice in these times of change. Her stance is unambiguous: there is more to the wisdom of the race than academic knowledge. This is the distinguishing belief.

The types of practical education that exist are almost endless, the specific form indicated in the language used to pick it out from other forms, as in family life education or vocational education. There are of course many different kinds of vocational education, such as education to be a carpenter or a motor mechanic, and there is the implication that it is in some sense different from professional education that is also associated with earning a living. Some forms of practical education are subsumed within broader forms, or they cross boundaries between different forms. Health education, for example, may be considered part of family life education and at the same time it may have a vocational or professional focus, as may home economics education. Practical forms of education take their distinctive focus and shape from a particular role or function or a set of related functions for which they are intended to prepare one. In this, they are unlike levels of education, such as elementary or higher education, in which the designation "elementary" or "higher" simply picks out the stage that a particular kind of education has reached or is aimed at reaching. If a naturalistic model of education is conceivable, practical education by its nature inevitably conforms to the production model of education.

It is in both the functionality and the kinds of learnings associated with it that the unique character of practical education primarily resides. Both dimensions set it apart from liberal education in which the learning is supposed to be free as well as freeing and in which the knowledge is supposedly pure or theoretical as distinct from applied. Practical education may be freeing but it is not free in the sense that it is shaped by the particular role or function to which it is tied. It may entail theoretical knowledge but typically calls for applied knowledge too. It is also concerned with action of some kind and it may have both physical and emotional dimensions. It is the absence of these non-theoretical components, and the opportunity for the learner to grow in the ability to make practical judgments through practice, that opens up the graduate of Hirst's liberal education to the charge of being an ivory tower type, of lacking common sense.

If practical knowledge is a key to tapping into the wisdom of the race not found in the academic disciplines, it behooves us to identify those forms considered necessary for a complete education. For Martin, family life education or home economics is clearly one. Others that come to mind and even overlap include civic and political education, moral education, health education, consumer education, driver education, communications and media education, and vocational and professional education. Forms such as scuba-diving education, day-trading education, art restoration education, are every bit as practical but they are also more specialized.

The knowledge, attitudes, and skills associated with the more general forms of practical education are in some cases transferable to functions other than those for which they were designed. It may even be that because they are more function-specific than those associated with liberal education—less versatile and hence in one sense less economical, educationally speaking—that they have been less favored in the past. Indeed, to the extent that the aim of traditional liberal education was to provide the broadest preparation for life, the subjects chosen for it may have been less the result of the epistemological fallacy, as Martin charges, than the belief that they were the most appropriate knowledge for the purpose. Over time they then came to be accepted as a given—the forms of Hirst being simply a contemporary formulation. Be this as it may, whether because students spend more time in school today than before, because of organizationally differentiated lifestyles, or for a variety of reasons pertaining to contemporary living, practical forms of education appear more educationally compelling than before. While this may be true, and while different forms of practical education such as business education, technology education, home economics education, and even community service have come to be accepted by schools, schooling has not yet properly adjusted to their particular requirements, the absence of suitable forms of testing and evaluation being an example of this. Other examples include programs of teacher education not designed to meet the new expectations, unsuitable curriculum and organizational arrangements, unexamined expectations for teachers, administrators, and costs, and the increasingly intrusive and sometimes counterproductive character of school law.

That institutionalized education—schooling—can ever cope with practical education of the kinds mentioned here has been questioned. As matters stand, it is unlikely that it can do so with ease, if at all. This is a situation likely to persist until the particular requirements of practical education can be more adequately provided for. The case made by Martin for more favorably valuing practical education and education for action is especially helpful in drawing attention to these requirements. It is but one instance of where her work points to new directions for curriculum theorists to explore.

CONCLUSION

A rigorous model for the comprehensive evaluation of educational ideals is one in which personal and social goals or purposes are identified and consideration is given to the provisions made for their attainment through curriculum, teaching, assessment and evaluation, organization and administration, and policy. Measured against such a model, it can be said that Martin accepts personal and social goals for education broadly in line with accepted societal expectations and has added an emphasis on the goals associated with the 3Cs. It is around this additional dimension that the distinctive character of her educational thought and curriculum-theorizing takes shape.

Turning to the distinctive character of Martin's educational thought and curriculum-theorizing, Decker Walker may be forgiven for not seeing in Martin's critique of Hirst's theory of a liberal education, and in particular in the short section in which she presented the outlines of a new paradigm for liberal education, the full extent of her educational ideal. In a series of articles published in 1981 in *Educational Theory* commenting on the Eightieth Yearbook of the NSSE, which was devoted to the philosophy of education and where Martin's critique of Hirst first appeared, Walker wrote, "all of the ingredients of her new paradigm have been actively under development in innovative schools and colleges since at least the Progressive era. Dewey, Schwab, and Broudy have all written on these themes in the same spirit."[16] If, after a century or so, it is only in innovative schools and colleges that the new elements of Martin's paradigm to which Walker refers are to be found, this alone lends support to her call for a new paradigm and to its elaboration. Martin would not acquiesce either in the thought that Dewey, Schwab, and Broudy have all written on the themes she focuses upon in the same spirit, or that her more fully developed theorizing should be described today as was her article on Hirst's theory when it first appeared, namely, as a piece of criticism and its burden largely negative.[17] She would be right.

Martin has extricated philosophical discussion of the curriculum from the rut to which it lured Hirst and the mainstream and she has charted a new course. She has identified promising new directions and generated a range of provocative yet sustainable themes for exploration by which feminist theory, the philosophy of education, and educational policy and practice may be greatly enriched.

NOTES

1. Henry A. Giroux, "Modernism, Postmodernism, and Feminism: Rethinking the Boundaries of Educational Discourse," *Postmodernism, Feminism, and Cultural Politics*, ed. Henry A. Giroux (Albany, NY: State University of New York Press, 1991) 52.

2. D.G. Mulcahy, "Personal Influence, Discipline and Liberal Education in Cardinal Newman's Idea of a University," *Internationale Cardinal Newman Studien*, Elfte Folge. Achter Newman–Congress, Freiburg; eds. H. Fries, W. Becker and G. Biemer (Heroldsberg: Glock und Lutz, 1980) 150–158.

3. Jane Roland Martin, *Changing the Educational Landscape: Philosophy, Women, and Curriculum* (New York: Routledge, 1994) 143.

4. Jane Roland Martin, *Reclaiming a Conversation: The Ideal of the Educated Woman* (New Haven, CT: Yale University Press, 1985) 193–199.

5. Martin, *Reclaiming a Conversation* 130.

6. Paul H. Hirst, *Knowledge and the Curriculum* (London: Routledge and Kegan Paul, 1974) 96.

7. Martin, *Changing the Educational Landscape* 180–184.

8. Jane Roland Martin, *Explaining, Understanding, and Teaching* (New York: McGraw-Hill, 1970).

9. Jane Roland Martin, "Reforming Teacher Education, Rethinking Liberal Education," *Teachers College Record* 88 (Spring 1987): 406–410.

10. "Book Review of *The Schoolhome*," *American School Board Journal* 179 August 1992: 34.

11. Benjamin Levin, "Book Review of *Changing the Educational Landscape*," *Journal of Educational Thought* 30 April 1996: 80.

12. She is cognizant of the limitations of her expertise, however, as well as of what it may contribute. Martin, *Changing the Educational Landscape* 9.

13. Levin, "Book Review" 81.

14. Martin demonstrates in a very early article that she is well aware of the kinds of difficulties involved in such assessment issues. Jane Roland Martin, "On the Reduction of 'Knowing That' to 'Knowing How,' " *Language and Concepts in Education*, eds. B. Othanel Smith and Robert H. Ennis (Chicago: Rand McNally, 1961) 67–70.

15. Martin, *Changing the Educational Landscape* 183.

16. Decker F. Walker, "Comments of a Curriculum Specialist on the Eightieth Yearbook," *Educational Theory* 31 (Winter 1981): 24.

17. Foster McMurray, "Animadversions on the Eightieth Yearbook of the NSSE," *Educational Theory* 31 (Winter 1981): 75, 84.

Bibliography

Aaronsohn, Elizabeth. *Going against the Grain: Supporting the Student-Centered Teacher*. Thousand Oaks, CA: Corwin Press, 1996.

Adler, Mortimer J. *The Paideia Proposal: An Educational Manifesto*. New York: Macmillan, 1982.

———. *Paideia Problems and Possibilities*. New York: Macmillan, 1983.

———. *The Paideia Program: An Educational Syllabus*. New York: Macmillan, 1984.

Apple, Michael W. *Cultural Politics and Education*. New York: Teachers College Press, 1996.

Arnot, Madeleine, Miriam David, and Gaby Weiner. *Closing the Gender Gap: Postwar Education and Social Change*. Cambridge: Polity Press, 1999.

Baca Zinn, Maxine. "Feminism and Family Studies for a New Century" in *Feminist Views of the Social Sciences*." (*The Annals of the American Academy of Political and Social Science* 571). Eds. Alan W. Heston and Neil A. Weiner. Special Editor Christien L. Williams. Thousand Oaks, CA: Sage Publications, 2000. 42–56.

Barrow, Robin. *Common Sense and the Curriculum*. London: George Allen and Unwin, 1976.

———. *Plato and Education*. London: Routledge and Kegan Paul, 1976.

Barrow, Robin, and Patricia White, eds. *Beyond Liberal Education*. London: Routledge, 1993.

Beecher, Catharine E. *Miss Beecher's Housekeeper and Healthkeeper*. New York: Harper and Brothers, 1873.

———. *A Treatise on Domestic Economy*. New York: Schocken Books, 1977.

Belenky, Mary Field, et al. *Women's Ways of Knowing*. New York: Basic Books, 1986.

Bereiter, Carl. *Must We Educate?* Englewood Cliffs, NJ: Prentice-Hall, 1973.

Bernard-Powers, Jane. "Out of the Cameos and Into the Conversation: Gender, Social Studies, and Curriculum Transformation," *Gender In/forms Curriculum*. Eds. Jane Gaskell and John Willinsky. New York: Teachers College Press, 1995. 191–208.

Bloom, Allan. *The Closing of the American Mind*. New York: Simon and Schuster, 1987.

Boyer, Ernest L. *High School*. New York: Harper and Row, 1983.

Broudy, Harry S., B. Othanel Smith, and Joe R. Burnett. *Democracy and Excellence in American Secondary Education: A Study in Curriculum Theory*. Chicago: Rand McNally, 1964.

Bruner, Jerome S. *The Process of Education*. New York: Vintage Press, 1960.

Bush, George H.W. "Remarks at the University of Virginia Convocation in Charlottesville." 28 Sept. 1989.

Bush, George W. "Inaugural Address." 20 Jan. 2001.

Carr, David. "Practical Pursuits and the Curriculum," *Journal of Philosophy of Education* 12 (July 1978): 69–80.

Casella, Ronnie. "The Theoretical Foundations of Cultural Studies in Education," *Philosophy of Education*. Ed. Steve Tozer. Urbana, IL: Philosophy of Education Society, 1998. 526–534.

———. *At Zero Tolerance: Punishment, Prevention, and School Violence*. New York: Peter Lang, 2001.

———. *"Being Down": Challenging Violence in Urban Schools*. New York: Teachers College Press, 2001.

Chambliss, J.J., ed. *Philosophy of Education: An Encyclopedia*. New York: Garland, 1996.

Clinton, Hillary Rodham. *It Takes a Village*. New York: Simon and Schuster, 1996.

Clinton, William Jefferson. "State of the Union Address." 27 Jan. 2000.

Connecticut's Common Core of Learning. Hartford, CT: Connecticut State Board of Education, 1999.

Cord, Robert L. "Church-State Separation and the Public Schools: A Reevaluation," *Educational Leadership* 44 (May 1987): 26–32.

Crittenden, Brian. "The Identity Crisis in Secondary Education," *Australian Journal of Education* 25 (August 1981): 146–165.

Davis, Hilary E. "Docile Bodies and Disembodied Minds," *Educational Theory* 46 (Fall 1996): 525–543.

Dearden, R.F. *The Philosophy of Primary Education*. London: Routledge and Kegan Paul, 1968.

Dearden, R.F., P.H. Hirst, and R.S. Peters, eds. *Education and the Development of Reason*. London: Routledge and Kegan Paul, 1972.

Dewey, John. *The School and Society*. Chicago: University of Chicago Press, 1956.

———. *Experience and Education*. New York: Collier, 1963.

———. *Democracy and Education*. New York: The Free Press, 1966.

———. *The Early Works, 1885–1898*, 5 vols. Carbondale, IL: Southern Illinois University Press, 1972.

Diller, Ann, et al. *The Gender Question in Education: Theory, Pedagogy, and Politics*. Boulder, CO: Westview Press, 1996.

Dwivedi, Kedar Nath, ed. *Enhancing Parenting Skills*. Chichester: John Wiley and Sons, 1997.

Eisenmann, Linda. "Reconsidering a Classic: Assessing the History of Women's Higher Education a Dozen Years after Barbara Solomon," *Minding Women: Reshaping the Educational Realm*. Eds. Christine A. Woyshner and Holly S. Gelfond. Reprint Series 30. Harvard Educational Review, 1998. 261–289.

Elvin, Lionel. *The Place of Commonsense in Educational Thought*. London: Allen and Unwin, 1977.

Eyer, Diane E. "There Is No Evidence That Mothers Harm Their Infants and Toddlers by Working Outside the Home," *Women, Men, and Gender*. Ed. Mary Roth Walsh. New Haven, CT: Yale University Press, 1997. 391–397.

Freire, Paulo. *Pedagogy of the Oppressed*. Trans. Myra Bergman Ramos. New York: Herder and Herder, 1971.

Gardner, Howard. *Multiple Intelligences*. New York: Basic Books, 1993.

Gaskell, Jane and John Willinsky, eds. *Gender In/forms Curriculum*. New York: Teachers College Press, 1995.

Gilman, Charlotte Perkins. *Herland*. New York: Pantheon Books, 1979.

Giroux, Henry A. "Modernism, Postmodernism, and Feminism: Rethinking the Boundaries of Educational Discourse," *Postmodernism, Feminism, and Cultural Politics*. Ed. Henry A. Giroux. Albany, NY: State University of New York Press, 1991. 1–59.

———. *Channel Surfing: Race Talk and the Destruction of Today's Youth*. New York: St. Martin's Press, 1999.

———. "Doing Cultural Studies: Youth and the Challenge of Pedagogy," *After the Disciplines: The Emergence of Cultural Studies*. Ed. Michael Peters. Westport, CT: Bergin & Garvey, 1999. 229–266.

Goals 2000: Educate America Act (PL 103–227). 31 March 1994.

Goodlad, John I. *A Place Called School*. New York: McGraw-Hill, 1984.

Goodman, Paul. *Compulsory Mis-education and the Community of Scholars*. New York: Vintage Books, 1964.

Grue, M. Elizabeth, Janice Kroeger, and Dana Prager. "A Bakhtinian Analysis of Particular Home-School Relations," *American Educational Research Journal* 38 (Fall 2001): 467–498.

Gutek, Gerard L. *Historical and Philosophical Foundations of Education*. Upper Saddle River, NJ: Prentice-Hall, 2001.

———. *Historical and Philosophical Foundations of Education: A Biographical Introduction*. Upper Saddle River, NJ: Prentice-Hall, 2001.

———, ed. *Historical and Philosophical Foundations of Education: Selected Readings*. Upper Saddle River, NJ: Prentice-Hall, 2001.

Hayes, Elisabeth, et al. *Women as Learners: The Significance of Gender in Adult Education*. San Francisco: Jossey-Bass, 2000.

Hewlett, Sylvia Ann and Cornel West. *The War against Parents*. Boston: Houghton Mifflin, 1998.

Hirsch, E.D. *Cultural Literacy: What Every American Needs to Know*. New York: Vintage Books, 1988.

Hirst, Paul H. "The Contribution of Philosophy to the Study of Curriculum," *Changing the Curriculum*. Ed. John F. Kerr. London: University of London Press, 1968. 39–62.

------. *Knowledge and the Curriculum*. London: Routledge and Kegan Paul, 1974.

------. "Education, Knowledge and Practices," *Beyond Liberal Education*. Eds. Robin Barrow and Patricia White. London: Routledge, 1993. 184–199.

Hirst, P.H. and R.S. Peters. *The Logic of Education*. London: Routledge and Kegan Paul, 1970.

Holt, John. *How Children Fail*. New York: Pitman Publishing, 1964.

------. *Escape from Childhood*. New York: E.P. Dutton, 1974.

Howard, V.A., and Israel Scheffler. *Work, Education and Leadership: Essays in the Philosophy of Education*. New York: Peter Lang, 1995.

Hutchins, Robert. *The Higher Learning in America*. New Haven, CT: Yale University Press, 1936.

Illich, Ivan. *De-schooling Society*. New York: Harper and Row, 1971.

Jagger, Gill and Caroline Wright. "Introduction," *Changing Family Values*. Eds. Gill Jagger and Caroline Wright. London: Routledge, 1999. 1–16.

------, eds. *Changing Family Values*. London: Routledge, 1999.

Johnson, Karen A. *Uplifting the Women and the Race*. New York: Garland Publishing, 2000.

Kallman-Roemer, Eleanor. "Harm and the Ideal of the Educated Person: Response to Jane Roland Martin," *Educational Theory* 31 (Spring 1981): 115–124.

Kelly, Ursula A. " 'The Feminist Trespass': Gender, Literature, and Curriculum," *Gender In/forms Curriculum*. Eds. Jane Gaskell and John Willinsky. New York: Teachers College Press, 1995. 96–108.

Kimball, Bruce A. *Orators and Philosophers: A History of the Idea of Liberal Education*. New York: Teachers College Press, 1986.

Kurz, Demie. "Physical Assaults by Male Partners: A Major Social Problem," *Women, Men, and Gender*. Ed. Mary Roth Walsh. New Haven, CT: Yale University Press, 1997. 222–231.

Laird, Susan. "Working It Out, with Jane Roland Martin," *Peabody Journal of Education* 71 (1996): 103–113.

------. "Jane Roland Martin," *Fifty Modern Thinkers on Education: From Piaget to the Present*. Ed. Joy A. Palmer. London: Routledge, 2001. 203–209.

Leach, Penelope. "Nurseries and Daycare Centers Do Not Meet Infant Needs," *Women, Men, and Gender*. Ed. Mary Roth Walsh. New Haven, CT: Yale University Press, 1997. 386–390.

Leavis, F.R. *Education and the University*. London: Chatto and Windus, 1948.

Levin, Benjamin. "Book Review of *Changing the Educational Landscape*," *Journal of Educational Thought* 30 (April 1996): 79–81.

Lipman, Martin. "Caring as Thinking," Internet at http://chss.montclair.edu/inquiry/fall95/lipman.html.

Lopez, Gerardo R., Jay D. Scribner, and Kanya Mahitivanichcha. "Redefining Parental Involvement: Lessons from High-Performing Migrant-Impacted Schools," *American Educational Research Journal* 38 (Summer 2001): 253–288.

Mann, Horace. *Annual Reports on Education*. Boston: Horace B. Fuller, 1868.

Maritain, Jacques. *Education at the Crossroads*. New Haven, CT: Yale University Press, 1943.

------. "Thomist Views on Education," *Modern Philosophies and Education*. Fifty-fourth Yearbook of the National Society for the Study of Education, Part I. Ed. Nelson B. Henry. Chicago: University of Chicago Press, 1955. 57–90.

Marshall, James O. "Education and the Postmodern World: Rethinking Some Educational Stories," *Educational Theory* 50 (Winter 2000): 117–226.

Marshall, J. Dan, James T. Sears, and William H. Schubert. *Turning Points in Curriculum.* Upper Saddle River, NJ: Prentice-Hall, 2000.

Martin, Jane Roland. "On the Reduction of 'Knowing That' to 'Knowing How,' " *Language and Concepts in Education.* Eds. B. Othanel Smith and Robert H. Ennis. Chicago: Rand McNally, 1961. 59–71.

———. *Explaining, Understanding, and Teaching.* New York: McGraw-Hill, 1970.

———. *Choice, Chance, and Curriculum.* Columbus, OH: Ohio State University Press, 1975.

———. "The Anatomy of Subjects," *Educational Theory* 27 (Spring 1977): 85–95.

———. "Bringing Women into Educational Thought," *Educational Theory* 34 (Fall 1984): 341–353.

———. *Reclaiming a Conversation: The Ideal of the Educated Woman.* New Haven, CT: Yale University Press, 1985.

———. "Redefining the Educated Person: Rethinking the Significance of Gender," *Educational Researcher* 15 (June/July 1986): 6–10.

———. "Reforming Teacher Education, Rethinking Liberal Education," *Teachers College Record* 88 (Spring 1987): 406–410.

———. "Transforming Moral Education," *Journal of Moral Education* 18 (October 1987): 204–213.

———. *The Schoolhome: Rethinking Schools for Changing Families.* Cambridge, MA: Harvard University Press, 1992.

———. "The New Problem of Curriculum," *Synthese* 94 (1993): 85–104.

———. *Changing the Educational Landscape: Philosophy, Women, and Curriculum.* New York: Routledge, 1994.

———. "Methodological Essentialism, False Difference, and Other Dangerous Traps," *Signs* 19 (1994): 630–657.

———. "Aerial Distance, Esotericism, and Other Closely Related Traps," *Signs* 21 (1996): 584–614.

———. "Home and Family," *Philosophy of Education: An Encyclopedia.* Ed. J.J. Chambliss. New York: Garland, 1996. 275–277.

———. "There's Too Much to Teach: Cultural Wealth in an Age of Scarcity," *Educational Researcher* 25, no. 2 (1996): 4–10, 16.

———. "Bound for the Promised Land: The Gendered Character of Higher Education," *Duke Journal of Gender Law and Policy* 4 (1997): 3–26.

———. "The Wealth of Cultures and the Problem of Generations," *Philosophy of Education.* Ed. Steve Tozer. Urbana, IL: Philosophy of Education Society, 1998. 23–38.

———. "Women, Schools, and Cultural Wealth," *Women's Philosophies of Education.* Eds. Connie Titone and Karen E. Moloney. Upper Saddle River, NJ: Prentice-Hall, 1999. 149–177.

———. *Coming of Age in Academe: Rekindling Women's Hopes and Reforming the Academy.* New York: Routledge, 2000.

———. *Cultural Miseducation: In Search of a Democratic Solution.* Forthcoming from Teachers College Press.

————, ed. *Readings in the Philosophy of Education: A Study of Curriculum*. Boston: Allyn and Bacon, 1970.

McClellan, James. "Response to Jane Martin," *Educational Theory* 31 (Spring 1981): 111–114.

McKernan, J. *Curriculum Action Research*. New York: St. Martin's Press, 1991.

McLaren, James. *Life in Schools*. White Plains, NY: Longmans, 1994.

McLaughlin, Terence H. "Paul H. Hirst," *Fifty Modern Thinkers on Education: From Piaget to the Present*. Ed. Joy A. Palmer. London: Routledge, 2001. 193–199.

McMurray, Foster. "Animadversions on the Eightieth Yearbook of the NSSE," *Educational Theory* 31 (Winter 1981): 73–89.

Middleton, Ann. *Disciplining Sexuality: Foucault, Life Histories, and Education*. New York: Teachers College Press, 1998.

Moir, Anne and David Jessel. *Brain Sex: The Real Difference between Men and Women*. New York: Dell, 1991.

Montessori, Maria. *The Montessori Method*. Trans. Anne E. George. New York: Robert Bentley, 1967.

Mulcahy, D.G. "Personal Influence, Discipline and Liberal Education in Cardinal Newman's Idea of a University," *Internationale Cardinal Newman Studien*. Elfte Folge. Achter Newman-Congress, Freiburg. Eds. H. Fries, W. Becker and G. Biemer. Heroldsberg: Glock und Lutz, 1980. 150–158.

————. *Curriculum and Policy in Irish Post-Primary Education*. Dublin: Institute of Public Administration, 1981.

————. "Is the Nation at Risk from *The Paideia Proposal?*" *Educational Theory* 35 (Spring 1985): 209–221.

National Association of Scholars. *The Dissolution of General Education: 1914–1993*. Princeton, NJ: National Association of Scholars, 1996.

National Commission on Excellence in Education. *A Nation at Risk*. Washington, DC: U.S Department of Education, 1983.

National Education Association. *Cardinal Principles of Secondary Education*. Washington, DC: Government Printing Office, 1918.

Newman, John Henry. *The Idea of a University Defined and Illustrated*. Ed. Charles Frederick Harrold. New York: Longmans, Green, 1947.

Noddings, Nel. *Philosophy of Education*. Boulder, CO: Westview Press, 1995.

Nussbaum, Martha C. *Cultivating Humanity: A Classical Defense of Reform in Liberal Education*. Cambridge, MA: Harvard University Press, 1997.

Oakes, Jeannie and Martin Lipton. *Teaching to Change the World*. Boston: McGraw-Hill, 1999.

Okshevsky, Walter C. "Epistemological and Hermeneutic Conceptions of the Nature of Understanding: The Cases of Paul H. Hirst and Martin Heidegger," *Educational Theory* 42 (Winter 1992): 5–23.

Olssen, Mark. *Michel Foucault: Materialism and Education*. Westport, CT: Bergin and Garvey, 1999.

Ozmon, Howard O. and Samuel M. Craver, eds. *Philosophical Foundations of Education*. Upper Saddle River, NJ: Merrill, 1999.

Palmer, Joy A., ed. *Fifty Modern Thinkers on Education: From Piaget to the Present*. London: Routledge, 2001.

Panel on Youth of the President's Science Advisory Committee. *Youth: Transition to Adulthood*. Chicago: University of Chicago Press, 1974.

Perkinson, Henry J. *Since Socrates*. New York: Longman, 1980.

Perry, L.R. "Commonsense Thought, Knowledge, and Judgement and Their Importance for Education," *Readings in the Philosophy of Education: A Study of Curriculum*. Ed. Jane Roland Martin. Boston: Allyn and Bacon, 1970. 187–200.

Pestalozzi, Johann Heinrich. *Leonard and Gertrude*. Trans. Eva Channing. Boston. D.C. Heath, 1891.

Peterat, Linda. "Family Studies: Transforming Curriculum, Transforming Families," *Gender In/forms Curriculum*. Eds. Jane Gaskell and John Willinsky. New York: Teachers College Press, 1995. 174–190.

Peters, Michael, ed. *After the Disciplines: The Emergence of Cultural Studies*. Westport, CT: Bergin and Garvey, 1999.

Peters, R.S. *Ethics and Education*. London: George Allen and Unwin, 1966.

———. "Moral Education and the Psychology of Character," *Philosophy and Education*. Ed. Israel Scheffler. Boston: Allyn and Bacon, 1966. 263–286.

———. "Reason and Habit: The Paradox of Moral Education," *Philosophy and Education*. Ed. Israel Scheffler. Boston: Allyn and Bacon, 1966. 245–262.

———. "Moral Development: A Plea for Pluralism," *Cognitive Development and Epistemology*. Ed. Theodore Mischel. New York: Academic Press, 1971. 237–267.

———. "Education and the Educated Man," *Education and the Development of Reason*. Eds. R.F. Dearden, P.H. Hirst, and R.S. Peters. London: Routledge and Kegan Paul, 1972. 3–18.

———. "The Education of the Emotions," *Education and the Development of Reason*. Eds. R.F. Dearden, P.H. Hirst, and R.S. Peters. London: Routledge and Kegan Paul, 1972. 466–483.

———. "Reason and Passion," *Education and the Development of Reason*. Eds. R.F. Dearden, P.H. Hirst, and R.S. Peters. London: Routledge and Kegan Paul, 1972. 208–229.

———. *Reason and Compassion*. London: Routledge and Kegan Paul, 1973.

———. "Ambiguities in Liberal Education and the Problem of Its Content," *Ethics and Educational Policy*. Eds. Kenneth A. Strike and Kieran Egan. London: Routledge and Kegan Paul, 1978. 3–21.

Phenix, Philip H. *Realms of Meaning*. New York: McGraw-Hill, 1964.

Plato. *The Republic*. Trans. Benjamin Jowett. New York: Airmont, 1968.

Power, Edward J. *A Legacy of Learning*. Albany, NY: State University of New York Press, 1991.

Pring, Richard. *Knowledge and Schooling*. London: Open Books, 1976.

Purpel, David and Kevin Ryan. "It Comes with the Territory: The Inevitability of Moral Education in the Schools," *Moral Education . . . It Comes with the Territory*. Eds. David Purpel and Kevin Ryan. Berkeley, CA: McCutchan, 1976. 44–54.

Reagan, Timothy G., Charles W. Case, and John W. Brubacher. *Becoming a Reflective Educator*. Thousand Oaks, CA: Sage Publications, 2000.

Reed, Ronald F. and Tony W. Johnson, eds. *Philosophical Documents in Education*. New York: Longman, 2000.

"Review of *The Schoolhome*," *American School Board Journal* 179 (August 1992): 34.

Scheffler, Israel. *The Language of Education*. Springfield, IL: Charles C. Thomas, 1960.

————. *In Praise of the Cognitive Emotions*. New York: Routledge, 1991.

Schwab, Joseph J. "The Practical: A Language for Curriculum," *School Review* 78 (November 1969): 1–24.

————. *Science, Curriculum, and Liberal Education: Selected Essays*. Eds. Ian Westbury and Neil J. Wilkof. Chicago: University of Chicago Press, 1978.

Shmurak, Carole B. *Voices of Hope: Adolescent Girls at Single Sex and Coeducational Schools*. New York: Peter Lang, 1998.

Siegel, Harvey. "Genderized Cognitive Perspective and the Redefinition of Philosophy of Education," *Teachers College Record* 85 (Fall 1985): 100–119.

————. *Rationality Redeemed: Further Dialogues on an Educational Ideal*. New York: Routledge, 1997.

————. "Israel Scheffler," *Fifty Modern Thinkers on Education: From Piaget to the Present*. Ed. Joy A. Palmer. London: Routledge, 2001. 142–148.

Simpson, Evan. "Knowledge in the Postmodern University," *Educational Theory* 50 (Spring 2000): 157–177.

Sizer, Theodore. *Horace's Compromise*. Boston: Houghton Mifflin, 1984.

Snow, C.P. *The Two Cultures: And a Second Look*. Cambridge: Cambridge University Press, 1965.

Spencer, Herbert. *Education: Intellectual, Moral, and Physical*. Totowa, NJ: Littlefield Adams, 1969.

Stein, Nan. "Sexual Harassment in School: The Public Performance of Gendered Violence," *Harvard Educational Review* 65 (Summer 1995): 145–162.

Stenhouse, Lawrence. *Culture and Education*. London: Thomas Nelson and Sons, 1971.

————. *An Introduction to Curriculum Research and Development*. London: Heinemann, 1975.

Stratemeyer, Florence, et al. *Developing a Curriculum for Modern Living*. New York: Bureau of Publications, Teachers College, Columbia University, 1957.

Straus, Murray. "Physical Assaults by Women Partners: A Major Social Problem," *Women, Men, and Gender*. Ed. Mary Roth Walsh. New Haven, CT: Yale University Press, 1997. 210–221.

Thayer-Bacon, Barbara J. "Review of *Coming of Age in Academe*." *Educational Studies* 31 (Winter 2000): 463–469.

————. *Transforming Critical Thinking*. New York: Teachers College Press, 2000.

Titone, Connie and Karen E. Moloney. *Women's Philosophies of Education*. Upper Saddle River, NJ: Prentice-Hall, 1999.

Waks, Leonard and Rustum Roy. "Learning from Technology," *Society as Educator in an Age of Transition*. Eighty-sixth Yearbook of the National Society for the Study of Education, Part II. Eds. Kenneth D. Benne and Steven Tozer. Chicago: University of Chicago Press, 1987. 24–53.

Walker, Decker. "Comments of a Curriculum Specialist on the Eightieth Yearbook," *Educational Theory* 31 (Winter 1981): 23–26.

Walker, J.C. and M.A. O'Loughlin. "The Ideal of the Educated Woman: Jane Roland Martin on Education and Gender," *Educational Theory* 34 (Fall 1984): 327–340.

Wallace, Kathleen. "Reconstructing Judgment: Emotion and Moral Judgment," *Hypatia* 8 (Summer 1993): 61–83.

Walsh, Mary Roth, ed. *Women, Men, and Gender.* New Haven, CT: Yale University Press, 1997.

Walsh, Patrick D. "The Upgrading of Practical Subjects," *Journal of Further and Higher Education* 2 (Autumn 1978): 58–71.

Weiler, Kathleen. "Freire and a Feminist Pedagogy of Difference," *Harvard Educational Review* 61 (November 1998): 117–145.

White, J.P. *Towards a Compulsory Curriculum.* London: Routledge and Kegan Paul, 1973.

Wollstonecraft, Mary. *A Vindication of the Rights of Woman.* Ed. Carol H. Poston. New York: W.W. Norton, 1975.

Woyshner, Christine A. and Holly S. Gelfond, eds. *Minding Women: Reshaping the Educational Realm.* Reprint Series 30, Harvard Educational Review, 1998.

Young, Eva and Mariwilda Padilla. "Mujeres Unidas en Accion: A Popular Education Process," *Harvard Educational Review* 60 (February 1990): 97–115.

Index

About the Author

D.G. MULCAHY is Professor in the School of Education and Professional Studies, Central Connecticut State University, New Britain, Connecticut.